DESTINATION BUCHENWALD

COLIN BURGESS

DESTINATION BUCHENWALD

The astonishing survival story of Australian and New Zealand airmen in a Nazi death camp

SIMON & SCHUSTER

London · New York · Sydney · Toronto · New Delhi

DESTINATION BUCHENWALD: The astonishing survival story of Australian and New Zealand airmen in a Nazi death camp
First published in Australia in 1995 by Kangaroo Press
This revised edition published in 2022 by Simon & Schuster (Australia) Pty Limited
Suite 19A, Level 1, Building C, 450 Miller Street, Cammeray, NSW 2062

10 9 8 7 6 5 4 3 2 1

Sydney New York London Toronto New Delhi
Visit our website at www.simonandschuster.com.au

NATIONAL LIBRARY OF AUSTRALIA

A catalogue record for this book is available from the National Library of Australia

ISBN: 9781761106712

Cover design by Luke Causby/Blue Cork
Cover image: *Gateway and gatehouse in Buchenwald concentration camp, Weimar, 1945* (2008.002.003) from the collection of The National WWII Museum, New Orleans
Typeset by Midland Typesetters, Australia
Printed and bound in Australia by Griffin Press

FSC www.fsc.org MIX Paper from responsible sources FSC® C009448

The paper this book is printed on is certified against the Forest Stewardship Council® Standards. Griffin Press holds FSC chain of custody certification SGS-COC-005088. FSC promotes environmentally responsible, socially beneficial and economically viable management of the world's forests.

This book is dedicated to the two airmen who never left Buchenwald:

Flying Officer Philip Derek Hemmens, RAF
First Lieutenant Levitt Clinton Beck, Jr, USAAF

'Only those who have been prisoners have any conception of the horrors of being a prisoner, or of the ineffable joy of release; of the terrible rise and fall of the spirit, the fluctuations between the delirium of happiness and madness of despair, attendant upon the fluctuating hopes and fears as the possibility of release advances and retreats.'

Percival Christopher Wren, *Beggars' Horses*

Other military history books by Colin Burgess

The Diggers of Colditz (with Jack Champ)
Prisoners of War (with Hugh Clarke and Russell Braddon)
Barbed Wire and Bamboo (with Hugh Clarke)
Australia's Greatest Escapes
(originally published as *Freedom or Death*)
Australia's Dambusters: Flying into Hell with 617 Squadron
Bush Parker: An Australian Battle of Britain Pilot in Colditz

CONTENTS

German boundary 1942
Concentration camp
POW camp
Hamburg
Ravensbrück
Belsen-Bergen
Sachsenhausen
Hanover
Berlin
NETHERLANDS
Sagan (Stalag Luft III)
GERMANY
Düsseldorf
Leipzig
Buchenwald
Weimar
BELGIUM
Oberursel
(Dulag Luft)
Frankfurt
Theresienstadt
BOHEMIA
Luxembourg
Nuremberg
FRANCE
Dachau
Munich
AUSTRIA
Berne
SWITZERLAND
ITALY

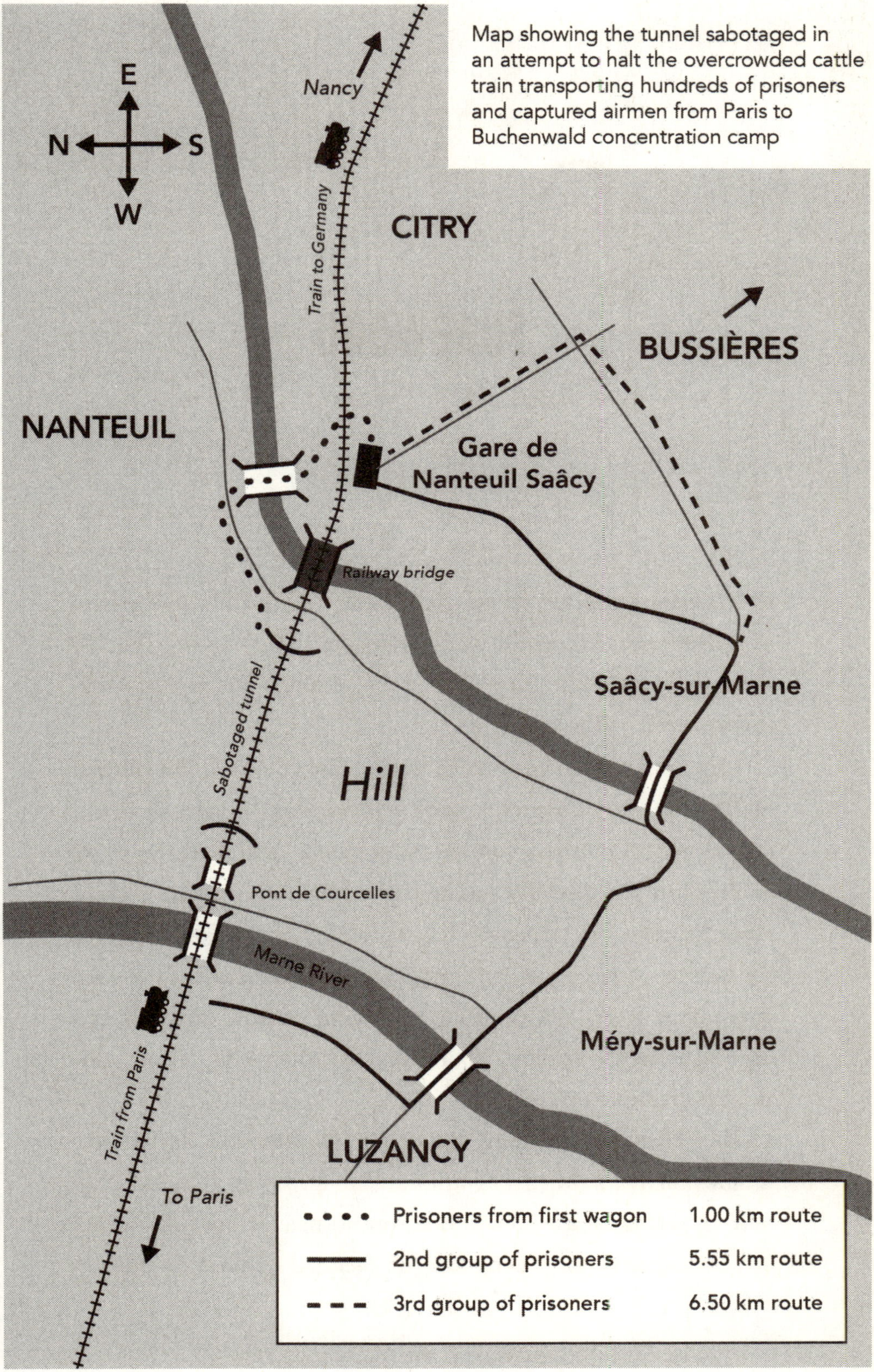

Map showing the tunnel sabotaged in an attempt to halt the overcrowded cattle train transporting hundreds of prisoners and captured airmen from Paris to Buchenwald concentration camp

FOREWORD

It is difficult to comprehend the totality of the evil which existed in Buchenwald, just as it is beyond human understanding to grasp the meaning of 'The Absolute' or the ultimate and unknowable. It was an evil as black as night.

I am honoured to be asked to write a foreword to Colin Burgess' excellent and well-researched book which opens the gates on one of Hitler's most notorious concentration camps, and leaves us in no doubt about the brutality and bestiality which caused tens of thousands to suffer the torments of Hell. We can feel the blows of the SS, hear the stamping of jackboots and the screams of the prisoners resounding across the Appellplatz [parade ground] through lice-infested huts, the stinking aborts [toilets], the places of execution and the crematorium.

The Allied airmen who arrived in Buchenwald during that summer of 1944, when our armies were sweeping towards Paris, were all young men who had been on normal air operations; they had no expectation, if sanguine, of eventual survival; if unlucky they could expect 'the chop' or if very unlucky they might end up in a prisoner of war camp – such was an airman's outlook during the war. Instead they were fated to undergo a nightmare experience which nearly had a macabre ending for them all. Shot down, often betrayed on the escape line, handed over to the Gestapo, imprisoned in Fresnes where they were beaten and tortured, packed tightly into cattle trucks, they were transported to Buchenwald, or 'Forest of Beeches' – surely the most euphemistic name for the death camp into which they were clubbed and kicked by demented SS guards.

The horrendous crimes committed in Nazi concentration camps have been well documented since the war. It is still difficult for most people to imagine how it felt to be subjected to such degrading and inhuman treatment, which left permanent physical and mental scars on many survivors, even destroying some. When the airmen were released and sent to Stalag Luft III they tried to describe their experiences, but the other prisoners of war had great difficulty in believing them. I spent over a year in the concentration camps of Sachsenhausen, Flossenbürg and Dachau, and so I know something of what the airmen must have suffered in Buchenwald. My experience came after I had been in normal prisoner of war camps so I was at least inured to barbed wire, but for all of us the dividing line between life and death was very thin.

The utter despair, exhaustion, starvation and death engendered by the deliberate Nazi system of brutality and sadism operated by the Kommandant, his vicious wife and the SS guards are described in horrifying detail; the murder of the gypsy children and the strangulation of the SOE agents are indelibly printed on the mind. Shafts of light relieve the blackness of this hell on earth; there is the resolute and wise leadership of the New Zealand Squadron Leader

Phil Lamason, the fortitude of all airmen under the most harrowing conditions, the humour, resource and heroism of Wing Commander Yeo-Thomas (the White Rabbit) and the final miracle of the release engineered by the SOE agent Christopher Burney who, himself, narrowly escaped a ghastly death.

Squadron Leader Stanley Booker describes his first return to Buchenwald after nearly 40 years: 'No birds sang and the ghosts of the past rose up to haunt me'. I returned to Sachsenhausen with Colonel Jack Churchill in 1975, 30 years after liberation; it was, like Buchenwald, a vast, bare and silent memorial. We went into the Zellenbau [cell block] where we had spent five months in death cells. The aura of evil had lingered on; I felt the cold hand of death once more on me, and suddenly the ghosts of so many tortured and murdered here seemed very close.

Should we not lay these troublesome ghosts of the past? It is traumatic, for those who experienced them, to recall the horrors of the concentration camps, but we feel we should remind the world, particularly those unborn at the time, that such things can happen in any country if freedom is not guarded.

Squadron Leader B. A. James, MC, RAF (1915–2008)

ABOUT THE FOREWORD WRITER

I WAS PRIVILEGED TO HAVE had a lengthy correspondence and friendship over many years with Squadron Leader Bertram Arthur James, MC, better known as 'Jimmy' James, and we even met once in London – a truly memorable day. Jimmy was one of the motivators and heroes of the so-called 'Great Escape' from Stalag Luft III, the German POW camp in Sagan, Lower Silesia, Nazi Germany (now Żagań, Poland). An incorrigible and determined evader, James had a long history of bold escape attempts before being sent off to Stalag Luft III, where he became part of the famed 'X' escape organisation under fellow squadron leader, Roger Bushell.

On the evening of 24/25 March 1944, a total of 76 prisoners managed to crawl through a top-secret, 120-yard tunnel codenamed 'Harry' before the sentries were alerted and shots were fired. Jimmy James was the 39th person to scramble out through the exit of the tunnel to begin his long and hopeful road to freedom. This time his bid failed when he was captured trying to make his way into (then) Czechoslovakia. Eventually all but three of the Great Escapers – two

Norwegians and a Dutchman – were rounded up and held by the Gestapo. When he heard about the enormity of the mass escape, Adolf Hitler was furious, demanding that all of those recaptured be shot. Fortunately for many, the chief of the Luftwaffe, Hermann Goering, intervened, fearing reprisals against captured German airmen. He persuaded Hitler to reduce that number. Hitler did relent, reluctantly, but only by reducing the number to be executed to fifty. Those recaptured, including Roger Bushell, were informed that they were being returned to the POW camp and were taken out to vehicles singly or in pairs. While enjoying a 'rest stop' during the journey they were callously shot down in cold blood. Only fifteen of the escapers were eventually sent back to Stalag Luft III, while another eight, including James, were illegally – under the terms of the Geneva Convention – sent to the concentration camp at Sachsenhausen, where they were interrogated under torture.

Despite where he was being held, James was resolute in trying to escape, and was soon involved in digging yet another tunnel – an activity in this camp punishable by death. He and five other prisoners managed to escape through the tunnel, but he was recaptured two weeks later and fortunately returned to Sachsenhausen, when he too could have been shot. He was eventually freed by troops of the American Army on 3 May 1945, just five days before the German surrender.

Post-war, Jimmy James was awarded the Military Cross (MC) and was Mentioned in Despatches for his many escape attempts before retiring from the RAF as a squadron leader in 1958. He subsequently became general secretary of the Great Britain–USSR Association and joined the diplomatic service in 1964, retiring in 1975. His self-penned escape story *Moonless Night* was published in 2001, and he also served as the British representative on the international Sachsenhausen committee for most of the remainder of his life.

Squadron Leader B. A. 'Jimmy' James, one of the war's greatest escapers, died in Royal Shrewsbury Hospital on 18 January 2008, at the age of 92.

INTRODUCTION AND ACKNOWLEDGEMENTS

In August 1944, 168 British and Allied airmen were herded together and locked into filthy, overcrowded railway cattle wagons and transported from Fresnes prison in Paris, where they had been subjected to brutal interrogation and beatings, to Buchenwald concentration camp – one of Hitler's earliest slave labour centres. The orders accompanying them were explicit: the transportation document stated 'Not to be transferred to another camp'. In less couched terms, they were to be secretly eliminated.

Counted amongst this number were eleven men from Australia and New Zealand who went to war with the customary pride of country and Empire, resplendent in their fine new air force uniforms, and ready to dish out a lesson to Hitler and his all-conquering Third Reich. Instead, they found themselves shot down and fleeing their enemy over the muddy fields of France and Belgium, relying on the goodness and fortitude of the local people.

In a collective sense, this is not a book about heroes, nor of heroic circumstance. It is a distressing and true story of a group of ordinary men who were forever touched by the most horrifying aspect of any war – the evil of mankind.

This book was originally begun in 1987 – a year designated the International Year of Peace. But for the men whose stories are told in these pages there has been no real peace. Post-war, many found themselves still struggling to comprehend the terrible things they witnessed in their youth, and the memories, vividly emblazoned in their minds, ensured that they would never know true peace within themselves. For them the war was not ennobling, and they were combatants who did not return from the war purified in spirit and soul. Rather, they came back scarred and skeletal, strangers to their loved ones, their sleep pervaded to the end of their days by terrifying nightmares.

I have presented here the stories of the nine Australians and two New Zealand airmen who, together with 157 of their fellow aircrew, made that harrowing journey into the vile jaws of Buchenwald. Their stories are meant to be representative of the rest – the men from Canada, Britain and the United States. Every incident in this book is factual, and the draft was meticulously read by many of the principals to ensure complete authenticity. Some liberties have, of necessity, been taken with conversations, but these are carefully based on the actual dialogue as recalled by the men involved.

I have several to acknowledge for their kind assistance and support for what I was doing in putting this story into book form. I could never hope to repay in kind the time, efforts and open hospitality they gave me, nor their trust in allowing me to intrude in deep-rooted personal memories and profound emotions, which gave me a rare and truly unforgettable insight.

Firstly, my thanks to the Australians and New Zealanders who, without exception, gave me their stories over many meetings and much correspondence, and to their wives and families who in many instances learned for the first time some of the horrors their men had witnessed and endured.

Thanks also to Art and Betty Kinnis from Victoria, British Columbia, Canada, both now sadly deceased, who twice threw their home open to their Australian visitor at short notice. Art, one of the Canadian airmen and for many years principal motivator of the KLB (Konzentrationslager Buchenwald) Club, not only gave me immediate support and much-needed information, but endorsed my efforts to other KLB airmen across Canada and the United States following our first meeting, initiating a welcome flood of valuable information and anecdotal material.

Other KLB members who assisted me were Leo Grenon, Willie Waldrum, Dave High, Ed Carter-Edwards and Bill Gibson from Canada. Additionally, Jim Hastin, Bill Powell, Joe Moser, John Crawford and Stratton Appleman of the United States readily replied to my every query, while in England, Stanley Booker MBE, Ian Robb, Bill Hegarty, Ron Leverington, Reg Joyce, Eric Davis and Ken Chapman were undaunted in their efforts to ensure I had all the facts I needed.

For providing information and tributes, I wish to acknowledge further sources: former Federal Minister Robert Tickner AO, in Australia, and ex-RAAF Pilot Officer George Mulvaney, as well as Barbara Yeo-Thomas, John Marpole, Phil Bear and Kevin Murphy in England. From France, former members of the Resistance Henri Theron and Madame Denise Lorach from the Musée de la Résistance et de la Déportation in Besançon, and French Ambassador Stéphane Hessel. Lorie Acton at the Smithsonian Institution in Washington, DC, Frederick Martini and Dr Thomas Hofmann at the

Bundesarchiv in Koblenz, Germany, and Chana Byers Abells from Yad Vashem in Jerusalem all provided much-needed information and photographs. Dr Bodo Ritscher from the Buchenwald Memorial Museum also proved to be of considerable and unstinting assistance.

I was pleased to allow the original edition of this book to be used as a source for a tribute book on the life of Squadron Leader Phil Lamason, who had assumed leadership of the 168 airmen in Buchenwald. This impressive and informative book was published in New Zealand as *I Would Not Step Back* in 2017, researched and written by Hilary Pedersen and associated writers. In turn, I recently requested permission to use some of the background information contained in that book, which was happily allowed.

Two long-time chums and avid POW researchers in England, Michael Booker and David Ray, gave me the same effusive and expert help as with my earlier books on the POW experience, while Jonathan Vance in Canada once again came up trumps with information and addresses. Author and military historian Alan Cooper was of tremendous help in London in guiding me to the correct documentary sources at the Public Records Office in Kew, while the late Don Charlwood, an outstanding Australian author and friend, read through the first draft of the manuscript and offered valuable suggestions for enhancing its structure and content. I was also grateful to the remarkable B. A. 'Jimmy' James, the author of the absorbing *Moonless Night*, who played an integral role in the ill-fated Great Escape from Stalag Luft III in March 1944. He kindly stepped in at my request and undertook the task of writing the foreword to this book following the sad and untimely death of Group Captain Leonard Trent, VC, DFC, who had earlier agreed to take on that task for me. He had been another surviving participant in the Great Escape.

Immeasurable thanks also to Paul Rea, one of the most dedicated and thorough journalists I have ever known, whose unswerving desire to see proper and grossly belated justice for Australian and New Zealand servicemen wrongly incarcerated in Nazi concentration camps saw him engaged in a quixotic search through records worldwide, and in the ministerial halls of Canberra. This book owes its origins to you, and to a chance remark you made that I should look into the Buchenwald story. Paul's superb 2007 book *Voices from the Fortress: The Extraordinary Stories of Australia's Forgotten Prisoners of War* is a necessary follow-on to his award-winning documentary *Where Death Wears a Smile*, revealing how captured Australian and Allied servicemen were wrongly sent to the infamous Theresienstadt concentration camp. It is a great and moving cry for long overdue justice.

I would also like to acknowledge yet again the excellent team at Simon & Schuster Australia for their ongoing support and appreciation of my efforts. As always, Managing Editor Michelle Swainson has been my guiding light throughout the preparation of this manuscript, ably assisted by Editor Rosie Outred and Copyeditor Mark Evans – thank you for your meticulous work in correcting my errors and your many helpful suggestions. Thank you also to Luke Causby for his brilliant cover design.

And finally to my wife Pat, for her inestimable support for what I was doing, my enduring love and gratitude.

AUSTRALIAN AND NEW ZEALAND AIRMEN IN BUCHENWALD

Australia:

Flight Sergeant Mervyn James Fairclough (1923-1964), Moora, Western Australia
Serial No. 427078. Buchenwald No. 78427

Flight Sergeant James Percival Gwilliam (1923-2002), Bathurst, New South Wales
Serial No. 432355. Buchenwald No. 78423

Flight Sergeant Eric Lyle Johnston (1922-2003), Northcote, Victoria
Serial No. 418951. Buchenwald No. 78421

Flying Officer Kevin William Light, DFM (1921-2008), Randwick, New South Wales
Serial No. 402447. Buchenwald No. 78381

Warrant Officer Thomas Alexander Malcolm (1921-2002), Hawthorn, Victoria
Serial No. 418755. Buchenwald No. 78379

Flight Sergeant Keith Cyril Mills (1924-2012), Mackay, Queensland
Serial No. 425954. Buchenwald No. 78426

Pilot Officer Robert Neil Mills (1924-1990), Salisbury, South Australia
Serial No. 417883. Buchenwald No. 78405

Flight Sergeant Raymond Walter Perry (1923-1997), Belka, Western Australia
Serial No. 415738. Buchenwald No. 78355

Flight Sergeant Lesley Keith Whellum (1923-2003), Kensington, South Australia
Serial No. 417545. Buchenwald No. 78442

New Zealand:

Squadron Leader Phillip John Lamason, DFC and Bar (1918-2012), Napier
Serial No. NZ403460. Buchenwald No. 78407

Flight Lieutenant Malcolm Ford Cullen (1918-2002), Maungaturoto
Serial No. NZ421963. Buchenwald No. 78388

1

INTO THE NIGHT

'Dear God in heaven, what is this place?' exclaimed the weary Canadian airman. Moments earlier, the solid wooden door of the railway cattle truck had been rolled open from the outside and a sudden burst of daylight had flooded the crowded, stinking interior. As he stared out into the vista that lay beyond the door, the young man's face seemed to sag. He shuddered and repeated himself, this time in an awed whisper. 'Dear God in heaven!'

Squatted uncomfortably beside him on a small patch of damp, filthy straw, Flight Sergeant Ray Perry, from the small wheatbelt town of Belka in Western Australia, took in the growing expression of horror on his companion's dirt-streaked face. He wondered if he presented a similar sight in the crushed motley of humanity. The man's rumpled shirt and trousers, ill-fitting on his trim, athletic frame, bore evidence of the nightmare five-day journey they had endured on a forced evacuation from the besieged city of Paris. Like everyone, he was soaked in sweat, covered in filth and scraps of straw, and stank of urine and faeces. As Perry's eyes swept around the other grimy, bearded faces, he finally decided that he and the Canadian would be quite indistinguishable from the others, all of whom were now blinking owlishly in the unaccustomed sunlight.

As they stared out at their destination, the expressions on the faces of the other men were rapidly changing from a glazed resignation to one of horrified incredulity. They did not want to believe what they were seeing.

Immediately beyond the siding platform was a high wire fence surrounding a cluster of squat buildings, but it was the sight of the men toiling within this fence that shocked the new arrivals. Emaciated men and boys with close-cropped hair shuffled around in ragged, striped pyjama-like tunics, wearily going about their appointed tasks. Stoically indifferent to anything but the frenzied shouts and unrestrained blows of the German guards, their expressions spoke of the inhumanities they had endured as they shuffled along.

A few metres from the hissing locomotive, a barely adequate army of these barefooted living corpses endeavoured to haul a rough wooden cart overloaded with newly quarried rocks along a dusty incline. As they strained and dragged and pushed the cumbersome vehicle, they were dispassionately flogged by two uniformed SS guards. Ferocious dogs snapped and tore at their legs, and they worked with a desperation that only fear of pain or death can induce.

Shrill cries and the guards' strident orders silenced the frightened hubbub of conversation in Ray Perry's cattle truck, and moments later three thick-set guards appeared at the open doorway, screaming and waving at the occupants to get out. Their faces red with exertion and anger, their tirade continued as they grasped those nearest the door and hauled them out head-first onto the concrete platform.

Eventually, the train had disgorged its human cargo, and the guards had whipped their charges into a long column, five abreast. Ray Perry was nursing a painful shoulder where the end of a club had connected. Tears stung his cheeks, but he suffered the pain with mute determination.

For the mass of captured airmen and French prisoners, this display of cruelty was a stark prelude to the living nightmare they were about the enter and endure – a place far more deserving of Tennyson's line, 'Into the jaws of death, / Into the mouth of Hell', than that to which the words had originally applied.

A sign mounted at the station had read Buchenwald – that is, Forest of Beeches. It was once a peaceful wooded area, where philosophers such as Goethe and Schiller had sat and mused, their thoughts nurtured amid the lush tranquillity and raw-scented beauty. But Buchenwald was now a corruption, a blasphemy encircled by centuries-old trees.

Eventually the column of prisoners was forced to move out of the railway siding at the double and onto a stony concrete road they would come to know as the Caracho Way, or the 'Street of Blood'.

It was 20 August 1944 – a day Ray Perry would never forget – and as he was shuffled along towards the gates of a large enclosure, he thought about the irony of the date. This day of pain and realisation, of terror and uncertainty, was also his twenty-first birthday.

More than three months had passed since that fateful day when Ray Perry had parachuted through the skies over France and found himself in the midst of the enemy he had flown over and bombed so many times. Earlier, back at their 466 (RAAF) Squadron base in

Leconfield, Yorkshire, there had been little to distinguish that day from so many others; breakfast with his crew, the ops briefing at which they learned of their target, and the usual nervous excitement that evening as he clambered aboard dear old Halifax Mk III, LV 943, given the identifier 'G-George'.

In the early hours of 7 May 1944, the crew took off from Leconfield, and the Halifax clawed a noisy passage into the almost cloudless night. Apart from English engineer Jack Dickens, they were an all-Australian crew under the command of Flying Officer Edmund (Ted) Hourigan. This was their thirteenth operation as a crew, and the portent of bad fortune evinced by that number was not lost on them. They were on ops that night as part of a 149-bomber force detailed to attack a railway marshalling yard at Mantes-Gassicourt (now known as Mantes-la-Jolie), 50 kilometres west of Paris.

In most respects the operation did not appear to be as dramatic as previous sorties, which had included four ops to the heavily-defended Berlin. Ground defences in their target area were reported to be light, but as they headed out over the Channel, bomb aimer Perry and navigator Chris Cullen talked for a short time on the less palatable aspects of the raid. They would be flying over France at 10,000 feet in bright moonlight, and the bomber force could easily be seen by prowling German fighters.

At this stage of the war, many small raids were being carried out on marshalling yards and similar objectives in north-western Europe, preparatory to the planned land invasion. Twelve Halifax bombers had taken to the skies that night from Leconfield, which lay 16 kilometres north of Kingston upon Hull, but only eleven of that number were destined to return. Operation No. 13 would indeed prove unlucky for Ted Hourigan and the crew of 'G-George'.

They managed to drop their bombs across the line of glowing markers, but as the aircraft swung for home it was pounded by cannon fire from an unsighted enemy fighter. Hourigan threw the lumbering aircraft into desperate corkscrewing manoeuvres, but when he finally levelled out to allow his crew a chance to assess the damage they were hit again, and this time the shattered Halifax erupted into flames. Hourigan ordered his crew to bale out. Ray Perry vividly recalls the ensuing moments:

> In the Halifax aircraft the escape hatch was in the floor of the plane near the front; in fact under the navigator's seat. The drill was for the navigator to tip up his table and shift his chair, put on his chest-type parachute pack, undo the hatch and jettison it before going out feet-first. As the bomb aimer, I was in the nose of the plane and went out second, followed by the wireless operator. During this time, the engineer put on his own pack and also the pilot's pack for him. The mid-upper gunner could either come up front or go out the back of the plane, while the rear gunner centred his turret to reach inside the plane to get his chute pack, then turned his turret hard to port or starboard and tumbled out backwards.
>
> I got about half out of the hatch when the back of my chute harness caught on the edge of the hatch. With the wind dragging on my legs I couldn't ease myself back up to free myself, but soon felt a heavy foot on my shoulder which quickly solved the problem, and I was out. Not knowing how much height we had lost, I quickly pulled the ripcord and was soon floating comfortably down, wondering what the future held. We were very fortunate, as the seven of us made successful landings and survived.

Ray Perry had landed in a field. Rapidly bundling up his parachute canopy, harness and Mae West inflatable jacket, he headed for a nearby wood where he quickly buried the lot under some leaves and fallen branches. Later that morning, having rested in the shelter of the wood, he approached some French people in a nearby farmhouse and though no one spoke English, he managed to convey his desperate situation to them. After enjoying some bread and a cup of thick, steaming coffee, he was shown to a bedroom and told to rest. He woke at midday and was told to take off his flying clothes, watch and identity discs. He was then handed a pair of well-worn trousers and a shirt, both of which were too large for him, but a length of string tied around his waist kept the baggy pants at full mast. Shoes, fortunately the right size, were produced, and finally a beret which had seen better days. He was given another small meal and then a newcomer arrived at the house, bringing with him two bicycles. Perry was instructed through words and gestures that he should pedal along behind this man, while maintaining a safe distance so they would not appear to be together.

> I was provided with a French identity card and knew then that I was in with the Underground. I gathered that if any Germans stopped my guide I would, if allowed, just ride on and would be on my own again. If I was stopped, my guide would just continue on and leave me to my own devices. If questioned, I would not divulge who had helped me get civilian clothes or where I had obtained them. I knew if I was caught I would become a prisoner of war, but if the French people were caught it would be a death sentence for them.

As it turned out, the cycle trip was uneventful, and even quite pleasant. The two men finally pedalled into the small town of Ivry. Here Perry followed his guide down a side path to the back of a house, which they entered through a rear door. They were expected, and Perry was introduced to a man and his wife, who made him understand that he was to stay there that night. The following day he was picked up in a car and once again enjoyed an uneventful trip to the village of Rouvres, where he was introduced to an elderly couple living in a petite two-storey house. As before, the couple did not speak any English, and his feeling of loneliness almost overwhelmed that of gratitude for these patriotic people.

Two days later, a spritely lass of about fifteen appeared at the house, and Perry was overjoyed when she addressed him in English. From then on, young Giselle visited the airman two or three times a week, and her visits were a welcome highlight of his days. During one visit she told him that she had received news of Ted Hourigan and Jack Dickens; they were safe and under the care of another Underground group.

After fifteen days, on 23 May, Giselle arrived with two bicycles and told Perry that he was to stay with her family in the neighbouring village of Boncourt.

> I met Giselle's parents Madame and Monsieur Wyatt, and her younger brother Noël. One of the first questions I was always asked was when the invasion of Europe would commence. I had been to Bournemouth on leave in April and had found out that one could only get to the south coast with a special pass, so realised that the invasion would be sometime in the summer, especially as we had been bombing rail targets near the north coast of France

and Belgium. I could only tell the French people that I thought it would be in a month or two.

Life there was quite pleasant, but I had to have a French lesson every day, and in a short time I always had to speak French at the meal table. My conversation was very limited at those times, but I'd like to think that I helped the two children with their English. The Wyatts had a radio well hidden in the house and at 1 pm every day would listen to the BBC French news service, following which I would be informed of the main stories. We always referred to it as the invasion of France, they always referred to it as the 'disembarkation', and on 6 June, within a few seconds of 1 pm, we knew that the invasion had begun. There was wild excitement in the house and a bottle of special wine, obviously saved for the occasion, was soon uncorked and glasses produced. Some friends arrived soon after and the celebrations continued into the night.

During July, Ray Perry was informed that there were two RAF men staying with the elderly couple back in Rouvres, and it was not long before they paid him a visit. They turned out to be Flying Officer Frank Salt and Flight Sergeant Eric Davis, both of whom had been shot down after the invasion.

With Bastille Day approaching early in July, the Wyatts decided to have a small celebration. Having been a farmer prior to joining up, we had always kept ourselves in meat by killing sheep, so I offered to help with the young goat. The kid was held on a table while its throat was cut so that the blood could be caught in a dish to make black pudding. The stomach and lungs were about all of the animal that was not used. The liver, heart, kidneys, brain, and even the testicles were to be used to bolster the meat ration. On 14 July, Frank Salt and Eric Davis were brought to the Wyatts' house, and another French family came to assist in the celebrations.

Following the D-Day landings, the Allies made very little progress into France, and the three airmen were becoming increasingly impatient. They could not comprehend at that time the vast amount of armaments and equipment which needed to be transported across the English Channel before the commencement of any major offensive. Eventually they conferred with the Wyatts, asking if the family could arrange for them to be moved a little closer to the front. This was finally done, and after a fond farewell they set off with a member of the Underground and were placed in an empty house in a wood. They stayed there for an exasperating eight days, receiving occasional supplies of food, but were understandably impatient to be on their way.

On 1 August, members of the Maquis (the fighting section of the Resistance movement) arrived and wanted to occupy the house, so the three men were moved to another village. The day after, another member of the Underground arrived and announced that he was to drive them to Paris, and they would soon be back in England. The trio broke into a round of cheers and slapped each other on the back. They would soon be home.

On 7 June 1944, a month after Ray Perry's aircraft had been shot down, seventeen Lancaster bombers from No. 15 RAF Squadron based at Mildenhall, Suffolk, were detailed for operations against Massy-Palaiseau near Paris. The operation would prove to be one of the most severe reversals suffered by the squadron, losing three aircraft over France and another shot down by enemy fighters over Friston as it crossed the coast into Sussex. Among the missing crews from the operation was that of Lancaster LM 575 'H' belonging to Squadron Leader Phil Lamason, DFC, the Commander of 'A' Flight.

The lanky, blue-eyed New Zealander was born in Napier on 15 September 1918, the third of six children for William and Violet Lamason. He grew up in the hardship years of the Depression, but his father's occupation as a surveyor meant that his father was always fully employed. Then, on Tuesday 3 February 1931, the family survived one of the most violent and catastrophic events in modern New Zealand history. Phil Lamason was only twelve years old that fateful day when an earthquake of massive intensity struck the peaceful coastal town at 10:47 am. It remains New Zealand's most destructive and deadly seismic activity, registering 7.8 on the Richter scale, and terrorising the local inhabitants over a period of two-and-a-half minutes. Napier and the city of Hastings to the south were devastated, and 256 people lost their lives. Hundreds of buildings were toppled, fierce fires broke out and bridges collapsed, while water and sewage lines were cut. The quake also resulted in coastal regions in and around Napier being lifted by six feet. Evidence of this activity is still quite visible in Napier today, although the town was essentially restored – rebuilt to its former art-deco glory.

Once the full ferocity of the quake had finally subsided, Phil's shocked parents gave him the task of riding his bicycle around the battered neighbourhood, checking if everyone was okay or needed help, while at the same time reassuring everyone they knew that his family was safe and unharmed.

The following year, Lamason attended Napier Boys' High School where he became interested in studying agriculture and began looking forward to a future in farming. A fiercely determined youth, he also revelled in the competition of school rugby and boxing, becoming the school's flyweight champion in 1932, his first high school year. For the rest of his life he would sport a twice-broken and misshapen nose as a legacy and reminder of his tenacity.

In 1936, the Lamason family would suffer a terrible tragedy. On 3 March, William Lamason was in a car with four other men, travelling to Hastings to attend to a church matter, when a goods train slammed into their vehicle at the Waitangi rail crossing. William was killed instantly and another passenger died soon after, while three others, including the driver, were badly injured.

Despite all that had happened in his young life, Lamason remained determined to become a farmer, enrolling in a Department of Agriculture course at the Massey Agricultural College in Palmerston North and then working as a livestock inspector. He had also developed a keen interest in flying, taking lessons at the New Plymouth Aero Club before joining the RNZAF to train as a pilot.

In March 1941, Lamason and his childhood sweetheart Joan Hopkins were married, but they would only have a short time together as man and wife, as he was about to begin pilot training with the RNZAF. Along with other volunteers, he was sent to Canada under the Empire Air Training Scheme (EATS) just four weeks after the wedding ceremony.

Following his training in Canada, Lamason was shipped across to England. His first operational posting was with No. 218 Squadron at RAF Marham, Norfolk, where he received further training on the twin-engine Vickers Wellington bomber. He then began flying bombing sorties over such well-defended targets as Berlin. In February 1942, the squadron would transition to the heavier, four-engine Short Stirling. Once the crew was familiar with the new aircraft, they were flying ops to such hazardous, flak-filled targets as Dusseldorf, Essen, Mannheim, Berlin and Bremen to deliver their bombs. Before too long they had chalked up thirty missions, with Lamason earning the first of his two Distinguished Flying Crosses.

His first DFC was won during an attack on the German city of Pilsen, a strategically important target in the Ruhr, in April 1942. During the return flight, his aircraft was attacked by an enemy fighter and sustained severe damage; the hydraulics were shot away and the turret rendered unserviceable, while a fire broke out in the mid-fuselage area. In the words of the citation: 'Displaying great presence of mind, Pilot Officer Lamason coolly directed his crew in the emergency and, while two of them dealt with the fire, he skilfully out-manoeuvred his attacker and finally shook him off. By his fine airmanship and great devotion to duty, Pilot Officer Lamason was undoubtedly responsible for the safe return of the aircraft and its crew. This officer has completed 21 sorties and he has at all times displayed courage and ability.'

The bar to his DFC, gazetted on 27 June 1944, also cited continuing 'courage and devotion to duty of a high order' and 'vigorous determination' in attacks on Berlin and other heavily-defended targets.

On 3 October 1942, now promoted to Squadron Leader, Lamason was appointed a training officer on Short Stirlings at No. 1657 Heavy Conversion Unit at RAF Stradishall in Suffolk. In December 1943 he became operational once again with a posting to No. 15 Squadron at

Mildenhall in Suffolk, which was then converting to the four-engine Avro Lancaster. Here he formed the crew with whom he would fly over the next six months. They were engaged in what was known as the Battle of Berlin, a crucial period of the war when aircrew losses were at their highest for Bomber Command. Never afraid to speak up, Lamason had an occasion to warn his station commander that heavy losses could result on a raid to attack Nuremberg on 30/31 March 1944. That evening, a massive raid was planned, with 795 bombers taking part, and Lamason was concerned about the route being taken, especially on a moonlit night. History records that the raid took place as scheduled and a terrible toll resulted, when 95 bombers were lost. Eventually Bomber Command's attention turned from these massive raids on Germany and their unsustainable aircraft losses to specifically identified targets in France, in preparation for the Normandy landings.

Looking back over more than fifty years, Phil Lamason's memory of the crew's final bombing raid – and his 45th sortie – on Massy-Palaiseau on the evening of 7/8 June 1944 is still clear in his mind. As he later revealed, they took off from RAF Mildenhall around 11:50 pm as one of 17 Lancasters heading into France.

> Our target was a bridge over the railway line, giving access to troops on their way to the front. There was some low cloud, and we flew in as the first wave of aircraft to attack at eight to nine thousand feet. Unfortunately, we arrived over the target area about half a minute early, before the Mosquitoes had dropped their flares, and I throttled back, not wanting to over-run our objective. It was a bad mistake because I presented the German fighters with an easy target. They attacked, and our right wing exploded into flames. I gave the order

> to bale out immediately, worked my way out of my seat wearing my navigator-style chute, and jumped. Our aircraft was well alight and as I watched, it just collapsed at the wing roots and went in.
>
> I landed in a field near Trappes about 0200 hours and hid my parachute, harness and Mae West in some bushes. I had sprained my ankle badly but was pleased to come across my navigator, Ken Chapman, a few moments later. We remained together from then on. We walked across country for about two kilometres until we heard some voices. We dropped to our bellies and crawled towards the voices until we recognised the French language. We approached the group who had been watching the raid and Ken, in his rusty French, told them who we were and asked for help. But they didn't appear to be all that keen to assist us, and pointed us in another direction where they said we might find some help. Soon after, we heard more voices coming from the courtyard of a house. The two of us approached a small group of two or three families who had also been watching and listening to the raid. We declared our identity and were at once taken to a nearby house, where we were given first aid for our injuries, which were minor, a strong alcoholic drink, and a light meal.

Lamason and Chapman were given some additional food which they placed in their pockets, and were escorted to a small wood a kilometre away. They remained hidden that night, and early the next morning a boy of about sixteen brought some more food and told the two men that members of the Resistance would come and arrange to give them shelter. A little later, two French women arrived, one of whom spoke reasonable English. Chapman, from Sussex in England, remembers their first day as evaders being a combination of confusion and uneasiness, but also recalled with fondness the French people who risked their lives to help.

> The woman who could speak English welcomed us and gave us a great deal of encouragement by telling us of the work of the French people as a whole against the Germans. She went away and returned later with the local postman, a member of the Resistance. Evidently he just wanted to look at us, but could speak no English. Again they left; we found a clearing in the wood and lay and rested in the sun. At 11 am the English-speaking woman returned with the French boy, carrying a sack of civilian clothes. We gave up our battledress for these, and although we looked a couple of tramps, we could reasonably pass as a couple of French labourers to a dim Jerry.

The two men were instructed to walk to a rendezvous where a car would be waiting for them. With his badly sprained ankle, Lamason had great difficulty and pain in walking the couple of kilometres to the rendezvous point through the wood, but he managed by taking his time and remaining alert. Chapman continues:

> After cautiously avoiding two German soldiers repairing telegraph wires, we reached the car containing the driver and his pal, who had been searching for us. The 'car' was a contraption with an engine of sorts, with a cab built of wood and numerous holes in the floor. I was to curl up in the back and cover myself with sacking. Phil, donning a beret, sat beside the driver.
>
> The ride was anything but comfortable, and in my position I could see nothing of the countryside. We dodged a couple of German motorcyclists who threw suspicious looks at the car,

> and arrived at a farmhouse. Here we were taken inside to a good meal. I produced a packet of Players [cigarettes] and our French friends went into raptures. Towards the end of the meal, the son, spying at the gate, ran in to announce a car of German soldiers was approaching and we had to make a hurried exit through the rear window, across the garden, and over an eight-foot gate, which Phil found some difficulty climbing. We ran across a ploughed field, jumped into a running stream, and hid under the stump of a fallen tree. Soon our friends came to say that the Germans had called for water for their car!

Next, the two airmen were taken to a barn near the house until it was considered safe for them to be driven to their first lodgings. They were covered with sacking in the back of the car and eventually pulled up in a side street in the small town of Montfort l'Amaury. Here they were welcomed by Roger Cuillerie, the town locksmith, and his wife Yvonne. Inside the comfortable house, a pleasant surprise awaited them in the shape of George Scott, an American airman. Yvonne produced some more respectable clothing and hid their personal belongings for them while they changed. They stayed with the Cuilleries for five days, never leaving the house except to use the outside toilet, and only then with extreme caution.

One sad event during their stay was the occasion on which the entire village turned out to bury several RAF crewmen killed during the recent raid. Two of Lamason's crew, tail gunner Flying Officer Tommy Duncan and mid-upper gunner Warrant Officer Robbie Aitken, had been killed in the fatal attack on their Lancaster. Tommy Duncan had died instantly in a hail of fire from the enemy aircraft, while Robbie Aitken left it far too late to bale out and perished when the doomed Lancaster broke up and slammed into the French countryside. The villagers reverently laid wreaths of red, white and blue flowers on the fresh graves in a gesture of respect. Lamason was not to know for some months that his three remaining crew members, Gerry Musgrove, John Marpole and Lionel George, had all managed to successfully evade capture.

George Scott left the house soon after to go to another hiding place. The three men were destined to meet again a few weeks later in less-pleasant circumstances. The day after Scott's departure, and amid great commotion, a badly burned American fighter pilot was brought to the house, suffering from shock and exposure. Yvonne fussed over the young pilot (whom they only ever knew as Jack, but was later identified as USAAF 2nd Lieutenant John Larkin), applying jelly to his burns and placing him in their double bed. Ken Chapman felt bad about taking up their only other bed.

> We implored Yvonne and Roger to take our bed, but they wouldn't hear of it. Yvonne slept on the divan, Roger on the floor. Next day Roger made a steel-arch affair to raise the clothes off Jack's badly burnt legs.

On 18 June, an attractive blonde-haired Belgian girl called Marie (real name Anne Marie Errembault), accompanied by two men, picked up Lamason and Chapman in the now-familiar motorised vehicle. She spoke excellent English and told Lamason that arrangements were under way to have them taken out of France, either by aircraft or by train to Spain. With luck, she said, they would be back in England within two weeks. Disguised as painters, sitting amid piles of paint pots, they were soon on the move again. 'This time,'

Chapman would later relate, 'we could view the countryside and the lines of German tanks and transport in the woods.'

They finally arrived in the village of Rambouillet and the home of Roger Prompsaud and his wife, who gave the airmen a cup of black-market tea and a huge bowl of strawberries. That evening they were handed over to Claude Lefebvre, the son of their next benefactor in Rambouillet, Christiane Lefebvre. Her husband had been a commandant in the French army, but he had been captured and was being held in a POW camp in Germany. A little later another RAF airman on the run joined them; he was Flight Sergeant Dick Rowe, who had been shot down a few days earlier. Although Rowe later went his own way, he too was destined to wind up in Buchenwald.

The three airmen remained with the Lefebvres until the morning of 23 June, when they were told to prepare for another move. They gave their sincere thanks to the benevolent mother and son, then were escorted a short distance away by Roger Prompsaud to await their next conveyance. And what a conveyance it turned out to be. They could hardly believe it when the local fire truck pulled up alongside them and the three men were instructed to don fire helmets and coats. Feeling incredibly conspicuous, but pleased to be on the move again, they noted with some alarm a few bullet holes in the canvas cab of the tender which Prompsaud casually explained were the result of a fighter attack.

Just outside the village of Chevreuse, on the side of a hill, the fire engine chugged to a halt by the wayside, where they were met once again by Marie, together with Maurice Cherbonnier, the village librarian. They removed the firemen's outfits and, trying their best to appear nonchalant, the party of five watchfully strolled into the quaint little village. After walking down a cobbled street, they reached the library and paper shop, where they were greeted by Madame Marie-Thérèse Guillou, the wife of Maurice, and her daughter Janine Cherbonnier. Upstairs, they were introduced to a couple of RAF airmen, Canadian Flight Sergeant Robert Davidson and Sergeant A. Hunter, as well as First Lieutenant Byron Phelps of the USAAF.

Conditions in the tiny flat were crowded, although generally amiable, but it was with a certain amount of relief that Marie arrived on 2 July and said she had to escort two of the airmen to another house. Lamason and Chapman elected to go, and bid the others good luck.

A brisk ten-minute walk soon had them arriving at a large elegant dwelling where they were handed over to Germaine Kalmanson and her two daughters, Denise and Colette. They were shown upstairs to their room, which contained two beds. Even here they had to exercise caution, according to Chapman.

> Denise and Colette spoke English fluently, easing matters considerably. Our stay here was very pleasant and we enjoyed it. An unusual thing – Monsieur [Gabriel] Kalmanson was 78 years old, and they did not inform him of our presence in the house. This procedure provided us with endless amusement, and we kept up a regular game of hide and seek!

The two men spent an idyllic fortnight at the house, eating breakfast in bed, sunbaking, and generally helping out in the extensive vegetable gardens at the rear. Eventually the aged Gabriel Kalmanson encountered Chapman going to the toilet, but after his initial alarm, he accepted the situation quite happily and allowed the men to stay.

On the morning of 18 July, word reached Lamason that they were to be moved on to Paris. The girls ironed and pressed their clothes and they all shared an early lunch with a little 'bon chance' wine. The Kalmansons were genuinely sorry to see their guests leave, but understood their desire to return to England. After many tears and handshakes, they set off from Chevreuse on foot, in the company of Gabriel and a woman named Janine. They walked for three kilometres until they reached the railway station, where Janine purchased their tickets. Marie was at the station and told them she would take over and escort them to a 'safe house' in Paris.

The train was crowded with people, particularly poor folk from Paris who had come to the country to buy, beg or even steal vegetables from the farmers. Lamason and Chapman stood patiently in the crowded carriage as the train slowly edged away from the platform. After a short journey, the passengers had to disembark at Massy-Palaiseau and walk to another train some three kilometres away. Lamason caught Chapman's eye and winked with a smile. Only weeks earlier they had been above this same place, trying to blow the rail bridge to pieces, and now they had to suffer the general inconvenience inflicted by RAF bombers. Their train was waiting at a bomb-damaged station and they clambered aboard with Marie.

Hours later, the train pulled into the Gare Université and despite their circumstances, the two evaders enjoyed their first sight of the elegant, ancient city of Paris. Liberation, they felt, was now tantalisingly close at hand.

Almost without warning, Jim Gwilliam crashed into the upper branches of a large tree, breaking a painful path downwards to the lower limbs. One branch caught under his parachute harness, slipped up the back of his battle jacket, and bowed under his weight. The red-headed tail gunner from Bathurst in New South Wales found himself in the ignominious situation of being suspended upside-down like a skewered apple, bobbing up and down as he struggled to hit the quick-release button. His whole left side felt numb, but self-preservation gave him strength. After several attempts, he managed to punch the button with sufficient force; the parachute clips disengaged and he fell to the ground, landing heavily just centimetres from a barbed wire fence. As he sat up, he was surprised to note that he was wearing only his right flying boot. Then he recalled the left boot becoming jammed in some twisted metal cladding in his gunner's turret. He had left it behind in his haste to leave the doomed aircraft.

Gwilliam released himself fully from his harness and was relieved to note that the worrying numbness had been caused by an incorrectly positioned strap. As full feeling and the realisation of his position coursed through him, he looked around in bewilderment and dismay, feeling but hardly noticing the stickiness of fresh blood on his mouth and chin. During his descent, the area around his mouth had been quite painful; he'd spat out blood and pieces of teeth all the way down. Swaying beneath the silken canopy, Gwilliam could not recall hitting anything in his frantic efforts to leave the blazing aircraft. However, the loss of a few teeth did not mean as much as the sight of a fierce fireball which had erupted below him as their brand-new Halifax bomber slammed into the ground. Now, safe and relatively unharmed on the ground, he wondered about the fate of the rest of his crew.

As he pondered his immediate movements, the chimes of a nearby clock tower rang out, and he found himself headed in the direction of the peaceful sound. The delusion of tranquillity was suddenly shattered by the howling sound of several enemy fighter aircraft swooping to a landing at the nearby Montdidier airfield. Gwilliam lay low for a short time, and pulled his escape kit from beneath his jacket. Every airman carried this survival pack, but he never imagined he'd be putting it to use. He stashed the kit in the trunk of a nearby oak tree, intending to retrieve it a little later. Then, settling back against the tree, he went over the events of the past few hours and decided he was lucky to be alive.

It had been the first operational foray for the crew aboard the newly delivered Halifax Mk V, EY.P ('Peter'), which displayed a mere four hours' flying time on the clock. They had taken off from Breighton bomber station in South Yorkshire at 2236 hours on the evening of 21 June 1944 as part of a 4 Group Bomber Command attack on Laon, in northern France. Their skipper, Bob 'Lofty' Mills, had previously flown a single operation with another crew from 78 Squadron, and was now taking an excited, albeit tense crew on their first bombing raid. The weather boys had forecast a low ceiling of cloud over much of England and France.

No problems were encountered as they passed over the French coast with Calais to port and headed inland. There was a little medium flak directed at them, but the crew were chiefly concerned about German fighters, which they knew were operating in vast numbers over the area. They dropped their load of high explosives and incendiaries and then flew out on a sweeping reciprocal course. Not long after, mid-upper gunner Doug Foden reported to Bob Mills over the intercom that he thought he had seen an aircraft below them. The skipper dipped the port wing, then the starboard, allowing the anxious crew to scan the night skies.

Nothing. Then, twelve flying minutes away from the target area, disaster struck.

With terrifying suddenness, the Halifax shuddered and shrieked as 75 mm shells from a Junkers 88 raked the aircraft from below, lancing the port wing tanks. The fuel erupted into flames, which streamed out behind the Halifax's wing in a fiery, 30-metre contrail. Realising their aircraft was doomed, Bob Mills gave the order for an immediate evacuation.

Navigator Keith Mills (no relation to the pilot) hurriedly stowed his navigation table and seat before donning his parachute. Together with bomb aimer Ian Innes, he attempted to open the escape hatch in the floor of the aircraft. Two hefty kicks finally cleared it and he told Innes to jump, following immediately behind.

Wireless operator Eric Johnston was seated in the front of the Halifax, forward of Keith Mills. With the bale-out order he began to stuff some precious items down the front of his battledress. In went his compact thermos flask, escape kit, and a small koala mascot he always carried as a good luck token. He patiently waited until Innes and Mills had evacuated, remaining with Bob Mills for a few seconds as their skipper initiated a steep dive in an endeavour to extinguish the flames. The attempt proved futile, so he clipped on his chest parachute as Mills scrambled out of the pilot's seat. Johnston then made his way to the escape hatch, pushed himself out into the fierce slipstream, and as he fell, watched with alarm the roaring display of fire and sparks above him as the tail of the Halifax rushed by. Bob Mills jumped clear just moments later.

Jim Gwilliam would later be reunited with Bob and Keith Mills and Eric Johnston, but he would not know until his eventual return from Germany in 1945 that the rest of his crew had survived.

Charlie Wright, the English engineer on an otherwise all-Australian crew, was taken prisoner after running into a German ack-ack battery, while Doug Foden managed to evade capture until the end of the war. Ian Innes established contact with the French Underground and joined forces with them. His efforts with the Underground would earn him a Military Medal for bravery – paradoxically an army decoration.

It had been a tumultuous few hours, but as dawn began to pale the sky, Gwilliam headed off once more on what he hoped might be his first steps to eventual freedom.

On the outskirts of the village whose bell chimes had attracted his attention, Gwilliam came across a small cottage and decided to chance his luck with the occupants. It was difficult sneaking up to the cottage in his single flying boot, but he was soon crouched beneath a window. He raised his head for a furtive glance and took in a small but cosy-looking room with a deal table, two chairs and a bunk in the far corner. A grey-haired man was stretched out on the bunk, fast asleep, his snores quite audible through the window. Raising his head once again, Gwilliam noticed a worn shirt draped over one of the chairs, beneath which stood a pair of muddied boots. It seemed to indicate the man was a farmer, so he decided to take a chance on the man's patriotism.

Quietly at first, he tapped on the window glass with his fingernails. Then he tapped a little harder with his knuckles. After a few persistent knocks the man's eyes suddenly snapped open and he looked around in bewilderment. It would be difficult to guess who received the bigger shock as their eyes locked through the window. The man looked in horror at the bloodied apparition outside his house and yelled in fright. Alarmed by the shout, Gwilliam took off.

After running a few paces he decided to go back, realising that he had probably frightened the farmer, and retraced his steps to find the man peering around the door. It was a few moments before the farmer took in the dishevelled flying suit and realised who had woken him. Overcoming his fear, he looked around and hurriedly beckoned the airman inside.

By now the farmer's wife was in the tiny room, clutching her clothes to her chest as she anxiously looked on. Her fear subsided a little when her husband explained their unexpected guest's identity. Gwilliam picked out the words 'Ahr-aye-eff' in the excited dialogue, but she was still wary as she invited him to sit at their table. She then examined the young airman's blood-streaked face, clucked a little, left the room, and returned with a water-soaked cloth, with which she carefully cleaned up most of the encrusted blood and grime. He was given a small cup of milk, which he drank gratefully, and a welcome mug of strong black coffee. The farmer's wife cut him a thick slice of bread, which he gingerly chewed on as he tried to communicate with his benefactors.

The small village into which he had stumbled was called Le Tronquoy, and as they began to explain where it was located another man suddenly strode in through the door. He took in the stranger sitting at the table and immediately broke into an animated discussion with the farmer and his wife. The young newcomer was quite suspicious and sat on the end of the bunk, lighting a small pipe as he eyed Gwilliam and his flying clothes. At one stage he pointed the stem of his pipe at the wing-encircled 'AG' insignia on Gwilliam's jacket and asked what was a fairly obvious question in French. After responding by pantomiming his role as an air gunner, the fellow looked at Gwilliam with fresh interest. It seemed he was not family but was a resident in the house. After a short conference, they indicated to their unexpected visitor that he should sit tight while the men went out to retrieve his parachute. He pointed out the direction he had come from and the two Frenchmen set off, returning half an hour later with the parachute bundled up in an old hessian bag. Their arrival was timely; as they walked in the sound of a Focke-Wulf filled the air for some minutes. It was sweeping low, obviously searching for any evading airmen on foot or parachutes in the trees.

At this sound, the husband and wife became quite agitated and the younger man was still uneasy with the airman's presence. The penalty for harbouring escaping servicemen was imprisonment or death, and even though Jim Gwilliam was still feeling giddy and tired from shock and the smashing blow to his chin, he declared his intention of moving on. They all looked considerably relieved at this, knowing foot patrols might soon be knocking at their door, and saw to it that he was well provisioned for his onward journey, with a little food and a battered pair of sturdy boots. Although reluctant to venture out into open territory once again, he bade them a gratitude-filled farewell and set off.

As he walked along in the morning sunshine, an incautious lethargy crept over Gwilliam – in all probability a traumatic reaction to recent events. Whatever the reason, he found himself wandering without concern down a road heavy with passing traffic, caring little for the German tanks, motorcycles and pushbikes as they passed by. Despite the fact that he was wearing an RAAF uniform with flight sergeant insignia and the word 'Australia' on his shoulder tabs, it can only be assumed that the Germans, inured to a vast array of uniforms throughout Europe at that time, did not even give him a second glance. Of course no one would expect an enemy airman to walk along a main road in broad daylight wearing full uniform – apart from his tattered boots.

When the folly of what he was doing finally hit him, Gwilliam snapped out of his torpor and quickly dashed off into a nearby wheat field, running heavily through the chest-high crop. Moments later he blundered into an unseen obstacle and fell heavily. His tumble was accompanied by outraged oaths from the naked couple whose lovemaking had been so violently disturbed. He quickly leapt to his feet and fled the scene as the flustered man continued shouting at him. As he ran, he saw the funny side of that little incident and a mischievous smile crossed his face. Then, hurrying up a rise into a clump of trees, he suddenly stopped dead in his tracks and his smile vanished. Right in front of him stood a massive, camouflaged German Tiger tank.

The shock of this unexpected encounter quickly disappeared when it became apparent the tank was unmanned and there were no Germans in the vicinity. The whereabouts of the tank driver was a mystery, although Gwilliam would later realise that he may have been the upper portion of the coupling he had so rudely interrupted. He had taken little notice of the language used by the man, merely the threatening tone. Inspired by his good fortune, he pressed on.

> In the distance I could see a small village, and I moved onto the road which ran towards a small cluster of outlying houses. I was more cautious now, and slowed my pace as I reached a tree-bordered bend on the outskirts of the village of Cuvilly. My caution was justified; just around the bend, four German lorries were parked and two of the drivers were enjoying a smoke. Another pair were

relieving themselves in a small ditch by the side of the narrow dirt road, not 30 metres from where I stood. I did an immediate about-face, but as I walked past a two-storey cottage I noticed a woman staring down at me from an upper window, her hand over her mouth in astonishment. She knew exactly what I was. Following this I made a wide circuit of the village, finally withdrawing to the temporary shelter of a huge elm tree on the outskirts of Cuvilly, where I contemplated my next move.

The serenity was shortly broken by the unmistakable sound of a British Merlin engine passing overhead. As Gwilliam peered through the foliage of the elm a solitary Spitfire passed to the north of Cuvilly at about 5,000 feet. His predicament came to him more potently than ever; in just an hour or so, the lucky devil in the Spit would be back at base, enjoying a hot brew with his mates. His stomach rumbled at the thought, but he settled down on the grass and began to nod off.

The rustling of footsteps woke him with a start, and he looked up in alarm into the face of a teenage boy. The lad spoke to him, but he had to indicate that he did not understand the French language. Through the boy's gesticulations he understood that he was to stay put, following which the young lad walked away, leaving Gwilliam to ponder this new situation. For all he knew the boy might give him away to the Germans. On the other hand, he needed to contact someone he could trust and who could pass him on to the Underground. The boy, he decided, was as good a start as any.

A short time later, the youth returned on a pushbike and urged Gwilliam to straddle up behind him once they got onto the road. The boy turned out to be the son of the woman who had earlier noticed the airman on the road. The ride was uncomfortable and awkward, but he felt that at last something was happening. He managed to enjoy the scenery throughout the 20-minute ride, during which they skirted back around Montdidier. Fortunately for both of them, they did not encounter any enemy soldiers. The pushbike finally crunched to a halt outside a huge house, where they were welcomed by an attractive woman in a simple cotton dress. After a brief exchange, the young guide beckoned Gwilliam to enter. The house was sparsely furnished. An ornate, polished staircase swept upwards to a second level.

The woman was an English schoolteacher whose late husband had owned several cafés in the devastated Pas de Calais area. Over the next four days Gwilliam was able to relax a little. A maid fixed his meals, and he caught up with a lot of missed sleep. He was supplied with a smart set of civilian clothes, and his uniform was taken away and carefully hidden.

The owner assured him that plans were under way to help him, but for the time being he must remain hidden. On the fourth day he noticed a suspicious character hanging around the house and told the woman. She became quite agitated and made arrangements for him to move to another house. That night the young lad took him to a smaller house beside the main road leading into Cuvilly. It had been recently ransacked, and the doors and drawers had been forced open, probably by bayonets. Outside, all manner of German personnel and vehicles passed directly by – all within a couple of metres of the house. It was not an entirely comfortable situation, but every day the maid arrived and brought him some food, while reassuring him in broken English that things were well in hand for his return to England. Apart from her brief daily visits, Gwilliam was alone during the long days and nights and he began to grow anxious; it was only a matter of time before someone came snooping.

On the fourth day in the house he noticed a suspicious-looking character across the road, then at eight o'clock that night he heard a muted knocking at the back door. His heart pounding with trepidation he opened the door, and in barged his young friend, closely followed by a small number of wild looking men, all members of the Maquis and armed to the teeth. These rugged individuals were soon dispersed around the small room, talking in low but animated tones. Some came over and shook Gwilliam's hand, muttering words of reassurance, while others thumped him heartily on the back. Thunder rumbled outside, and heavy drops of rain began slapping at the dusty windows. Finally it was dark enough to move out, though by now the rain had intensified and occasional sheets of lightning illuminated the room and its occupants with startling clarity.

As thunder boomed all around them, the Frenchmen began turning up their collars and shouldering their Sten guns. The young lad came over to Gwilliam and said, 'We go now!' The prospect of walking out into a fierce electrical storm filled him with dread, but he understood the urgency of the situation and reluctantly followed the Frenchmen. The sky was alive with ripping sheets of lightning, while thunder continually crashed and rolled menacingly as they moved along. Feeling cold and miserable, Gwilliam plodded through one of the most terrifying nights of his life.

> Even today I refuse to go outdoors when it rains; that's how bad it was, and how badly that shocking night in the French countryside affected me for the rest of my life. Storms absolutely terrify me now. But eventually we reached the outskirts of a small village named

> Ployron where I said goodbye to the blokes from the Maquis. I was still trembling from the walk, but managed to wave goodbye and thank the men. Not long after, an elderly peasant came along on a horse and dray and pulled up. The youngster led me to the dray and told me to climb up beside the old man. Once I was settled in the seat my young helper wished me 'Bon chance!' and shook my hand. I owed him so much, but by the time I had begun to thank him he'd already turned and started back the way we'd come. The old man smiled at me and said, 'Bonjour monsieur', then he clicked his tongue at the horse and we moved off.

By now the electrical storm had abated, and as they moved along, the early morning sun was beginning to colour the sky before rising and peeping through the clouds. The old peasant appeared to be dozing, so Gwilliam relaxed, enjoying the freshness of the post-storm air and the tranquillity of the passing countryside. An hour later the horse pulled up at a small house by a rail siding, which appeared to be the gatekeeper's cottage. The old man indicated to Gwilliam that he could get down, and as he did so a slim woman in her mid-thirties opened the door, looked around and then waved him inside. He had to duck his head as he entered a cosy, well-furnished room. While he waited for the woman he looked around, and with a start noticed three small photographs propped on the sideboard. They were the escape-kit photos of three of his crew: Bob Mills, Eric Johnston and Keith Mills. The photos, taken back in England, showed the men in civilian clothing and were intended for possible use in making fake passes.

With a combination of excitement and relief, he could barely contain himself as he called the woman over and pointed at the photographs, then at himself. 'This is my crew,' he said. 'These men are from my aircraft!' The woman's face broke into a wide smile. 'Oui, monsieur; je comprends. Attendez, monsieur; attendez.' She then showed him into a small room and as he slumped onto the single bed he gratefully shed his sodden boots. He was exhausted after the adventures and dangers he'd faced since landing on French soil a few days earlier. As he removed his damp jacket, he heard the front door close and then the heavy clump of footsteps in the next room. He heard voices, and the door was suddenly flung open. Framed in the doorway was a huge, moustachioed Frenchman in a check shirt and flannel trousers. Having ascertained that Gwilliam did not speak any French, he introduced himself in broken English. His name was Pierre, and he revealed that the others on the crew had been at the house but had since moved on. He did not know their current whereabouts but said he would try to find out. Gwilliam thanked the man, who smiled broadly through his bristling moustache. He was a big brute, over two metres tall, and he really had to stoop low as he left the room.

Over the next few days, Gwilliam spent much of his time both in and on the small bed, waiting for any news. Pierre visited once or twice a day to bring food, but his news was always the same – please wait. German rail trucks and other armaments were constantly clanking past the small cottage, but the guards on board paid little attention to the dwelling by the rail siding.

Several days later, he was dozing in his room when Pierre entered. He apologised for the intrusion and then, lifting the cover, began to search for something beneath the bed. 'Excuse me,' he said, dragging out a heavy, cloth-covered bundle. 'I must bury somewhere.' To Gwilliam's amazement, the bundle was unrolled to reveal several Bren guns, grenades and boxes of ammunition. He had been sleeping on top of this little arsenal for a week! Pierre rewrapped the bundle after carefully checking the weapons, gripped it in his massive arms, and after a further apology, calmly strode out.

> Later that day Pierre took me to a neat farmhouse a quarter of a mile up the road, where I was greeted by a French couple who invited us in and gave me some bread and wine. They did not know where the other three men were hidden, but promised to ask around. The husband happened to tell me that the crash site of our aircraft was quite near, and asked me if I'd be interested in looking at the wreckage. I said I would, and we all walked to a small clearing nearby. On the edge of this clearing, with broken bushes and fresh mounds of dirt everywhere, lay our once-beautiful Halifax. It was just a twisted, broken heap of scrap metal. I really felt quite sad as I looked over the remains of what had been virtually a brand-new aircraft, and Pierre was most sympathetic. He said, 'C'est dommage, monsieur. Quel gaspillage.' (Such a shame, sir, such a waste.) None of us spoke a word as we returned to the farmhouse.

Over the next few days, Jim Gwilliam enjoyed some very pleasant times with the family, and often played cards with their young daughter. Sometimes they had visitors, but he was instructed not to speak to anyone. Pierre told him that the visitors assumed his guest to be mute. Nobody paid particular attention to him in the time he spent at the farmhouse.

Then came some very welcome news. Keith Mills was in the nearby village of Coivrel, and arrangements were being made for him to pay a visit. Later that day Gwilliam was picked up by a young farm worker on a pushbike and doubled along the narrow dirt road.

They passed several Germans on the way, but were left alone and unchallenged. Though dressed in peasant clothes, he had taken the precaution of wearing his perforated metal identity tags concealed beneath the collar of his shirt. As well as being called 'dog tags' they were commonly known to aircrew as 'dead meat tickets'. If killed, the tag was removed and forwarded to Allied headquarters so relatives could be notified and the wearer's death recorded. In Jim Gwilliam's case, it was the only means by which he could identify himself as an airman, should he be captured. He knew from briefings that any serviceman captured in civvies could be executed as a spy, and the knowledge made him more than apprehensive.

Finally the young farm worker pedalled into Coivrel and pulled up at a small corner café. They dismounted and strolled over to a battered door, where the youth knocked after carefully looking around. The door swung open, revealing an elderly man with a trim white moustache. He greeted the youth, sized up the stranger beside him, then urged them to enter. Inside sat Keith Mills, who leapt to his feet with a whoop of joy and shook his crewmate's hand vigorously, then launched into a gleeful barrage of questions.

Later, when the initial excitement had died down, the two men sat at a round table over cups of coffee brought to them by the diminutive grey-haired Madame Eugenie Tempez, wife of the café owner, Omer Creton. Keith told Jim that the elderly couple had been very good to him and had not asked him to leave even when it was discovered that a local, known to be a collaborator, had started asking questions of his benefactors. The previous evening, the collaborator had been intercepted and escorted out of town by a small, hostile group of villagers. They returned soon after, but the collaborator did not. No one spoke of his fate, but it seemed certain he would never betray anyone again. His other news was of a Lysander aircraft being organised to pick them up, along with Bob Mills and Eric Johnston, who were apparently being sheltered nearby.

Though understandably anxious to see his friends again, Gwilliam had to contain himself while cautious arrangements were made, and the next five days passed slowly for the two Australians in their small room above the café. Monsieur Creton kept them supplied with food and coffee, occasionally chatting with them about his habit of rabbit breeding. From time to time they could hear German voices in the café below, but were never disturbed.

Finally the evening came when the two airmen were taken to meet Bob and Eric, who were hiding in a small dwelling at the rear of a large house on the other side of the village. The property was owned by the patriotic Mayor of Coivrel, Paul Omnes, and here a joyful reunion took place. When all the back-slapping was over, the four men settled down around a polished antique table and began to take stock of their position. Everything seemed to be going so smoothly and Jim Gwilliam was looking forward to their return flight to England.

On 28 July, the men were told a Lysander would soon land at a nearby location. At noon the following day, a petrol-driven covered truck squealed to a halt outside the Mayor's house. Bob Mills and Eric Johnston made their farewells and climbed into the back, where two young Frenchmen were already seated. The truck rumbled around a few corners and pulled up outside the café, where Jim Gwilliam and Keith Mills piled in, each clutching a farewell gift of a bottle of local wine.

They headed off in a westerly direction as the six men in the covered cabin at the rear chatted happily and drank from the bottles. Outside the sun was shining and the Australians' mood was almost festive. They were on their way home; with a bit of luck and good planning they could be back in England in time for breakfast.

The truck stopped briefly on the outskirts of the town of Maignelay where one of the young Frenchmen, Ronald, wished everyone good luck and clambered out. Ten kilometres on, the truck pulled over to the side of the road near the village of Chepoix. One of the two men in the driver's cabin came around the back of the truck, beckoning the airmen to follow him. It was a pleasant day for a hike; the four men and their guide strolled through a thin forest and trekked across some fields, heading towards the town of Breteuil at an easy gait. On their way they saw the top half of a stationary locomotive just over a distant rise. Their guide told them that it had been there for some time after being severely damaged by Allied fighters.

Eventually they entered a thick wood where the guide said they should make themselves inconspicuous, stating he would return as soon as possible with another vehicle. The four men sat down and enjoyed some cigarettes, eagerly discussing what they would do once they'd reached England. About an hour later a horn tooted a prearranged signal and they made their way down onto the road, where a small black sedan with two men in the front was waiting. They were told to squeeze into the back seat and were assured that the trip would only be a short one. Uncomfortable but happy, the Australians watched as the lush countryside swept by.

Suddenly their mood changed from elation to alarm as the driver swung around a corner and drove straight up to a roadblock. A squad of armed German soldiers ordered them to get out of the vehicle and raise their hands. A further surprise came when the boot of the car was opened and another man scrambled out carrying an automatic rifle, which he quickly trained on the airmen.

Once they had been searched, the men were handcuffed and ordered back into the car. An armed soldier covered them from the front seat as the sedan roared off again, this time following another car. After a long drive suffered in silence they were driven into the forecourt of Beauvais gaol.

They had fallen into a trap laid by two traitorous collaborators named André Cauchemez and Paul Villette, who had given them up to the Germans in exchange for reward money. The Australians were stunned but at the same time deeply concerned; they hoped that reprisals would not befall any of the kindly villagers who had aided them over the past few weeks.

The captured airmen underwent interrogation, at which time they were informed that, having been captured in civilian clothing, they had given up their status as prisoners of war. Eventually they were transported to Fresnes prison in Paris for a further bout of even more brutal interrogation. All four had begun their nightmare journey to Buchenwald.

Footnote: In 1995, during a holiday visit to France, the author and his wife Pat located the village of Coivrel and spoke to an elderly couple who knew of the airmen hiding in their village during the war. They pointed out the village cemetery where we noted that Madame Tempez and her husband Monsieur Creton had died several years after the war. This news was later conveyed to Jim Gwilliam back in Australia, who had always been deeply concerned that the family might have been killed as a reprisal for harbouring them while on the run. When shown the photos of the gravestones, Jim broke down, crying tears of relief. He said it was a long-endured and massive weight off his shoulders.

2

BETRAYAL AND CAPTURE

It was Monday 24 July 1944. Air raid sirens began wailing as Phil Lamason and Ken Chapman sat uneasily on a wooden bench in the heart of German-occupied Paris, waiting to be picked up by the next contact in the escape line. They looked up, hoping to see some Allied aircraft flying overhead, but none seemed interested in flying over the French capital that day. Parisians, by now largely inured to the constant sound of these sirens, chose to ignore them and scampered about on their daily business. A few metres from the bench stood a nervous Frenchwoman, the helper who had brought them to this spot. Standing at a discreet distance she watched and waited as well, but she was observing the pedestrian traffic, looking for her contact or for any signs of trouble.

On their arrival in Paris two days earlier, the Belgian girl Marie had guided the airmen to a two-storey house at 66 Rue d'Assas, overlooking a school by the magnificent Luxembourg Gardens. Here Marie had handed them on to their next hosts, the Werths. Despite the acute shortage of food in Paris, Madame

Josephine Werth had generously provided them with good, nourishing meals.

After a pleasant weekend, Madame Werth had guided Lamason and Chapman to their next rendezvous. She rode her bicycle a slow, cautious 100 metres ahead of them as they followed her through the streets of Paris until she pulled up alongside a small bench where she indicated they should wait while she watched from a short distance away for the next link in the Underground chain to make an appearance.

The air-raid sirens were still sounding when a portly Frenchman strolled over to Madame Werth. They talked in muted tones for a few moments and then she subtly beckoned the two men over. With obvious relief but tears in her eyes, she wished them a safe journey and indicated they should go with the man, named Georges Prevot. As they watched Josephine Werth remount her bicycle, she smiled, crossed her fingers as a sign of good luck, and pedalled away.

The routine was the same as before. They followed Prevot at a safe distance as he strolled towards yet another place of hiding. They crossed the Seine at the Île de la Cité, enjoying their first sight of the spectacular Notre Dame cathedral in spite of their precarious situation. Next they passed the Préfecture and the Palais de Justice before entering the Boulevard de Sébastopol. A few brisk strides took them to an apartment opposite Demoy's Restaurant, where they followed Georges up a narrow flight of stairs to the top apartment. Here they were greeted by a young, short and fair-haired man wearing thick-lensed glasses, who introduced himself in lightly accented English as Captain Jacques, an officer in the French Intelligence. He assured Lamason and Chapman they were now on the final stage of their journey and would soon be back in England. As Lamason recalled, the contact's words were quite heartening.

> The man claimed to be working for the chief organiser of the escape route to Spain [the Comet Line]. He had a detailed story of how the journey would be accomplished, and claimed to have made the journey seven times.

The two men relaxed and were all smiles as they were introduced to Georges' sister Genevieve. Ken Chapman felt quite at ease and remembers every effort being made to ensure their comfort and make them feel they were safe and among friends.

> We had good meals here and had a comfortable double bed to sleep in. We were given clothes to wear so that our own could be pressed, and we could go out onto the balcony overlooking the Rue de Sébastopol to watch the throngs of people go by. Georges and Jacques provided us with tobacco, so we were fairly well supplied. That night Georges and Genevieve came in with two bottles of champagne, which we soon disposed of!

The following day, Jacques returned to the apartment with a young RAF evader identified only as Bob, who was actually Flying Officer Ralph Taylor. Later, while conducting a question session he said was quite routine, Jacques asked the three airmen for the names of those who had helped them in their journeys across France. Immediately all three became suspicious, and Lamason asked Jacques why he needed such delicate information.

'Many of these people are very poor and need money,' he explained. 'If you prefer not to tell me their names it is all the same to me, but it is usual for us to show our gratitude by rewarding such patriotism with an amount of 200 francs for each day you were with them.'

It all seemed perfectly reasonable. Jacques' credentials and authority seemed to be in order, so the three men divulged the names and locations of their past helpers. The following day, Lamason and Chapman left the apartment building with Georges and Jacques and were handed over to Jacques' assistant, an unsmiling woman with copper-coloured hair and spectacles. Jacques would not divulge her name, but they later discovered she was known as Madame Colette Orsini. She took over responsibility for the welfare of the two airmen and guided them along the banks of the Seine, through the beautiful gardens of the Tuileries and on to the Place de la Concorde. Here they waited for an hour until they were picked up by two men in a black Citroën. Both spoke good English with strong American accents.

The passenger in the front seat, who reminded Lamason of a Hollywood gangster, introduced himself as Jacques' chief in the Resistance network. He was a tall man of average weight with brown hair and blue-grey eyes. Lamason's first impressions were actually borne out when he told them something of his background. In response to their surprise at being picked up by agents who seemed to be American citizens, he claimed to have lived in Chicago for twelve years, and to have known Al Capone!

The driver was an even taller fellow in his mid-twenties. A ruggedly good-looking man, he had fair hair, blue eyes, and bore a faint scar along his forehead, just below the hairline. He told them he had been born in California and had joined the French air force in 1939. In what appeared to be an easy conversational manner, he tried to cajole Lamason into a discussion of the comparative air defences of Britain and Germany, but the New Zealander was firmly non-committal and would not be drawn into talking about such a provocative subject with someone he had just met.

As their journey continued, they drove past the Eiffel Tower and pulled up in front of a block of apartments near Bois de Boulogne. Here the two airmen were temporarily separated; Lamason occupying one room and Chapman in a small children's bedroom. On the surface, things seemed to be going smoothly, but Chapman later admitted he was beginning to feel somewhat ill at ease with their situation.

> I felt terribly lonely, and I had plenty of time to think. Swastikas were scrawled on the walls and to me this seemed strange. However, the tall American came in and reassured me.

That night they shared an uninspiring meal before retiring, although the news that they would be on their way back to England the following day brightened their outlook. Both spent an uneasy night wondering about what the morning would bring, and the hours crept by until it was time for breakfast. Chapman made his way downstairs, where he found Lamason already chatting with six other downed airmen who were moving in prior to their own departure for Spain and hopeful freedom. The hours now passed quickly.

It was not until lunch was over that their move was fully organised. Ken Chapman was to ride on the pillion of a Frenchman's two-stroke motorcycle to the prearranged rendezvous, while Lamason was to go by Metro with another Frenchman. They set off, and just after two o'clock were reunited at their rendezvous point near the

Champs-Élysées. Both men were dubious about the wisdom behind this move, as they now found themselves almost directly in front of a German barracks, and the area was swarming with enemy guards. Chapman takes up the story:

> We were left in the company of my escort. We crossed the road to a café and ordered some beer. Meanwhile we watched the passers-by. Many German troops were passing, but no private vehicles. All French people used cycles, of which there was a multitude. At 1500 hours I paid the bill and we returned to our rendezvous point across the road. A quarter of an hour passed and no one had arrived, and I was uneasy – there were too many Germans about who might recognise us for what we were.
>
> Soon two strangers came up, shook hands with our guide and with us, and led us to a car. We got in and thought we were at last on our way. We drove some five minutes then suddenly entered what later proved to be Gestapo headquarters with two guards outside! We were covered by guns, removed from the car, and led up several flights of steps to a room where we were searched and handcuffed together. Our Frenchmen had betrayed us, and we were in the hands of the Gestapo.

Almost two weeks after Lamason and Chapman had unwittingly fallen into enemy hands, Ray Perry, Frank Salt and Eric Davis also fell victim to the traitorous actions of the so-called 'Captain Jacques' after they had been driven into Paris by their Underground helper. Their journey was incident-free and they were told they would be placed into safe houses over the weekend. Subsequent plans called for them to be picked up and taken somewhere south of Paris.

Here they would be given passage aboard an aircraft secretly bringing in supplies for the Maquis, which would convey them back to England. Ray Perry picks up their story:

> After Frank and Eric were dropped off, our guide took me on the Metro to the suburb in which my house was situated. I had one nerve-racking experience when we were crammed in a carriage on the Metro and a German soldier, speaking in French, asked what the time was. Having been warned not to speak to anyone, I thought quickly enough to show my left wrist, on which there was no watch. Much to my relief, he immediately turned to someone else and asked them the time.
>
> I was duly picked up in the car on 7 August which, besides containing Frank and Eric, also had three Americans, two of them being on the floor in the back. As it was then only early afternoon, our Underground friend said he would take us to see some of the sights of Paris, so we drove around the Arc de Triomphe and passed the Eiffel Tower before driving through a narrow archway off a street into a courtyard where we stopped. The driver immediately jumped out, pulled a revolver from his pocket, and told us this was Gestapo headquarters and we were now prisoners of the Germans. We didn't want to believe it as we got out of the car, but knew by the number of armed Germans that our dreams of being back in England that night had suddenly turned into a nightmare.

Australian Warrant Officer Tom Malcolm from Hawthorn in Victoria was the bomb aimer on Lancaster LM 571 (JO.E) which had taken to the skies on 24 June 1944 as part of a 112-aircraft attack on the Prouville Road junction, a heavily-defended V-1 missile site some five kilometres to the north-west of Bernaville in the Pas-de-Calais area of northern France. The aircraft, from No. 463 (RAAF) Squadron, was flown by the affable Pilot Officer Tony Martin, a former gold refiner from Mount Lawley in Western Australia.

Moments after dropping their bombs on the target area, their aircraft was set upon by swarms of enemy fighters. The Lancaster burst into flames, and a few moments later exploded. By incredible good fortune Tom Malcolm was already wearing his parachute and was blown clear of the aircraft; the rest of his crew were killed in the explosion. Despite the shock of being thrust into the night sky amidst a massive fireball, he had enough sense to pull the ripcord as he headed towards the ground. After landing he set off, hoping to meet some friendly and sympathetic French people who could put him in touch with local members of the Resistance.

Eventually he made his way into the large town of Beauvais, located some 70 kilometres to the north-west of Paris. In his travels he had passed through the area known as Flanders Field, where, in that summer of 1944, the fields were blanketed with sweeping beds of the famous red poppies. Beneath the flowers and green grass lay the muddy earth in which Australian and New Zealand and other Allied troops had fought for so long and so desperately nearly 30 years before. At almost every road junction, he passed small graveyard plots filled with white crosses bearing the names of French or Allied servicemen, each generally surmounted by a simple shrine above the well-tended graves. The sight of so many shattered houses along the way served as a further grim reminder of the war.

Once in Beauvais, Malcolm drifted into an ancient cathedral, where he decided to gamble on asking for help from a pleasant-looking woman sitting passively in a wooden pew near the altar.

At first she was startled when he addressed her in English; although they were the only occupants of the church, she was decidedly uneasy. However, she indicated that he should stay where he was while she went to seek the assistance of some friends.

Left alone to ponder his fate, Tom actually dozed off, waking with a start when the woman returned accompanied by a tall Frenchman. The man began firing questions in broken English, which Tom answered, apparently to his satisfaction, as he then identified himself as the captain of the local Maquis. He took Tom to a nearby house where he was shown to a cellar filled with rack upon rack of dusty bottles of champagne. The Frenchman swept his hand around. 'Console yourself when the bombers come,' he said, with a twinkle in his eye. 'And if they don't come, console yourself anyway!' With that, he was gone. His words were quite prophetic. The bombers did come not long after, and explosions shook the cellar floor as the nearby railway yards were pounded. The Australian needed no further urging and, uncorking a bottle, he consoled himself. As Tom Malcolm explained, his path to hopeful freedom was soon organised.

> The captain arranged transport to Paris in a furniture van and, after a few miles, the largest of my fellow passengers enquired if I was English. I said 'Yes' and waited. He told me that the others had decided I was, and as we were to be stopped just outside Paris by the Germans, for the purpose of checking identification cards, it would be advisable if I concealed myself. I followed his suggestion and under cover of a few boxes and coats managed to pass through the roadblock. My large benefactor turned out to be no less than Monsieur [Robert] Thieblemont, chief of the Beauvais gaol. He had held a similar position in the Paris gaol, but didn't suit the Germans.

> I went with him to his house, still within the walls of this Paris gaol, met his wife and daughter, received more French greetings, and spent my first night in Paris in gaol!
>
> Monsieur Thieblemont had contacted my Underground address and after a stroll round Paris in the morning, I met the man who was finally to place me with the 'Organisation'. This was Monsieur [Andre] Girand, a quiet little grey-headed man who spoke perfect English and soon escorted me across Paris to his home. From there I moved to several different apartments in Paris, always under the noses of the Germans. The ordinary, happy young people who watched and risked their lives for us were known as the 'Pericles' Resistance group.

On 19 July 1944, Tom Malcolm was transferred once again, to the house of a portly policeman named Georges Prevot, where three downed airmen were already hiding. They were crewmembers Pilot Officer Michael Guilfoyle and Sergeant Doug Jordin of 12 Squadron, RAF, and Staff Sergeant Arthur Pelletier of the 8th Army Air Corps. It was at this apartment that Tom and the others first met the young man calling himself Captain Jacques, who told them he was with the British Secret Service.

Having questioned all of the airmen to his satisfaction, Captain Jacques informed them they would be driven to the south of France by truck. Elated with their apparent good fortune and impending freedom, Tom and the others started talking eagerly about what they would do once they reached England.

A short time later Jacques returned and told the waiting airmen that a truck had been organised and would be waiting at a fixed rendezvous. The four men followed Jacques down the street, walking briskly behind him along the windswept footpaths bordering the Seine. All around him, Tom could see historic buildings and colourful shop facades, and he revelled in the feelings of excitement and wonderment at the passing pageant of wartime Paris. Along the banks of the mighty river he saw some plane trees with their white bark scarred (or perhaps glorified) with the Cross of Lorraine. When they arrived at their rendezvous point, Jacques motioned his charges into the back of the waiting truck, closed them in and then climbed into the driver's cab with a large, fair-haired man wearing an ancient leather jacket. Inside the rear of the truck were another thirteen men – all of them airmen on the run.

As the truck moved out into the light traffic, the men in the back settled down in anticipation of a long, uncomfortable ride. A couple of them had expressed some uneasiness at the news that they would be driven to southern France. They had been warned back in England not to accept rides in petrol-driven vehicles as gasoline was strictly rationed, although German collaborators were known to have a ready supply. The argument was dismissed in light of their confidence in 'Captain Jacques'.

A few minutes later, the truck pulled up and the motor was switched off. The men had no idea what was happening until the two doors at the rear of the truck were suddenly thrown open, revealing a pair of Germans soldiers armed with machine-guns, ready to fire at the first sign of trouble. It was a crushing blow for Tom Malcolm and his dismayed companions.

> Our truck was in an enclosed courtyard, strangely enough called the Court of Sausages, and most of the available artillery was trained on us. Our friend Captain Jacques had cleverly passed us

on to the Germans. Thus ended my chance of escape at that time, and the joys of life under the Nazi heel were to be mine for a few months.

It becomes necessary at this point to tell a little of the history and deeds of the so-called 'Captain Jacques'. This man, responsible for the capture of dozens of fugitive airmen and the imprisonment, torture and even execution of unsuspecting Resistance workers, was in fact a double agent in the employ of the Germans.

Jean-Jacques Desoubrie, to give him his real name, was the rotten apple situated at the end of a long line of brave but oblivious patriots. A devoted admirer of Adolf Hitler, Desoubrie had been operating successfully as a German agent for some months under the aliases of Jean Masson and Pierre Boulain. 'Captain Jacques', as he preferred to be known, was the person most responsible for the capture of the majority of the 168 airmen who later ended up in Buchenwald.

Born on 22 October 1922 in Luinge, Belgium, Desoubrie was the illegitimate son of a Belgian doctor. Never having a proper home, and abandoned by his mother at an early age, he became a drifter and later took up a trade as an electrician. When war broke out, the Belgian teenager eagerly swallowed the Nazi propaganda, readily adopting their doctrines. Fluent in English, he foresaw a worthwhile occupation as a collaborator for his new masters, and soon became a key figure in the French Underground, passing valuable information back to the Gestapo. In April 1943, believed to be above suspicion, he was recruited as a guide for the Comet escape line, on the Brussels to Paris section. Little did the French Underground workers realise that Desoubrie, who received large sums of money from the organisers of the Comet Line to assist escaped prisoners of war and evading airmen, belonged to an elite Gestapo team headed by the infamous Prosper Desitter.

Desitter and his mistress Florentine Dings worked with Masson/Boulain/Desoubrie to destroy the Comet Line in Paris during 1943–44, and successfully penetrated other Allied escape lines. Desitter would inject members of the German Abwehr (Military Intelligence) into the Underground system, disguising them as airmen on the run, and was responsible for sending an untold number of evaders and members of the Resistance into Fresnes prison in Paris, and often to their death in one of Hitler's concentration camps. At war's end, Desitter and Dings were both sentenced to death by firing squad for their traitorous actions. It was reported that the night before he was executed, Desitter was heard howling in terror in his cell.

Jacques Desoubrie's favourite ruse in gaining confidence with unsuspecting Resistance workers was to pass himself off as a British agent, and he was reported to have conspired in many dozens of betrayals. He was responsible for the arrest of around fifty French and Belgian Resistance workers, almost all of whom were executed.

A short, stocky man with piercing grey eyes set behind a pair of moderately thick-lensed spectacles, Desoubrie dressed quite smartly, and his light brown hair was always immaculately combed. An easy smile revealed bright gold fillings in his front teeth. Many an evader was taken in by his excellent English, oily charms and smooth reassurances. His assistant or secretary – but also believed to be his mistress – was the waspish Colette Orsini, simply introduced to the Allied airmen as Madame Orsini. Married to the manager of the Buffet Hotel at Chartres station, she was thin and short, had a sallow complexion and copper-coloured hair, and wore dark-framed glasses. During a heated argument following the fall of Paris, Desoubrie shot

Orsini so she could not tell of his traitorous activities. Unfortunately for him, she did not die, and following some intense questioning by Allied interrogators, Orsini was imprisoned at Fresnes, charged with sedition. In May 1946 she was brought to trial in Paris but was eventually acquitted. It is believed this travesty of justice came about because the prosecution's principal witnesses failed to attend the trial. But that was all in the future.

Once Desoubrie had penetrated the Comet Line and established himself with many of the Resistance workers, more and more British and Allied airmen were taken in by his smooth charms. He laid his intricate web with ease, and his operation was in fact remarkably easy. The airmen were placed in convenient apartments or hotel rooms where they were promised rapid despatch to Spain or England. The people who gave them this information were genuine members of the Resistance living in fear of discovery and execution, so their anxiety and precautions were very real.

The man called Captain Jacques would then interview the evaders and, before their suspicions were aroused, try to learn as much as he could of their activities, their background, and the names of those who had helped them. He would then send cars or small buses to the hideouts and the generally trusting airmen would clamber in, eager to be on their way. It seldom crossed their minds that they had been sold out to the Germans, who simply gathered in the victims as they were delivered directly into their hands in the forecourt of Gestapo headquarters in the Avenue Foch.

Other evaders fell prey to similarly unscrupulous collaborators who had infiltrated the Resistance. These traitors were everywhere, and through the French Milice – a paramilitary force of Fascist collaborators – the Gestapo would lull their aircrew victims into a false sense of fraternity and security. In many cases the airmen became incautious and talkative. A favourite ploy of the Milice was to have one of their men burst into the room where an unsuspecting airman was undergoing an apparently harmless interview. The Frenchman, one hand bandaged and ostensibly wounded, would blurt out that there had been an ambush and one of the so-called airmen had to be a planted German traitor. The situation was both dramatic and unnerving in its presentation. Once the distraught man had been calmed down and ushered out, the concerned interrogator would point out that the integrity of the airman before him was easily resolved. Just a few answers to some 'harmless' questions that no German could possibly know, and this would quickly establish and confirm his bona fides. Nothing of a military nature, or course, just everyday things such as the name of the pub favoured by the lads in his squadron, their favourite beer, the name of the publican, and what one would see when looking south from the bar. Harmless stuff indeed, but once such information was passed on to the German Intelligence officers at the Dulag Luft interrogation centre at Oberursel, it could have a demoralising effect when casually mentioned to a newly captured airmen from that squadron. The airmen asked to supply such 'trivial' information were generally more than willing to talk in order to demonstrate their innocence in the matter of the purported 'ambush'.

Jacques Desoubrie served his masters particularly well, but his traitorous actions were finally uncovered. Suspicions were aroused when scores of evading and escaped airmen entrusted to his care mysteriously vanished from the normally secure Comet Line. Following the war, 'Captain Jacques' was put on trial in Lille under his real name. He was found guilty of collaboration and treason and executed on 20 December 1949 in Fort Montrouge in Arcueil, near Paris. It was reported that as he was lined up before the firing squad, his last defiant words were 'Heil Hitler!' But that was in the future.

Remarkably, it was only through research carried out by Frenchman Franck Signorile as late as 2017, the information came to light that there was not just one person using the alias of either Captain Jacques or Captain Jack, but two. According to Signorile, Guy de Marcheret – also known as the Count of Marcheret and Glebe d'Eu – was posing as a British Intelligence Officer, but was in fact a member of the Nazi-run counter-evasion service in Paris who had successfully managed to infiltrate and gain the trust of the French patriots operating the Comet Line. 'This man claimed to be working for the chief organiser of the escape line to Spain,' as Lamason, who fell into Captain Jack's clutches, later recalled. 'He had a detailed story of how the journey would be accomplished, and claimed to have made the journey seven times.'

Under the guise of Captain Jacques (or sometimes Jack), Marcheret had managed to infiltrate the Comet Line, and was covertly operating out of the Parisian home of Georges Prevot, Prevot's sister Genevieve and brother-in-law Jean Rocher, all of whom had been completely taken in by Marcheret. Both Prevot and Rocher were policemen, while Genevieve worked as a bank cashier. They shared a top floor apartment located at 20 Boulevard de Sébastopol. They had been hiding refugees and evaders as well as providing false ID cards for the Resistance. Prevot was able to do the forgery work as he did similar official work for the police. At some stage, deep undercover work by Abwehr and SS counter-intelligence agents discovered the operations taking place at the apartment and Marcheret was able to make himself known to

Prevot and Rocher and work his way into their trust. Once this had been established, he was able to move freely in the Line and secretly inform his superiors of their activities.

Guy de Marcheret was born under the name of Gleb Lizov in Moscow in 1914 to a French father and Russian mother. He grew up in Shanghai, China, before his family moved to France in the 1930s. Becoming proficient in foreign languages, he was eventually fluent in Italian, German, French and English. In 1940 he joined an Army division led by the young French General Jean de Lattre, but was captured by the Germans and thrown into prison. He was able to secure his release in June 1940 and made his way up to Paris where, for a time, he accumulated a small fortune dealing in the black market. An avid social climber using several different names, he had soon made important contacts in the Nazi hierarchy and offered his linguistic skills to the German Service of Information (SRA), an intelligence service connected to the Abwehr (German military intelligence) and the Gestapo.

The SRA quickly realised Marcheret's potential as a spy and was able to use him to devastating effect once he had managed to worm his way into the French Resistance, presenting himself as an Oxford-educated Englishman who maintained strong connections within the British Secret Service. Throughout the course of Germany's occupation of France, he became increasingly expert in setting traps for unsuspecting Resistance workers and evading Allied service personnel. Operating under the code name 'Captain Jack', he was ultimately responsible for betraying hundreds of French patriots and Allied airmen by deluding them with his smooth promises and skilfully guiding them into the hands of his German superiors, with often brutal consequences.

When the war ended, Marcheret fled to Denmark where he was captured and handed over to the French police on 25 October 1945. Four years later, he was finally brought before the Paris Court of Justice where he was convicted of treason and multiple cases resulting in the death of countless victims of his treachery. On the morning of 20 April 1949, just like Jacques Desoubrie, Guy de Marcheret would be executed by firing squad at Fort Montrouge.

Although many of the airmen in Paris were similarly duped into giving the names and addresses of those who had aided them in France, Belgium and Holland, it was fortunate that they gave this information to Marcheret and other traitors and their henchmen after D-Day. With the whole of Paris in turmoil, the Germans had enough on their plates without worrying about rounding up hundreds of relatively harmless villagers across Europe. This was especially true after the attempted assassination of Adolf Hitler on 20 July, when members of the Gestapo were arrested and dumped into an already overflowing Fresnes prison. The bloodbath that followed undoubtedly saved many of the airmen from the brutal interrogations conducted in the Avenue Foch. Several airmen and Resistance workers still fared badly at the hands of the Gestapo, but given the general confusion following the invasion at Normandy and the bungled assassination, and in the face of an anticipated assault on Paris, it is probable that many might otherwise have been tortured to death.

There are many stories and reports from the airmen who were rounded up and despatched to Buchenwald, and most of them demonstrate the extent to which the Gestapo had infiltrated the French Underground. Flight Sergeant Les Whellum from South Australia is one who can attest to the scale of the deception.

Whellum was a wireless operator with No. 102 (Ceylon) Squadron RAF, operating Halifax III bombers out of Pocklington, Yorkshire. On the evening of 28 June 1944, under the command of RAAF Pilot Officer George Mulvaney, they were detailed to bomb railway yards in Blainville, France, as part of a 230-strong bomber force sent to attack railway installations at both Blainville and Metz. Flying just west of Beauvais, as Whellum later recalled:

> The aircraft was attacked by a night fighter from under and raked us across the wing and the engineer's compartment. The engineer was killed and the aircraft set on fire. The Captain ordered abandon aircraft and then the intercom went dead. All the crew baled out except the engineer, height about 17,000 feet. The aircraft was turning in a large circle and losing height. The aircraft was on fire in the engineer's compartment and also under the wing. The aircraft crashed about 10 miles from Beauvais.

Those killed were the Flight Engineer, Sergeant Dennis Smith, RAF, and Air Bomber Flight Sergeant James Duell from Semaphore, South Australia (who drowned in a lake after becoming tangled in his parachute), while four crewmembers managed to parachute to safety and successfully evade capture. After a time, Whellum was able to locate some members of the French Resistance and soon felt he was also on his way back to England.

> I had been at a woodcutter's house for a few days when word reached me that I was to be moved on quite hurriedly. I was rather disappointed, as arrangements had been made for me to meet up with my skipper, who was hiding up in the village of Le Becquet

Saint-Paul, 14 kilometres away towards Beauvais. But questions had been asked around the village recently, and it was generally feared that a collaborator was trying to locate our whereabouts.

A battered truck called at the house the following day, containing two other Allied airmen being evacuated from the area. The truck headed southwards, making for the Gisors area, from where we were told we would ultimately join an escape route through Paris. Along the way we encountered two German roadblocks, but these did not present any undue problem. We were all dressed as French peasants, and we simply got out of the truck and ambled past the roadblock as the truck proceeded and was searched. The Germans were most methodical in searching any vehicles that reached the roadblocks, but did not worry about anyone walking through. Once out of sight of the Germans we simply jumped back in the truck. It was strangely exhilarating to stroll so casually by our enemy who did not give us a second look.

Sadly, my bid for freedom came to an end at Georges Prevot's apartment in the Rue de Sébastopol at the hands of Captain Jacques. The three of us joined several other British and Allied airmen at the flat, from which we were eventually taken in pairs, ostensibly to a new address, but in reality to Gestapo headquarters by Jacques' secretary.

A random group of MI9 reports prepared post-war by many of the Buchenwald airmen further reveal the extent of corruption in the escape line at that time.

Flight Sergeant Edward Phelps, 207 Squadron, RAF:

I was taken by car to a flat somewhere in the outskirts of Paris where I stayed for two days with three men and a girl. A well-dressed man tried to pump me for information by asking me to fill out a spurious Red Cross form. On the Thursday, he said I was going to be driven to the Spanish border. I got in a car, but was driven straight to Gestapo headquarters.

Flying Officer S. A. (Splinter Adolph) Spierenburg, 582 Squadron, RAF:
I was staying in a house when I was introduced to a man called Jacques who moved me to another home. Later I was taken to the Hotel Étoile and stayed there for three or four days. On 14 July another man came to the hotel and told me to get ready to go to Lyons. We went out to the car and I realised by looking at the driver that I was in the hands of the Gestapo. I was taken to the Palais de Sécurité, and then to Fresnes.

Flying Officer Stuart Baxter, 514 Squadron, RAF:
A Monsieur Jacques came to the flat and told the three of us [all from the same crew] that he was English and a member of the Secret Service. He interrogated us as to our true identities and said he would get us to Spain. He told us he would send his secretary to collect us. At 1500 hours a woman arrived and took us by car to Gestapo headquarters.

Flight Sergeant Terry Gould, 10 Squadron, RAF:
At the end of our six weeks' stay in Saint-André I was moved in the company of three Americans. We were moved by car to Paris where we were all driven to a private home. Here we found about 20 Allied personnel and all of us were told that we should be moved in the direction of Spain the next day. We were all fed that night. The next afternoon we were taken out, being told that we were to meet

our transport at six o'clock. At six we met this transport, which collected 33 of us altogether. To our disbelief, we were all driven straight around to Gestapo headquarters.

Flying Officer Douglas Percy, 630 Squadron, RAF:

I stayed in the house of a man who kept the local garage in the village of La Villeneuve-en-Chevrie. I met three American airmen at the house. On 28 July our host handed us over to a guide who took us by car to Paris, where we were taken to a house. There we met Squadron Leader Lamason and his navigator, who told us they were leaving that day and everything seemed all right. When it came our turn to be taken out of Paris we were stopped, asked for our identity papers, and taken to Fresnes prison.

First Lieutenant James Hastin, 374 Fighter Squadron, USAAF:

American Air Force Sergeant George Scott and I were moved to the Post Office in a nearby town where some people said that we would be flown out. There was a lot of confusion about where the plane was going to pick us up. We should have smelt a rat here because we were taken by car to the town together with two English chaps at a time when the only people driving cars were the Germans. We were then taken to Paris, to meet with some other people, and to wait for news of our plane. After a meal, we were taken to the Piccadilly Hotel, where we stayed for three days. While we were there, a man who spoke excellent English came and asked us to complete Red Cross forms. On these forms were a lot of trivial questions, such as marital status, name of mother-in-law, do you own a dog, and so forth. But there were also questions relating to the type of aircraft you had flown, where your group was stationed, the missions you were on when shot down, and others. It was a standard type of Red Cross form that the Germans used, and which we had been briefed on back in England.

On 28 June a French-Italian chap came and told us to be ready to go in five minutes. He was going to take us to Orleans, as our plane had been cancelled. He gave us papers saying we were Belgian workers. Sergeant Scott, plus one of the RAF airmen and I got into the car and we drove off in the direction of Orleans. However, we were stopped at a roadblock and asked for our papers. A couple of Germans got into the car and proceeded to search us. One of them found my dog-tags, and that was it for us. We had been sold out.

Flight Lieutenant Peter Taylor, 158 Squadron, RAF:
The man who said he was working for the British Intelligence was called Robert Moulet. He fetched me from the chateau on about the 27 April 1944 and took me to a village called Breteuil, leaving me in a café owned by a Monsieur [Andre] Duboille. Here I met two other RAF types named Sergeant Dowdeswell of the same squadron as myself, and Sergeant Hegarty of Snaith RAF station. We stayed here for about a fortnight. Moulet then fetched me and took me to a small village called Lachaussée-du-Bois-d'Écu, where he left me at the house of a family called Anty. I stayed here for about two months. By this time our invasion had started and they said they had instructions not to try and get people away, but to wait until the British overran the place. On 28 July a representative of Moulet came and asked me if I would like to fly to England. I naturally jumped at the chance and we set off for Moulet's place in the nearby village called Caply. On the way we picked up two American airmen who appeared to be waiting; they were Lieutenant Hunter and Sergeant Edge.

> After a short journey, Moulet stopped and a little later a car drove up with two civilians in it who told us they were going to take us to the plane. All three of us boarded the car which finally struck a main road and set off towards Beauvais. We had not gone far before I saw another car parked at the side of the road with two men tinkering with the engine. They signalled us to stop, and when we did so we were surrounded by armed Germans, and that was that!

A little clarification is needed here, as the author must emphasise that both Robert Moulet and his assistant (Guy Brillé) were actually genuine and active members of the French Resistance, but they were sadly taken in by German collaborators who arranged to collect these and other airmen from the unsuspecting Moulet. Then, instead of organising the airmen's onward journey to possible freedom, the collaborators promptly turned them over to the Germans. As with previous betrayals, the two men who were the chief instigators of this traitorous activity were André Cauchemez and Paul Villette. Post-war they were both arrested, charged with treason and sentenced to death. Both sentences were later commuted to 'hard labour in perpetuity' and still later to just 20 years' imprisonment.

3

FRESNES PRISON

The vast and forbidding Fresnes prison, situated nearly 20 kilometres south of Paris and close to the present-day site of Orly Airport, was built in the late 1890s. When completed, it was made up of three massive blocks or divisions, each containing five storeys of cells, and was the largest criminal penitentiary in the country. But as German troops swept into Paris in June 1940, the SS replaced the incumbent police guards with their own men, and many of the cells were soon filled with political prisoners, foreign agents, and others loosely labelled as undesirables and enemies of the Reich.

Entrance to the prison was gained by driving through a set of heavy gates off the main road to Paris, then down a cobbled private road straddled by magnificent poplars until reaching twin statues of the Sisters of Mercy, which were positioned either side of a huge pair of iron gates. However, many of the men and women brought to Fresnes prison were only too aware that the quality of mercy had very little place in the SS doctrine, unless it was the swift mercy of a bullet.

The majority of prisoners held in Fresnes were French citizens, although some were from the occupied Channel Islands, gaoled for sedition and non-cooperation. Several British subjects, a small number of them captured secret agents, were also held in the stark cells. Among the agents imprisoned there were Odette Samson, who was held in solitary cell 108 in the 3rd Division, and later cell 337; Peter Churchill in cell 220 in the 2nd Division; and Wing Commander Forest Frederick Yeo-Thomas in cell 293, also in the 2nd Division.

Division One was for male prisoners of the SS and the Wehrmacht, usually German deserters. The second was also for males – Frenchmen, political prisoners, agents, saboteurs and other categories. Division Three, in which the airmen were held, was a mixed block holding both men and women.

The cells, measuring four by two-and-a-half metres, had stone walls partially covered by crumbling plaster, into which were scratched dozens of messages proclaiming both hope and despair. A large, hinged, frosted-glass window, through which thick bars could be seen, was set high in the wall opposite the steel door. These windows were usually left ajar so the occupants could hear other prisoners shouting out messages and news to prisoners in other cells. A lavatory was situated beside the door, as well as a tap and a small enamel basin secured to the wall. There was also a wooden shelf and pegs to hang clothing. A single bed frame lay folded against a wall. When this was lowered, a shapeless palliasse served as a mattress.

The prisoners were regularly inspected through a small oblong slit and spy hole set into each door. The majority of cells had no lighting, and prisoners were checked by guards shining a torch through the inspection slit. The lights in those cells that had them were kept on all night.

Over several weeks, the captured airmen were delivered to Fresnes prison in handcuffs, transported in company with French prisoners, and sometimes one or two fellow aircrew. They were not to know for some time the actual number of airmen sent to Fresnes, nor the enormity of the deception that resulted in so many being picked up through the actions of double agents and traitors such as Jacques Desoubrie.

On arrival they were taken into the nearest building, where their handcuffs were removed. They were counted as they entered, and found themselves in a long, broad corridor where the walls rose to an arched ceiling four storeys above their heads. Each floor was indicated by a narrow steel balcony, secured to the concrete walls by stays and bolts. These were connected vertically by steel ladders, and horizontally by slightly arched walkways which spanned the chasm between balconies at each level.

Next the men were shepherded into a large interior room containing a number of German clerical staff seated behind broad desks. One at a time they were made to strip naked and thoroughly searched. The guards confiscated their belts, ties, shoes, matches and the contents of their pockets. It was here that most of the men had the dog tags ripped from their necks by guards shouting abuse and calling them 'Terrorflieger' (terror flyers). Any signs of disobedience or defiance would earn a savage blow to the head, or a swift kick to the shins with a heavy jackboot. Anyone wearing wedding or other rings and jewellery were forced to remove these and hand them over, hating the fact that this would probably be the last time they would see them. They were then locked into one of a series of small wooden cubicles for an indeterminate time, until it was their turn to be questioned.

Flying Officer Kevin Light, DFM, was kept in one of the cubicles throughout the day following his arrival. He filled in some of that time carving his name and service number into the wall with a tiny knife he had managed to conceal under his armpit. At a time when Bomber Command crews could take their discharge after 20 operations, he had decided to continue beyond that point and had flown an extraordinary 53 operational sorties before being shot down. As he carved his name into the wooden wall, he had time to reflect on the events which had brought him to this place.

Educated at Marist Brothers College in Randwick, New South Wales, Kevin Light enlisted in the RAAF on 19 August 1940 and received his initial training at Bradfield Park before attending Empire Flight Training School in Edmonton, Canada. Arriving in England in March 1941, he became a Navigation Officer with the RAF's 142 Squadron, then operating on Wellington bombers.

One tragic night, during a training exercise at Binbrook field, Lincolnshire, in misty rain and poor visibility, he was involved in a horrific crash. The crew's usual skipper, the well-liked Billy Brill, was operating as second dickie to another pilot who was experiencing great difficulty in landing a near-new bomber on the repaired strip. At his third attempt, the man came in too high and thumped it down halfway along the strip. The Wellington raced towards a field at the end of the runway, and as the pilot desperately hauled the lumbering bomber into the sky once again, it became evident they would hit a cluster of trees. The aircraft tore a path through the topmost branches, gained some altitude, and then began to plunge uncontrollably to starboard. Kevin Light braced himself for impact as best he could before they hit the ground.

The doomed aircraft rolled beyond the vertical and slammed into the field, tearing in two and erupting into flames on impact. He blacked out momentarily, and when he came to, his hair and jacket were smouldering, and the air around him was filled with noise, thick smoke and fire. Somehow he fought his way out of the twisted fuselage, slapping at his hair and jacket as he jumped clear, then collapsing in total shock. A young soldier, quickly on the scene, hauled him to safety away from the blazing wreckage and he was soon receiving treatment for his burns, which were fortunately not serious. Meanwhile the rest of the crew had been killed in the crash or the subsequent fire.

Light could have opted to resign from the air force but decided to stay on, and entered an air gunnery course. Having served on postings with several operational units, including No. 460 (RAAF) Squadron, he was eventually assigned to the famed No. 9 Squadron, then based at RAF Bardney, Lincolnshire. Along the way he picked up a well-deserved Distinguished Flying Medal and a new bride – his English sweetheart Brenda, an attractive WAAF from Derbyshire. They had been married for only five weeks when he and his Lancaster crew, under Flying Officer Jim Smith, took off on Light's fifty-third and final sortie over enemy territory.

It was the evening of 18 April 1944 and their target was the railway marshalling yards at Juvisy, south of Paris. Flying too far south of the area, Smith made a late run over the target well after the other aircraft (including some from the now-legendary 617 'Dambusters' Squadron) had dropped their bombs and headed for home. They managed to release their bomb load from 7,000 feet, but moments later a devastating explosion shook the Lancaster, which had been hit by anti-aircraft fire. Jim Smith called up all the crew on the intercom and received acknowledgements from everyone apart from rear gunner Dudley Bates. Two of their inboard engines were on fire, and the aircraft was filling with dense smoke. Despite engineer Ron Wilson's best efforts, he could not feather the engines and extinguish the flames. Now rapidly losing height, Smith ordered the crew to don their parachutes and bale out just before the intercom became unserviceable. A third engine then erupted into flames. Smith held the aircraft as steady as possible for around three minutes before assuming everyone had safely evacuated and baled out himself at 3,000 feet as the aircraft began to curve towards the ground. The stricken Lancaster crashed onto the railway line just outside the village of Longjumeau, south of Paris.

Kevin Light had managed to hurl himself out of the blazing aircraft and landed safely by parachute. He would later learn that only his pilot Smith and English bomb aimer Charles Martin had managed to leave the crippled aircraft. Both would evade capture and make it back to England. The remaining four crewmembers, rear gunner Dudley Bates, wireless/air gunner Frank Heath, navigator Dennis Moss and flight engineer Ronald Wilson had failed to leave the aircraft and were killed. All four would later be interred at Clichy Northern Cemetery, Hauts-de-Seine. Fortunately for Kevin Light, some local help would soon offer to shelter him from German search parties.

His story of evasion across France over the next few weeks is similar to that of many of the other Buchenwald airmen. After landing, he made his way to the village of Longjumeau (Essonne), where he asked for help and was taken into the house of the mayor, Jean Rodier. He stayed with this family for eighteen days before heading south, teaming up along the way with an American evader. Several weeks later, they fell in with a group that identified themselves as Resistance workers. The two men were taken into Paris and lodged at the Picardy Hotel, but to their misfortune they had fallen into the clutches of Jacques Desoubrie, who questioned the airmen and then, after assuring them they were on their way back to England, delivered them into the hands of the Gestapo.

Soon after Kevin Light had finished carving his name into the wall of the cubicle at Fresnes, he was taken out and searched once again, then marched across to one of the German clerks. Like many of the others, he was quite surprised when he was simply asked to supply his name, rank and service number – nothing else – and before he knew it his clothes, but not his other possessions, were returned to him, before he was escorted out of the room again and placed in a cell.

Every downed airman entering Fresnes prison had a truly dramatic story to tell. When Flight Sergeant Mervyn Fairclough was brought to Fresnes some weeks later, he found himself occupying the same cramped cubicle as Kevin Light to await questioning. Mervyn, from Moora in Western Australia, had been on the run since April, and like so many of the airmen, he had fallen into the hands of the Gestapo through the activities of a traitor.

A rear gunner with 51 Squadron RAF based at Snaith in South Yorkshire, Fairclough was aboard Halifax III LV880 on the evening of 10 April 1944, as part of a massive bombing raid on rail marshalling yards at Tergnier in northern France. Having dropped their bombs over the target area, they were subjected to a head-on attack over Montdidier by Luftwaffe fighter ace Gerhard Friedrich in a Messerschmitt Bf 110. Raked by 20 mm cannon fire, the Halifax's port wing erupted into flames. Pilot Officer Mervyn Hall attempted to extinguish the flames by placing the aircraft into a steep dive, but this would prove unsuccessful. Shortly after, he ordered the crew to don their parachutes and bale out. Moments later the bomber was torn apart in a massive explosion. 'I went forward to see if the abandon order had been given as I couldn't make contact,' Fairclough later recalled. 'I was thrown to the floor and couldn't get up, but [was] finally blown out when the aircraft exploded.'

Only three of the crew had managed to evacuate the aircraft and all landed safely a few miles north of Montdidier, although Mervyn Fairclough ended up stuck in a tree. Fortunately, a local Frenchman, Baud Fernand, had seen the airman's parachute become entangled in the tree's branches and helped to extricate him before a German patrol could reach the area. Fairclough was soon reunited with his RAF mid-upper gunner Bill Hegarty. They would later learn that four of the crew had been killed in the explosion and subsequent crash. Those who died were Pilot Officer Mervyn Hall (RAAF), flight engineer Sergeant Gordon Peck (RAF), air bomber Flying Officer Charles Hartley (RCAF) and wireless operator/air gunner Warrant Officer John Osborn (RAAF). Their bodies would be interred at the nearby Davenecourt Communal Cemetery.

Meanwhile, RAAF Navigator Fred Kirkwood had landed in a field, hidden his parachute and headed off in a south-easterly direction, hoping to reach Spain. He would remain on the run until 20 August, when he managed to make contact with A Troop, connected to the US Third Cavalry.

Mervyn Fairclough and Bill Hegarty now found themselves in friendly French hands and were sheltered in a number of locations as attempts were being made to get them back to England. At one stage they were hidden by some sympathetic French families in the village of Breteuil for more than ten weeks, by which time they had been joined by more than a dozen airmen under the care and watch of a local Resistance group. Much to their disgust, they were sold out to the Germans by a traitor working in the local Underground, and were captured on a road near Beauvais. Both would end up in Buchenwald. After the war, Fairclough received a letter from one of his French helpers informing him that the traitor had been 'dealt with'.

On arrival at Fresnes, Fairclough was astonished to see Kevin Light's name scratched on the wall of the wooden cubicle, as the two men had trained together back in Australia. The familiar name gave him a welcome uplift of spirits. Afterwards, when searched, he was wearing a gold ring on his right hand, engraved with his name and that of his wife Elaine. He protested loudly when a guard began to wrench it from his finger, and for his trouble received a stinging blow to the face. The guard slipped the ring into his pocket, then spat on the airman and hurled abuse. He grabbed Fairclough's arm and sent him on his way with a savage kick to the back of his legs.

Eric Johnston was carrying his small, furry koala mascot – a good luck charm he had risked his life retrieving from the cockpit of their blazing Halifax before baling out. At Fresnes, a guard seized the little mascot, dropped it on the floor and deliberately crushed it beneath his heavy jackboot. Eric gritted his teeth and glared at the man, but wisely held his tongue. His silent insolence was still enough to earn him a sharp belt across the mouth.

Jim Gwilliam found himself locked in a cell with an Englishman sporting an angry-looking stye on his left eye. Once they got around to talking, his companion revealed that he had been picked up in a brothel, where he had earlier been placed by the Underground.

He told how he had taken advantage of a little carnal delight by peeping through keyholes as the girls cavorted with their clients. Jim prudently refrained from asking the fellow if the stye was a form of penance for his voyeuristic activities.

Very few of the airmen who entered Fresnes escaped brutal physical beatings and the constant threats of death. The living conditions were totally degrading, while the food was both appalling and irregular. The tiny cells were overcrowded, there were no facilities for exercise, no contact with the outside world, and the men were forced to wear the same clothing throughout their imprisonment. Fleas, lice and other bugs thriving on filth were a constant source of aggravation. Like the other prisoners, the airmen were forced to clean their cells daily.

There was a much-feared torture chamber in the basement, where the men were sometimes taken to be beaten and questioned, then left totally naked in a cold, dark cell for days and even weeks. More than this, however, the inmates feared the trip up to Paris and the notorious Gestapo headquarters. Prisoners called out for interrogation were placed in a long police vehicle and transported under escort to the Avenue Foch. These trucks had small, windowless, cage-like compartments on either side of a central corridor. Prisoners were locked into these cramped cells where a tiny grille provided the sole means of light and comfort. An armed guard sat on a folding seat below the wire-covered rear window and kept close watch on the cell doors.

Gestapo headquarters was located at Nos. 82 and 84 on the Avenue Foch. An elegant building with ornate iron gates, it had once been a private residence – a stately home on one of the most picturesque tree-lined avenues in Paris, which runs from the Arc de

Triomphe to the greenness of the Bois de Boulogne. The illusion of nobility soon vanished as one entered this building, for the principal activities at No. 84 were interrogation and torture.

Members of both sexes were at the complete mercy of the Gestapo torturers. Those conducting the interrogations wore civilian clothing and performed their tasks methodically, stopping only when they had learned enough, or had caused the death of their victim. If the primary interrogation was considered unsatisfactory, further beatings, whippings, burning and submersion in icy water followed. Fingernails and toenails were torn from their sockets using pliers. The genital region was a particular favourite for the attention of the interrogators, and often the mere threat of severe and even permanent damage brought the desired response from the victims.

Second Lieutenant Jim Hastin, USAAF, had been picked up after hiding out in the notorious Piccadilly Hotel. The young pilot, from 374 Fighter Squadron, was shot down on 8 June 1944 while on his 70th combat mission, his second for the day. Among the effects he had when turned over to the Germans was a towel he had taken from the hotel. A French barber called in to give some of the Fresnes prison inmates a haircut noticed the towel and asked the American if 'a red-headed woman and a Belgian wearing a leather jacket' had brought him into Paris. He further asked if a short man wearing rimmed glasses had been responsible for his arrest. When Hastin confirmed all of this, the barber shook his head and said, 'Then you were sold to the Germans!' He went on to say that the identities of these people were known, and they would pay at the time of liberation.

Flying Officer Thomas Blackham, DFC, from Dunoon in Scotland, was shot down by a German fighter long before D-Day while on a raid with 50 Squadron over Mailly-le-Camp, France.

He managed to keep the Lancaster bomber flying until all his crew had baled out safely, and then a sudden explosion knocked him senseless, hurling him through a glass panel. He recovered consciousness to find himself surrounded by flames and jumped clear moments before his aircraft blew up. Parachuting into Maquis territory near Saint-Mesmin, the young airman narrowly escaped being hanged or shot as a German spy. Fortunately, another British airman already in the vicinity was able to vouch for him.

For months, Blackham lived and fought with the Maquis, until he was sent on to Paris for a return to England. He too was betrayed by Jacques Desoubrie and was eventually imprisoned in Fresnes. He recounts some of the maltreatment he received at the hands of the Germans – particularly the day he was in a group which faced a firing squad manning a machine-gun, and he looked squarely into the faces of the men who were about to take his life.

> The machine-gun was never fired. The Nazis were master craftsmen in mind torture [and] they left us standing for several hours. All the time the three Germans were preparing the gun, and every moment we expected to hear the order given for them to shoot. Instead we were hustled off to the prison dungeons, stripped of our clothing and put under cold showers. Some of the group were very feeble and one old Frenchman next to me was on the point of collapse. I tried to speak to him – and was hit over the head by the Nazi guard. He hit me with a filthy broom. The wound it made festered and my throat afterwards swelled so that I could only eat and speak with much pain.
>
> Each one of us was then put in a cage-like steel locker with no room even to raise an arm. After leaving us there for some time, we

were 'gently' interrogated about our Resistance comrades. We told nothing and, after one or two more questionings at intervals, I was separated from my fighter pilot friend [RAF Lieutenant Henry Mutter] and other prisoners, and put in a cell by myself. Throughout the night I could hear men and women screaming as they were tortured. From there I was moved into another cell – all part of the ceremony to make me talk – with a little Frenchman who had been terribly tortured. He had been whipped with knotted thongs and the knots had broken two of his ribs. It was an agony for him to breathe.

I was here for two weeks, living on weak sauerkraut soup and sleeping on filthy lice-infested straw. The lice, however, provided a useful diversion; we spent much time betting each other how many of them we could catch in a given time. Neither of us received any medical attention, but by this time my throat had healed quite unexpectedly.

Unlike the majority of airmen swept up by the Gestapo, Malcolm Cullen was a fighter pilot. From Maungaturoto in the Northland Region of New Zealand, he flew Typhoons with No. 257 (Burma) Fighter Squadron. On the night of 24 May 1944, six of the squadron's Typhoons had joined forces with eight others from 193 Squadron, with whom they had been engaged for several weeks in pounding the invasion coastline from west of Cherbourg to east of Amiens. Their objective that night had been a large concentration of camouflaged petroleum vehicles in the rail sidings south of Amiens. Cullen's aircraft was hit by flak as he flew out of the target area and, after gliding to a safe landing in a field near a small forest, he fled his blazing fighter for the safety of the woods.

Cullen then spent several weeks on the run, living with sympathetic families across France, but ended up in Paris, where he too fell prey to Jacques Desoubrie. He and an American Marauder pilot were placed in a 'safe' flat and questioned by Desoubrie, following which they were told they would be driven elsewhere. Instead they ended up in the clutches of the Gestapo. Cullen's cell in Fresnes contained a Frenchman and, as he would soon discover, thousands of bed bugs.

> As I was spreading the rough palliasse on the floor I noticed something which cheered me immensely. On the wall, scratched into the soft mortar, was the name of an American with his service number and the annotation 'USAAF'. I don't remember that name; I wish I could, for it was that which made me straighten up my shoulders and grin. I wasn't the only sucker – others had been caught. I laid down and tried to sleep, but as soon as I hit the blanket I had thrown over the palliasse, they were onto me – all over me – and I must have caught a hundred before I fell asleep. I didn't sleep long, but spent the early morning scratching. When finally the light started through the bars I stood up and I made an inspection around the cell, and of myself. I received a shock; I must have been bitten in at least 300 places. Great white welts stood out all over my body, and around the area covered by the top of my trousers, they were almost touching.
>
> That day I was shifted first to a shower and delouse, and from there to the fourth floor where I was extremely relieved to be greeted in my own language. There were two others in the cell when I entered, one French and the other American. The American informed me that he had been there for close on five months and

he could not understand it. Others had come in and been sent to Germany within four weeks. I hoped fervently that I would fall under the latter category and made up my mind to settle down and wait with all the patience I could muster.

The days slipped slowly past, each with its own small diversity. Every day we received news of the outside world from Frenchmen who went out on working parties. This was conveyed to all and sundry by the heating system which ran up the inside wall of the cells. Each had an opening into this pipe about seven feet up the wall, and by climbing up onto our one and only stool we could shout into this primitive means of communication and receive our replies. The cry of 'Avez vous du nouvelle?' (Have you any news?) could be heard every morning. This was not the only method however. Morse code was used to a large extent, and with a spoon in one hand to make the 'dits' and a small piece of iron in the other hand for the heavier 'dashes', news was passed around the whole floor.

Stanley Booker, a 10 Squadron air observer on Halifax bombers, came from Gillingham, Kent. He and several others had been hiding out in the Piccadilly Hotel near the Arc de Triomphe, and had also been duped into capture by Desoubrie. At Fresnes he was searched, questioned about his false identity card (supplied to him by Resistance helpers), given a fierce beating and locked away in solitary cell 429, on the upper floor of the 3rd Division of the prison. He picks up the story:

Each day was the same – the soup trolley on its noisy track made the same noise as it approached your cell down the long metal corridors. Monday or Sunday, there wasn't really anything to distinguish one day from another. Rumours prevailed; life after D-Day was much easier as there was so much activity, and the Allies had set foot on the continent and were approaching Paris. Fresnes was an anti-climax. Having overcome the initial shock of being shot down and established a new pattern of life as an evader, it came as a profound shock to be caught, given a thorough beating up – not the nicest experience when you can't retaliate – and thrust into a dark, bare cell; confused, angry, and wondering just what was going to happen next. All the time you were thinking of your loved ones at home; every day you wondered how they were taking the fact that you were missing; praying, willing yourself somehow to communicate just the fact that you were alive – eager, anxious to return.

The early days were in many ways the worst – alone with your thoughts. The shock came when the German guard threw open the cell door and shouted in a pitched, hysterical way, 'Tribunal – Raus!' Then down the many staircases from the upper floor, down through the maze of underground corridors and out into the open, to be shut up in a very confined metal cupboard in the special black prison coach, and driven across Paris to the dreaded Avenue Foch. Then the awesome experience of being gathered as a bunch at the foot of a vast staircase, guarded tightly, watching the hapless, bleeding and battered prisoners dragging themselves down, or being dragged down the staircase to take their place in the line, suffering from the effects of their interrogations. The apprehension, wondering how you will react, the dreadful responsibility of knowing the names and locations of those brave families that have risked so much to give you – a complete stranger – shelter and food and clothing, and take terrible chances in escorting you in trains and public transport. Now their lives are in your hands – not a happy situation!

The hours spent afterwards back in your cell, nursing your hurts, your pride, and wondering what the next 'tribunal' would be like and how you would be able to react. As the days passed and the call didn't come, a hope was cherished – perhaps they had forgotten about you. And then all is shattered, and the screaming voice again destroys your little silent world: 'Tribunal – Raus!'

After D-Day, things began to get a little hectic in Paris, and obviously they had to follow a different policy as the pressures grew and the Allies approached Paris. Whether you were called to interrogation probably depended on what documents or other compromising materials one carried when caught. The Gestapo were always sensitive about forged papers, especially identity cards which, although they could be stolen, had to be authenticated somewhere. I was unfortunate because, apart from a set of forged travel papers with my name and photograph, I had been given a large sealed envelope when I left my little Resistance group. I was supposed to hand it over when I made rendezvous that night with the aircraft that had allegedly been organised for me. What the envelope contained I don't know to this day, but it certainly was a source of interest to the interrogators, which didn't make life any the pleasanter at the time.

In retrospect, I wonder whether the actual beatings were perhaps not as bad as the periods of sheer fear, when your imagination runs wild in the confinement of your cell, nursing your aches and pains, wondering if the next visit would involve the real specialist torture for which the Gestapo had a reputation amongst the prisoners in Fresnes. Perhaps I came off lightly, with only two missing teeth, a badly busted nose, and a painfully swollen groin – an area to which a particularly sadistic interrogator paid very unwelcome attention.

Other men suffered severe cruelty, pain and torture during their time in Fresnes, and the terrifying sounds of men and women screaming and sobbing rent the air at all hours. Canadian Leo Grenon was hit murderously hard on the head with a Luger after being kept in a death cell for seven days, during which time he was extensively beaten. Post-war treatment for his physical afflictions took ten years, and medication was required until he died in 1994.

Another Canadian, Bill Gibson, spent thirty days in solitary confinement, with food every third day. Whenever gunfire was heard in the courtyard, the guards would tell Gibson he was next for 'the chop'. Another two of the Canadian contingent would also suffer permanent legacies of their time in Fresnes: Don Leslie lost his two front teeth, while Art Kinnis had his right eardrum broken, and did not receive any treatment for shrapnel wounds in both legs.

The airmen tossed on their bunks and pondered the awesome question: would they be next? Slowly they began to shed weight with their inadequate diet, but more than anything it was the precariousness of their situation that caused the greatest anxiety.

As August progressed, news of the approaching Allied armies raced through the prison grapevine. As well, the men were sometimes able to pick out a snippet or two of news from the rough squares of German newspaper the guards supplied as toilet paper. The prisoners began to allow themselves a glimmer of hope when reports put the American 3rd Army under General George Patton at Chartres, while others said they were moving in on Versailles. The Free French forces under General Philippe Leclerc were also said to be nearing Paris. Much of these had to be rejected as hopeful exaggeration, but one thing was abundantly clear – Paris would soon be liberated.

In the early morning hours of 8 August, the corridors at Fresnes suddenly came alive with a babble of voices and the strident screaming of the guards. The airmen's hearts sank. Evacuation could be the only reason for such mass activity so early in the day, but surprisingly they were not amongst the first evacuees selected. Soon the din abated as the evacuees moved out, and each of those left behind breathed a sigh of relief. The Americans were coming, and they would all soon be free.

The final evacuation of Fresnes took place on Tuesday, 15 August – a hot, sticky and hazy day over Paris. Worried that roads and railways leading out of the French capital would be cut before they could evacuate their prisoners, the Germans decided to give this task priority. They stormed into the prison and emptied the cells of the civilian prisoners first, packing them off to the nearby railway yards for transportation. Ray Perry remembered the day well:

> Our 'café' and food arrived at breakfast time and at about 9 am a guard came along and informed us that we were being moved and be ready to go at any moment. We knew then that the evacuation of the prison had been going on for some hours. Soon after our food was delivered we could hear shooting going on downstairs and it didn't take too much imagination to think that the prisoners were being taken downstairs and shot. I think we all had the same thoughts and an uncomfortable silence fell among us. Soon after being told we were to move out, the shooting stopped and this relieved the tension somewhat. It was not until sometime later we found out the shooting was some of the guards having revolver practice.

> Most of the windows were now either opened or broken and from a shouted conversation, the three Americans sharing my cell discovered that their first and second pilots were also in the prison and soon made their presence known. I heard Frank [Salt] calling my name and discovered he was okay in a nearby cell on our floor. At about 11 am (we had no watches) we were taken from our cell and lined up on the staging outside. There were already about 20 chaps there and we could not help laughing at one another's clothes as there were all sorts, from well-tailored suits to the cheapest of peasant-style clothing, with many berets in evidence. Some had not had haircuts for weeks, and one must remember that in those days it was short back and sides, with a haircut every two weeks in the forces. Many had beards coming along nicely and I had not shaved for over two weeks nor cleaned my teeth in that time. It was ten days since I had used soap for a wash, and after ten days in the hot cells we all had a good dose of BO.

The airmen were among the last to be taken out and assembled in the covered quadrangle. Each man had assumed that there might be some others in Fresnes, but as more and more bewildered faces emerged into the daylight, the surprised shouting and conversation swelled, as men recognised friends and fellow crewmen and realised the number of aircrew who were in the same predicament. As a result of their sojourns to the Avenue Foch, many bore black eyes and facial wounds, but they had come to regard these as symbols of their defiance, and they even laughed at each other's bruises. Finally, 169 airmen, not one in uniform, were formed into some sort of order under a guard company of seventy armed Germans.

A slender Prussian SS officer made his way to the front of the group and asked if any of them could act as an interpreter. A Dutch pilot from the RAF named Spierenburg hesitated, then stepped forward, and the officer addressed him for two minutes. Following this the officer turned on his heels and strode off, leaving Spierenburg to relay his message.

'We are going to be taken across Paris by bus, and placed on a train for our next destination. He did not say where this would be. I was instructed to tell you that anyone attempting to escape will be shot, and a hand grenade will be thrown into the back of the bus he came from. He has further told me to stress that he is very serious, and no attempts should be made to test his word.'

A few minutes later, vats of thick bean soup were wheeled in and ladled into bowls. As the men chatted and ate the welcome soup, another column of prisoners was escorted to a waiting green and yellow bus. Among those forced to squeeze aboard was the bulky form of Georges Prevot, his face now pale and drawn. Several airmen wondered if he and his sister had been in some way responsible for their betrayal to the Germans. The sad truth was that Prevot had also been badly taken in by Desoubrie, and when his usefulness came to an end, he and his sister Genevieve Rocher were turned over to the Gestapo. While his sister managed to survive Ravensbruck, Prevot died in Buchenwald. Both would later receive an award for bravery and for assisting evading airmen, although his was sadly a posthumous honour from the French government.

As the bus roared away from the prison, another two pulled up and the first batch of airmen was ordered to climb aboard. Soon both vehicles were crammed full and a contingent of armed guards on each kept a close watch on the occupants as they were shunted in batches to the Gare de l'Est station. They did not enter the station itself, pulling up instead at the nearby Pantin freight yards alongside a long train of French cattle trucks. The installations at the Gare de l'Est had been destroyed by the French Resistance on the evening of 12 August, which necessitated the change to the Pantin yards, where cattle were normally loaded. The platform was already crowded with detainees from several places of imprisonment in the Paris region; not just Fresnes, but Cherche-Midi and Compiègne prisons, and the Fort de Romainville.

Hundreds of prisoners were milling about and the guards were kept busy shoving them into the dank, open boxcars. The women had been segregated and were placed in five separate cars at the rear of the train. More than thirty of the cattle trucks were linked together with some carriages and guards' vans, forming a train 400 metres long. Wooden placards on the side of each boxcar stated '40 hommes/8 chevaux en long', but this restriction to forty persons or eight horses was completely disregarded by the Germans, who crammed as many as a hundred prisoners into each wagon. A 20-litre water pail sat in the middle of each car together with an empty one intended for use as a toilet. They were actually British-manufactured canisters dropped from Halifax bombers, containing food and supplies for the Resistance, and the irony was not lost on the airmen. Once again the prisoners were informed that any attempt to escape would be punished by death, and then each person was given a small hard loaf of bread commonly known as knäckebröd. They were not told that this was meant to last them several days.

The attitude of the SS guards towards their prisoners was made abundantly clear when Squadron Leader Lamason tried to protest their treatment. By way of reply he received a hard punch to the face.

Elsewhere, surprisingly, one of the elite guard responded readily to Jim Hastin when he asked about their destination.

'You are all being sent to a labour camp in Germany,' he was told. 'That is as much as I am able to tell you. But you are an American, no? I don't understand why you choose to fight against us. In the next war America will be fighting with us against the *verdammt* Russians!' Hastin was about to reply when another guard's rifle butt propelled him towards the door of his boxcar. The airmen were loaded into three crammed wagons behind those carrying the women.

Lights flickered in the sky to the west and south, and the distant sound of artillery reached the men as they reluctantly clambered aboard what would prove to be the last train to leave Paris before its liberation. During the day, more busloads of prisoners reached the station to join the general melee and were forced into the already overcrowded wagons until all were packed full.

On 20 August, five days after the evacuation of Fresnes prison, British and American forces entered and liberated Paris.

A total of 2,453 men and women and some children would be evacuated to Germany on this final train. Apart from the airmen, only 300 would ever live to see France again.

It was the dogdays of August. Even before the heavy doors were rolled shut and padlocked, conditions in the unlit, overcrowded cattle trucks were unbearable, with the sun beating down relentlessly on the black roof just half a metre above the heads of the occupants. Conditions worsened once they were closed in, as the interior temperature climbed and the air became stuffy and fetid.

A drag of heavy barbed wire was arranged behind the train to deter any foolhardy escapers planning to break loose and lie down between the tracks while the train was moving slowly. Every fifth wagon was a guards' van, each one equipped with a raised wooden observation box from which they could see all the wagons and watch for any signs of escape activity.

The French Red Cross had managed to distribute a little food and some cigarettes to a few of the prisoners, but their supplies did not go far amongst the crowded and hungry multitude. Little did the prisoners know that the cattle trucks would be their homes for the next five days, or that the many discomforts they would endure were merely a prelude to the greater hells of the concentration camps in Germany.

As part of the growing passive resistance to German occupation, members of the French railway network had gone on strike, and it was only after a delay of several hours that the Germans came up with a locomotive capable of drawing the crowded train away from Paris.

Time dragged by, and the prisoners perspired freely in the stuffiness, cursing the Third Reich while trying to get comfortable. Some could sit down, but the majority had to remain standing. In every car, agreements were reached as to how many could sit down at any one time and the rest time they would be permitted before another group took their places. Nobody talked much about the coming night or their prospects of sleep. Finally a steam whistle sounded down the line, followed moments later by a sudden clang and lurch as the locomotive mated with the train.

After ten minutes' activity, the carriages jerked, couplings rattled and the train began to surge forward. The heavily overladen convoy of cattle trucks slowly laboured its way out of the freight yards a little before midnight. Although it was only moving at a sluggish pace, some fresh air began to flow into the wagons through four small ventilator windows which had been laced with barbed wire. Everyone ate a portion of their food, although no water was permitted: it was being strictly rationed in each wagon and those who protested their thirst were shouted down by their fellow travellers. The train rumbled on into the night, although it would jerk to a stop from time to time before resuming the nightmare journey.

Men and women alike, many suffering terribly from dysentery, had to endure the degradation of performing their toilet functions in the middle of the crowded boxcars. The stench, compounded by a lack of substantial ventilation, was appalling. As the toilet pail filled, it began to slop about in the dark interior, and the clothes of those unlucky enough to be crammed nearby were saturated by its foul contents.

The train trundled slowly on that first night, heading due east towards the city of Nancy. Sleep was almost impossible for the occupants, most of whom eventually dozed while standing, rocking back and forth while supported by those around them. Several tried lying down, but there was insufficient room. Many harsh words were spoken as people fought to protect what little space they had, but in time everyone became resigned to the fact that they were all going to suffer equally, and a grim silence prevailed.

Realising that they were moving further away from the scene of possible freedom, some of the men in Tommy Blackham's cattle truck car began prising three boards from a half-rotted wall. At three o'clock they were still hard at work when the train stopped unexpectedly. Shots rang out further down the train as a squad of guards moved towards them, checking for any signs of escape activity.

When they saw the damage to the wall, the men were ordered out and made to strip naked while the damage was repaired. They were then directed back into their wagon, their clothes returned, and a general warning issued that if so much as a hand was seen outside, the train would be stopped and a hand grenade tossed through the door into the offending wagon. When the train moved on again, the guards would fire a volley of shots every so often to demonstrate their alertness and to serve as a warning.

At dawn, the train's locomotive was attacked and strafed by an Allied fighter. Fortunately there were no injuries and little damage on this occasion, though there were subsequent attacks and the added dread of strafing or bombardment made the prisoners' lot even more unendurable. The airmen knew well that any trains moving across France by day at this stage of the war presented a fat target to the swarms of fighters and bombers from England.

Later that morning, having travelled around 70 kilometres from Paris, the train hauled into a long tunnel at Nanteuil-Saâcy where it screeched to a halt. Outside the unlit cattle trucks, the Germans began shouting and there was a lot of loud activity. Beyond the tunnel lay a rail bridge over the shallow river Marne, but both the bridge and the exit to the tunnel had been destroyed by Resistance operatives making a last-ditch effort to halt the train.

The exhausted prisoners suffered for a while in resigned silence, unaware of the cause of the delay, but as the locomotive continued to belch pungent smoke into the blocked tunnel, a new problem arose, as the smoke found its way into the darkened boxcars. Panic started to set in as the occupants began to cough and choke on the thick fumes. Packed into trucks towards the rear of the train, the airmen and the women were comparatively fortunate, but the hordes crammed into the leading boxcars began to beat the walls and cry out into the darkness. As the noise swelled, the Germans, who also found conditions in the tunnel quite unbearable, shouted back even louder and fired shots through the upper walls of the closed trucks.

After much shouting and panicky jostling, the frightened occupants were finally relieved to feel the train slowly shunting backwards out of the tunnel. Later estimates of the time spent in the suffocating blackness varied from one to three hours, but the darkness, heat and fumes made each minute an eternity of fear and uncertainty. Several of the men and women had fainted standing up.

Eventually the doors on all the boxcars were rolled open and the prisoners informed that the train could go no further. Their initial excitement was dashed when it was explained that they would be transferred to another train located in a tunnel on the far side of the river. Originally positioned at a siding near Nanteuil-sur-Marne, this train had been emptied of its livestock to make way for the evacuees. The prisoners were further informed that it would be necessary for some of them to carry all items of baggage, the guards' packs, and other stores across the remains of the bridge to the other train.

One wagonload of men were detailed to this task, with six of their number kept under guard as hostages in the event of trouble. Everyone in the detail was warned that any escape attempts would result in the six men being shot dead. The occupants of an adjoining wagon were ordered to cross over to the waiting train and load it with the baggage and other freight as it arrived. Meanwhile all the empty wagons were locked up and the prisoners ordered to assemble by the train and await further orders.

Later in the day, as the transfer continued, the male prisoners were permitted to jump down and relieve themselves on the embankment by the train, followed soon after by the women, who were forced to line up and urinate while squatting facing the train, in full view of the guards and the men moving the equipment. Bob Mills, who made four crossings of the damaged bridge, recalls averting his eyes from this humiliating spectacle. In order to prevent any spontaneous escape bids, the prisoners were all ordered back into their wagons. The Germans then allowed each wagon to empty its toilet pail – the only time this would be permitted throughout their entire journey – and to refill the water containers, all of which would be transferred to the other train. Les Whellum and French-Canadian Leo Grenon volunteered their services as water carriers, and were able to drink their fill from the river as they replenished each of the containers.

Throughout the afternoon, the work detail made repeated crossings of the Marne. When their work was done, the remainder of the prisoners were ordered back out of their wagons in staggered batches and marched down the embankment to the fields beside the track. Here they were told through interpreters that they would have to take a detour of around six kilometres, as the Marne had to be crossed more safely by a bridge at a village further downstream. The officer in charge ordered that several of the guards' packs and some other remaining stores be carried by the prisoners, and reminded them that any disobedience could result in those offenders being shot.

As the exhausted prisoners moved out of the culvert they encountered a fresh threat – a muscled SS guard who began lashing out indiscriminately with a long, thick baton. The men had to pass by this brute as hurriedly as possible, but few avoided the stinging blows he handed out. Phil Lamason was horrified at the sight of this bully beating his men, especially when he saw a young Englishman, Philip Hemmens, hanging back from the screaming German. Hemmens had a broken arm which had received only cursory treatment and binding. Without hesitation, Lamason strode over to Hemmens, grasped him by his good arm and walked him out of the column. He took the young man up to one of the senior guards, who was watching the proceedings with obvious interest.

'You must tell that man to stop beating my men!' Lamason demanded. 'We are prisoners of war, and cannot be beaten by rotten bastards like him!' He pointed a shaking finger towards the culprit. The German surprised Lamason by speaking reasonable English. 'You are *not* prisoners of war,' he stated firmly. 'You are *Terrorfliegers* – child murderers. No, you are not prisoners of war.' Nevertheless he cast a look at Hemmens' arm. 'This man is injured?'

'Yes, dammit!' Lamason replied.

'Then I will have a word with my colleague,' the German promised. 'But every man, no exceptions, must help us to move. Perhaps your man can carry some straw for the compartment floors?'

Lamason looked at Hemmens, who exhaled with relief and nodded. The German strolled over to the red-faced guard and spoke to him in a stern but muted tone. The man scowled but lowered his baton. Malcolm Cullen remembers the temporarily uplifting detour that followed:

> The journey was slow but made a pleasant change after the night in the truck. At least we could breathe fresh air again. The road led through a village and the people were very sympathetic and showed contempt for our guards at every chance they got. They threw us bread and fruit and some of our boys managed to get a drink of cider. Water pumps along the roadside were besieged and the guards had to become threatening to move the boys on.

> After making about five or six kilometres in the shape of a horseshoe, first down the river and across, then back up the other bank, we came to a place opposite the tunnel where the hill sloped straight down into the river. In the cutting, a line of cattle trucks were backed down to the bridge approaches and stood awaiting passengers. Into this train we went and the doors were again locked.

Art Kinnis recalled that it was not long before the airmen began sizing up escape opportunities from their new train.

> We were all repacked into the all-too-familiar boxcars, some of the chaps finding as many as 90 aircrew and French civilians in one car. We were lucky, for our car still contained 70. The French Red Cross were again on the spot and we got some sour milk, bread and coffee. Some of the cars were fortunate and received roasted potatoes. At this point one of the guards handed one of our chaps a hammer, telling him to fix the nails holding the barbed wire over the windows. With this object in his hand, and the previous knowledge that one of the floorboards was loose, it took but a quick bend and the board was made easily movable and ready for future use. The window nailing was completed to the guard's satisfaction and the tool was handed back. This was the start of an advantageous and disastrous time for that car.

The journey was soon resumed and, contrary to expectations, the train made good progress. That night followed the same pattern as their first, with many prisoners falling asleep on their feet and collapsing in exhaustion on top of their disgruntled companions. Two surprise stops were made while the guards checked underneath the carriages with torches. Their diligence would be dramatically rewarded on the second inspection.

Once they had left the river Marne behind, and following some work on the floor of Art Kinnis' cattle truck, a handful of men prised up the loose floorboard and the one next to it. They began slipping out while the train was travelling slowly up an incline, darting away into the darkness from the tracks once their carriage had passed. Flying Officers Dave High from Edmonton, Alberta, and Joel 'Tex' Stevenson, his skipper from 419 Squadron, were followed into the night by some equally desperate Frenchmen. Unfortunately one of these men was spotted by an alert guard and shot down by a wildly spraying machine-gun as the train shuddered to a halt and pandemonium erupted. One squad was despatched to round up the escapees, while the rest of the guards stood watch along the tracks, ready for any further commotion.

The majority of the escapees, including Dave High, were soon rounded up and dragged back to the train, but Canadian airman 'Tex' Stevenson was not among them. Stevenson had been captured in Paris on 14 July and sent to Fresnes prison. He had somehow managed to conceal a small serrated knife from his captors, which he used to assist in loosening the floorboards in their boxcar on the morning of 18 August. 'I dropped out while the train was travelling at about 25 miles an hour,' he later recalled. 'Two French officers escaped with me and made for the undergrowth. It was about 0240 hours when we left the train and we were about 40 kilometres east of Paris.' After making sure they were no longer being pursued, the three men walked to the village of Mézy-Moulins where a sympathetic family took them in. The two Frenchmen decided to head off for Paris, but Stevenson would spend two nights in the house.

'The owner fetched a woman who arranged for me to go to Chateau-Thierry and I hid above a shop until the Americans arrived on August 28. I returned to the UK on September 4th, 1944.'

All the occupants of the damaged truck were shoved to one end and counted. Their latrine pail was kicked over, potatoes and other saved food items were squashed underfoot, and there was heated talk of shootings. Surprisingly, however, the Germans did not seem anxious to take any immediate reprisals. Once the offending boards had been nailed down securely, the men were left alone, although High did not entirely escape the wrath of his captors. 'I was beaten with a rubber hose. I was struck mostly on the head, shoulders and arms, and was able to move about only with great difficulty for three or four days. I was black and blue for weeks.' But to his satisfaction he noted that his skipper had not been one of those brought back.

As the train moved off, the door of their wagon was left open, but with two German guards stationed at the far end of the boxcar keeping a close watch on the tightly-packed occupants. The men were still expecting some form of reprisal, and their fears increased a little after dawn when the train slowed and stuttered to a stop in the middle of the countryside. They heard the ominous crunching sound of approaching footsteps and then an officer, his face scarlet, addressed the prisoners through the open doorway. The Dutch pilot Spierenburg was one of the occupants, and he squeezed forward to translate. The officer roared at the Dutchman for the best part of a minute, during which time the pilot's face tightened and paled. Even those who did not understand German heard the word *geschossen* (shot) punctuating his tirade. When the German had finished, he moved off and Spierenburg turned slowly to face the others, badly shaken. 'I've been instructed to tell you,' he said, and then paused for a moment, 'that to prevent any further escapes and by way of punishment, thirty-five RAF airmen and twenty Frenchmen from this carriage are to be shot!'

At this a loud howl of protest went up, and the guards stiffened themselves for action. The prisoners randomly selected to die were quickly separated from the rest and ordered down from the carriage, the Frenchmen cursing and shaking their fists at the Germans. Two machine-guns were set up on tripods a short distance from their carriage, following which the men were ordered to form three lines parallel to the train. Many of the airmen and most of the Frenchmen began to mutter prayers, and several quickly discussed a revolt against their would-be killers. They were prepared to charge the guards the moment any shot was fired. Many would die, but they would not lay down their lives without a fight. Then the first line of twenty men was ordered to step forward a few paces, and the machine-guns were trained on them. South Australian Les Whellum, one of those in the front row, looked down the barrel of death and shivered.

> I thought, this is it, Les; goodbye to sweet life. I was staring straight down the business end of a machine-gun, and my Lord that hole looked huge. I can't remember whether I was frightened or just somehow resigned. It really comes as a dreadful shock when your enemy points a weapon at you, and you suddenly realise that your life might end right there and then.

Tense seconds passed, then a minute had gone by. The air was thick with emotion as the guards waited for the order to open fire, and the line of prisoners shook involuntarily and even wet their trousers with fear and anticipation. The officer in charge stood stock still, his eyes roaming up and down the line. All was quiet, and to the condemned men, every second spent waiting for death was an agony.

Suddenly the German barked an order. The prisoners tensed, but watched with incredulity as the guards behind the machine-guns rose and stood to attention. Spierenburg was called over and the officer spoke to him briefly. With that he strode off, issuing orders to his men as he departed.

The relieved Dutchman approached the group standing apprehensively by the train. 'He's decided not to shoot you after all,' he said. 'He feels the lesson has been learned, but that the next escape will bring the most severe punishment. He has ordered you to remove all your clothes, together with everyone else in this carriage, and give them to the guards. They will be returned once we get into Germany.'

The men, still shaking, quickly divested themselves of their clothing, which was gathered up and removed. They had been fortunate, and knew that they had come within an ace of being slaughtered. Once they were back inside their carriage, their water pail was removed, the repaired floor inspected once again, and then the door was rolled shut and padlocked. Their collective nakedness now added to the men's misery, but they realised that further protests would not only prove futile but could provide the Germans with a further excuse to shoot them.

That same day, 18 August, the train pulled up for yet another snap inspection. In the cattle truck from which the escape had taken place, a naked fourteen-year-old French boy grasped the ledge of one of the small ventilation apertures, intending to pull himself up so he could see outside. He had either forgotten the order to keep his hands away from the window, or was just being foolhardy. As he hauled himself up to peep out, a guard watching for any such movement opened fire with his Schmeisser. As everyone instinctively tried to drop to the floor of the truck, one of the guard's bullets hit the youth across the knuckles, shattering his hand. He fell to the floor, screaming as he clutched his bloodied hand against his chest. The bullet that hit the boy's hand had also grazed Bill Gibson's forehead. Years later, as a direct result, he would lose the sight in his right eye.

Shortly after, the door was unlocked and flung open and the guards demanded to know which of the naked occupants had disobeyed their orders. The grimacing youngster came forward, stumbling through the mass of huddled bodies to the door, his hand covered in blood. By this time the officer had arrived at the doorway and ordered the youth to get down from the carriage and move to the front of the train. Canadian Harry Bastable, a first-aid man, demanded the boy receive medical treatment, but his entreaties fell on deaf ears.

'From where we were crouched on the rough wooden floor, we watched the naked boy hesitate before jumping down,' recalled Canadian John Harvie. 'No doubt he was looking for a spot to land which would not be too cruel on his bare feet. He disappeared through the opening and those nearest it saw him start towards the front of the train.'

The French boy stopped by the Feldwebel, who asked the tearful youth if he was French or English. He stammered that he was French, following which he was motioned to proceed down a slight incline by the railway tracks. When he reached the bottom he turned to see if he should stop there. The Feldwebel motioned him to continue forward along the train, and as he moved off, the German unclipped his Luger and shouted an order at the guards. They lifted their Schmeissers and fired at point blank range into the boy's back. The youngster threw his arms wide and then slumped forward, landing face down on the hard ground. The Feldwebel walked down the incline and stood over the prostrate form, aimed his Luger, and fired two bullets into the back of the boy's head.

The faces of the men watching were a study of incredulity; not a person moved as they stood in shock at what they had just witnessed. The German calmly swung around and ordered two men to step down from those watching through the open doorway. The guards grabbed the two closest, Canadian Leo Grenon and Englishman Dick Rowe, and the Feldwebel ordered them to bury the body. The men, still naked, were given small field shovels with which they hacked out a shallow grave in the hard road ash of the embankment. Dragging the youth's body up to the grave, they buried him as best they could before they were ordered back, silent and grey-faced, to their cattle truck. They stopped briefly to wash their hands in a puddle of water beside the tracks.

As the train slowly pulled away from the scene, those peering through cracks in the boxcar wall could see the dead boy's hands and feet protruding grotesquely from his shallow grave. Several of the men felt ill. They too had touched the lacing of barbed wire over the small window, and had even emptied pails of excrement through it.

When the train finally passed out of France and into the Fatherland, now heading for Saarbrücken, the tension felt by the guards eased noticeably. Although their vigilance did not relax on the infrequent stops, they were visibly pleased to be away from French soil and the prevailing risk of attacks by the Resistance. The naked men now had their clothes returned.

For two more days and nights, punctuated only by unsettling surprise searches by the guards, the train rolled on. The Germans need not have worried excessively about further escapes. The prisoners had grudgingly accepted that such attempts would only bring a swift and terrible retribution.

The occupants of the boxcars grew dirtier, more despondent and miserable with every passing kilometre. Every wagon stank of human waste, vomit and body odour. The prisoners itched and perspired incessantly, and were ravenously hungry and thirsty. Added to this, the burning need for sleep had sapped the last of their energy.

Rumours began to sweep the cattle trucks. The train seemed to be heading towards Frankfurt, and all aircrew knew that outside Frankfurt was Dulag Luft – the Luftwaffe interrogation centre where captured air force prisoners were taken for questioning prior to their conveyance to proper POW camps. On the fourth day, lookouts peering through wall cracks reported that the train was indeed approaching Frankfurt. Hopes rose but quickly faded as the long train roared into the station and then swept out the other side without stopping.

On the fifth morning, the train slowed once again and a station signboard came into view. Word of their whereabouts quickly swept around the boxcars – Weimar. The airmen held brief discussions as to their location and it was decided that they were some eighty kilometres south-west of Leipzig.

Once there, the railway staff switched the rail tracks 100 metres behind the train, following which another locomotive backed out of a siding, linking up with what had been the last cattle truck. The five boxcars carrying the female prisoners were then uncoupled and the locomotive moved off, transporting the women to what would prove for most to be their final destination – the concentration camp at Ravensbrück. Once again the tracks were switched and the shortened train now containing all the male prisoners began to back up, made its way onto a side track, and began to pick up speed. The prisoners felt they were now close to their destination. Finally the train braked and slowly came to a stop.

Outside, emaciated men dressed in filthy striped clothes were working beside the railway tracks. Spierenburg stood up to the window and started to question them in German. When he finally lowered himself the others were keen to know their location.

'It's a place called Buchenwald,' he said. The men muttered amongst themselves – nobody had ever heard of the place.

'I'm afraid it's one of the worst concentration camps in Europe,' Spierenburg continued. 'Not a prisoner of war camp, but a punishment camp. I rather fear we are all in big trouble.'

No one moved, no one spoke. Finally someone cleared his throat and uttered a heartfelt expletive.

A few shouts came from outside, then the train began to move once again. The clank of steel on steel seemed to break the spell, and the boxcars were soon alive with conversation. The French prisoners were visibly nervous, while the airmen were angry that they were not going to a Luftwaffe camp under the protection of the Geneva Convention. The engine crawled up a long incline then coasted downhill until it finally rolled into a temporary platform surrounded by barbed wire.

The doors were unlocked and rolled open, and the occupants were ordered to get out. If the prisoners thought their guards on the train had been harsh, they soon discovered that the SS guards from the camp were infinitely worse. As the weakened prisoners were dragged from the cattle trucks, those who fell to the ground were brutally kicked until they got up. Anyone slow to respond received a boot to the back or a punch in the face. Vicious, near-manic dogs snapped at the men's bodies and tore at those on the ground.

The bewildered prisoners were formed into five ragged lines before being herded away from the railway sidings and onto a crumbling concrete road. The SS guards, screaming and shouting, moved everyone along at double time, whipping and beating those who moved too slowly. They were finally halted in front of what Canadian John Harvie later described as 'a formidable, multi-tiered gate structure surmounted by a clock tower. Long, low wings reached out on each side.'

The beatings continued as the large gates, bearing the ominous words 'Buchenwald Konzentrationslager', were opened and the men shuffled through them into the camp. One American flight sergeant who had suffered a badly sprained ankle when landing by parachute had his walking stick kicked from under his arm. 'There are no cripples in here!' growled the guard. The airmen had hoped their final destination would be a properly administered prisoner of war camp, but that forlorn hope was rapidly fading, as John Harvie recalled.

> Beyond the gate I could see people dressed in the now-familiar blue-and-white-striped prison garb of the work gangs. To me, this looked more like a place of internment than a Luftwaffe-run POW camp. At that time I knew there were civilian internment camps in Germany, although I didn't know any of their names. Perhaps this was one of them. Perhaps it would only be a temporary stopover before the POWs were transferred to a proper camp. This certainly

couldn't be Stalag Luft III, nor any other prisoner of war camps of which I had heard, not with people in striped prison suits and SS guards everywhere.

Further along the road, they passed the Kommandant's office and the Political Department where selected inmates would undergo Gestapo interrogation. The men finally passed through another iron gateway, which opened up beneath a large tower. On either side of this tower were brick wings lined with steel shutters, which they soon learned were the bunkers, or punishment cells. Next they entered into a large compound, where they were made to turn right and then halted outside a large brick building. All around the new arrivals were hundreds of skeletal, weary-looking men dressed in ragged striped garb, who sat or stood pensively watching them from a cobbled area. The new intake of prisoners was made to sit down in columns, taking the opportunity of this break to finish off any scraps of food they had been saving, as well as passing around a few precious cigarettes. The French even managed to produce some chocolate. The established inmates, kept at a distance by the guards, watched every move and every morsel consumed with craving in their eyes.

After a while, the new arrivals were ordered to stand and wait in the scorching sun as the French prisoners were separated and ushered roughly into the brick block, having been told to remove and carry their clothing.

A pungent, sickly smell hung over the entire camp, drifting around with the thick smoke belching from a tall chimney atop a squat building on the far side of the barrack area. The men innocently assumed this building to be some sort of incinerator, but all too soon they would come to know of its more evil function as the camp crematorium.

The official International Red Cross Excerpts from Documents, issued by the International Tracing Service at 3548 Arolsen, Germany, states that the 'Polgende Häftlinge' (police detainees) prisoners arrived in Buchenwald on 20 August 1944. The salient comment on this document is the acronym 'DIKAL (Darf in kein anderes Lager)' – Not to be transferred to another camp – an instruction that the airmen were never to leave Buchenwald. It is considered a blessing that none of the men were aware of this fact at the time.

The arrival date at Buchenwald is further authenticated by a document from the SS archives in the Buchenwald Museum. Dated 28 August 1944 and signed by the SS Hauptsturmführer (a paramilitary commander), the Camp Medical Officer, there is a complete breakdown by camp registration number of the entire intake of prisoners who 'arrived from Paris on the 20th August 1944 and were placed in the Zeltlager [tented camp] within the Kleine Lager [Little Camp]'.

Against the serial numbers 78266 to 78423 (some numbers were not allotted to the new arrivals) appears a heavy handwritten annotation: 'TERRORFLIEGERS'.

4

BLOODY, BLOODY BUCHENWALD

On 28 February 1933, Germany's new Reichschancellor Adolf Hitler introduced into his arsenal of power the Reichsgesetzblatt or Presidential Emergency Decree, which allowed – among other harsh measures – for the 'protective custody' of political opponents to the Third Reich, in order to safeguard and enlarge his new and expanding regime.

Heinrich Himmler, who had been appointed Reichsführer of the Schutzstaffel (SS) in 1929, was installed into the position of Chief of the German Police, and the decree gave him unlimited and non-accountable power to set his feared SS and Gestapo to the task of rounding up anyone they deemed to be enemies of the state, including gypsies and Jews, who were referred to in the decree as 'inferior races'.

Hitler and many of his followers harboured a manic hatred of the Jewish people, as evidenced in Point Four of the Nazi Party program, which declared: 'Only a member of the race can be a citizen. A member of the race can only be one who is of German blood, without consideration of creed. Consequently, no Jew can be a member of the race.'

This volatile doctrine was preached across Germany virtually from the moment Hitler took power, and was used by the Nazis as a means of implementing their master-race policy. First the German people were encouraged to boycott any Jewish enterprise, and then a series of laws were passed which effectively displaced Jews from every department of public administration. They were ejected from the civil and armed services and forbidden to hold posts in higher professions such as education. Soon Jews were no longer permitted to own businesses or make purchases in gentile stores, and were prohibited from marrying gentiles.

A single Jewish grandparent was sufficient ancestry to qualify as a member of this so-called 'inferior race'. Brilliant Jewish academic Albert Einstein was ousted from his position as Director of the Kaiser Wilhelm Physical Institute of Berlin, following which he sailed to America, while Sigmund Freud was forced to flee Vienna in 1938 for exile in Hampstead, England. He died of cancer the following year.

Germany's Jews were not arrested as a matter of general policy. In the formative years of the Nazi regime, many were picked up by the Gestapo on vague and often spurious changes and finally sent to work in the concentration camps, where they were treated as vermin. Tens of thousands of ordinary citizens were thrown into these camps, from where there was very little chance of return.

Gypsies were similarly being rounded up before the war, and placed in the camps as part of the Nazi campaign against those they referred to as shirkers and asocials. Previously they had simply been moved on, but Himmler prohibited the customary wanderings of these nomadic people, and their encampments became subject to constant raids and arrests. Himmler reasoned it was better to get rid of this 'scum', as he called them, by sending them to the work camps. Later, in 1942, orders were promulgated which stated that any gypsies remaining in Germany, irrespective of age or sex, were to be sent to the camp at Auschwitz for extermination. With very few exceptions, Germany's gypsy population perished within the confines of Auschwitz or other concentration camps.

The Gestapo and SS worked in collusion: the Gestapo rounded up the prisoners, while the Allgemeine department of the SS was designated the responsibility for staffing and administering the camps.

Buchenwald concentration camp, which later became the first large extermination camp to be seized intact by Allied advance troops, was located eight kilometres to the north-east of the historic and cultural city of Weimar, capital of Thuringia, and was built on the lower slopes of the often fog-shrouded Ettersburg – a mountain rising 700 metres above sea level.

The camp was one of those first planned by the SS Totenkopfverbände (Death Head Unit) for permanent sites as early as 1936, and ultimately operated for eight years. The other main camps were located at Dachau, near Munich, and Sachsenhausen, near Berlin-Orianienburg. Dachau was located in southern Germany, Sachsenhausen the north, and Buchenwald the central region. As with later camps such as Ravensbrück, Auschwitz and Belsen-Bergen, they were administered from Berlin. By the time Hitler invaded Poland in 1939, there were six camps in operation, containing some 20,000 inmates. Soon there would be nearly a hundred, as the shadow of Nazi domination swept across Europe.

Pre-war, the massive influx of dissidents, political prisoners and other 'undesirables' meant that the new camps had to be built quickly, but forced labour was easily obtainable. And so to the worksite at Buchenwald went the Jews, gypsies, Jehovah's Witnesses, homosexuals and the so-called feeble-minded. The devastating Holocaust, with its promise of 'racial purity' had begun.

The site for Buchenwald camp was a former estate, bequeathed to the SS by its allegiant owner, which covered 140 hectares of rugged and well-wooded, previously uninhabitable beech and pine forest. The camp was opened on 15 July 1937 as KZ (Konzentrationslager) Ettersburg, but less than two weeks later the name was changed to the less austere Buchenwald – Forest of Beeches. On 27 July more than a thousand concentration camp inmates, mostly convicts and political prisoners, began arriving under escort from the established camps of Dachau and Sachsenhausen to commence the mammoth, back-breaking task of clearing the woodland slopes. Standartenführer Karl-Otto Koch, a mid-ranking commander in the SS, was appointed by Himmler as the first Kommandant of Buchenwald, and he brought with him his new wife, Ilse, who would go on to achieve a notoriety far exceeding that of her husband.

Koch had impressed Heinrich Himmler as far back as 1934, when he was appointed Kommandant of Sachsenburg, a concentration camp located close to the city of Chemnitz. He quickly gained a reputation within the SS for carrying out orders, however inhumane they might seem. Koch subsequently held a number of posts at other concentration camps, which included Esterwegen, Lichtenburg and Dachau. As his power increased he familiarised himself with brutal interrogation techniques, instructing his underlings accordingly in methods of extreme mental and physical torture. With Himmler, and elsewhere within the SS hierarchy, he rapidly gained a reputation as a ruthless and even sadistic administrator, seemingly unrestrained by any signs of human decency. Following his appointment as Kommandant at Buchenwald, he ensured all the SS officers and staff lieutenants under his control were equally brutal monsters, and like Koch completely lacking in humanity.

The prisoners were forced to work fourteen hours a day under the most primitive of conditions, and with very few tools. They were subjected to continual torment by their guards, who kicked and beat them with little compunction. Guards who shot any prisoners, ostensibly on the flimsiest excuse of an escape attempt, were usually rewarded with additional pay, promotion and leave passes. Labour was easy to come by, and fear made the prisoners work without pause, in the terrible knowledge that even the slightest hint of flagging or rebellion was keenly looked for – and even manufactured – by the guards.

Parties of workers were taken to the nearby stone quarry, where they were subjected to further harassment from their foremen – generally convicts who had elected to work in this supervisory post for extra rations. These foremen would sometimes snatch a cap from one of the prisoners, toss it away and order the unfortunate man to run and pick it up – at which a sentry would shoot the man for making an 'attempted escape'. The sentry and foreman would later share the bounty. If the sentries decided that work in the quarry was progressing too slowly, they would roll or throw huge rocks onto the frightened workers below them. Those not fast enough to evade the rocks suffered fearful injuries or death.

Water for the workers was scarce during the autumn of 1937, and sanitary provisions consisted of two massive open pits, each eight metres long by four metres wide and deep. Over these lay several indescribably fouled logs, on which squatted as many as fifteen dysentery-stricken men at any one time. One hideous and common sport practised by the guards was to rush the toilet area without warning to see how many prisoners would fall in panic from their precarious perch. Those who fell tried to scramble to the earthen banks of the pits but many, too weak to extract themselves, died in the thick excrement, the laughter of their tormentors the last sound they ever heard. To go to their aid involved the risk of sharing their fate.

In clearing the terrain of trees and vegetation, many of the massive tree roots were painfully and unnecessarily dug out by hand. The SS guards did not issue any digging implements, preferring to watch the prisoners clawing at the hard earth with their hands. However, one massive oak, known widely in the area as Goethe's tree, was spared the fate of the lesser pines surrounding it. According to local legend the revered poet had once meditated beneath its branches, so German officials not only spared the tree, but planned that it would eventually dominate the centre of the new camp. It seemed to take on even more imposing proportions as the ground around it was cleared and exposed.

In fact Goethe's tree was seemingly so indestructible that the inmates quietly developed an improbable superstition concerning the mighty oak. When the tree fell, they declared, so too would Hitler's despised Third Reich. The expectation that this would occur was almost impossibly remote. Incredibly, however, the tree did actually fall towards the end of the war without the hand of man touching it, and in death it became an embodiment of hope and freedom to those who witnessed its destruction.

The site workers in 1937 had little time for such superstitions and were indifferent to the future of Goethe's tree as they slaved on into the extreme cold of the winter months, when temperatures on the newly-exposed slopes would sink as low as a soul-destroying -22°C. As planned, the SS quarters were finished first, so Germany's soldiers could spend their evenings in comfort while freezing prisoners tried to sleep in wretched, inadequate shelters.

Farcical rollcalls were held, during which the prisoners stood for hours on end in the sub-zero temperatures. Every prisoner, living or dead, feverish or badly beaten, had to be marked being present; the only exceptions being hospitalised inmates or those on detached work details. The rollcall on 28 October 1937, with the temperature recorded at -15°C, lasted an absurd 18 hours and 20 minutes, and was drawn out until the Germans were satisfied that the tally of living and dead was correct. The following year, during evening rollcall on 14 December, the count was down by two and the lightly-clad prisoners were forced to stand for 19 hours through a bitterly cold night. By morning, 25 men had frozen to death. When the prisoners were finally dismissed at midday, the number of dead had risen to 70.

On occasions the guards would search prisoners at rollcall. All pockets (if they had them) had to be emptied and the contents examined. This was generally an excuse for the guards to confiscate any money or tobacco they found, but at times they carried out full strip searches simply as an act of humiliation. The prisoners were compelled to stand completely naked for several hours, during which time Ilse Koch and the wives of some of the SS officers would often inspect the prisoners through the wire fence of the compound, pointing out different men, laughing and making lewd comments.

In desperation, a number of prisoners attempted to escape, but generally these were futile bids, and the mandatory penalty was death. In the spring of 1938, a gypsy was recaptured after making an unsuccessful break for freedom and Kommandant Koch decided to use the man to set an example. The gypsy was shoved into a wooden box so small the man could only crouch, and the open side of the box was covered with chicken wire. It was then placed in a prominent position in the rollcall area. Under Koch's orders, several long nails were driven into the sides, back and top of the box, which meant that the man was unable to change his cramped position without piercing his flesh. For two days and three nights the gypsy's agonised screams and pleas for mercy rent the air. On the third day he was given an injection of poison to put an end to his suffering.

On 15 June 1938, a group of around five-hundred Jewish prisoners arrived at Buchenwald. Following the standard delousing process, these men were consigned to a sparse blockhouse commonly known to the inmates as 'the sheep shed'. They were worked to the limit of their physical endurance, existing on a pint of thin soup and a small loaf of bread to be divided amongst five men every day. Many times even these rations were stolen and sold by barracks orderlies. The Jews began dying of exhaustion and maltreatment, with pernicious abuse a daily ordeal. Within eight weeks, 150 of these men had died or had taken their own lives, while the rest were physically incapable of continuing the strenuous work. Then a fresh intake of 2,200 Jewish workers, mostly Austrians, arrived from Dachau.

The November 1938 assassination of German Embassy Secretary Ernst vom Rath in Paris by 17-year-old Polish Jew Herschel Grynszpan resulted in a massive retaliatory round-up of Jews across

Germany. A further 9,800 Jewish workers were sent to assist in the construction of the camp at Buchenwald.

By 1939, over 40 hectares had been clawed bare from the landscape and building was well under way. A typhus epidemic caused the camp to be quarantined for a time in February, but work went on. Only a small part of the site was actually allocated to hold the planned 20,000 male inmates – the greater area had been set aside for the lower SS ranks and for an impressive headquarters building. Apart from the extensive administration building and barracks were such incongruous showpieces as carefully tended zoological and botanical gardens, a game preserve, falconry court, a cinema, and even a riding academy.

On orders from Kommandant Koch in 1938, a small zoo was constructed in an area near the entrance to the inmates' camp, in which several monkeys and other small animals were caged, and a birdhouse erected. Further fuelling Koch's vanity, the zoological garden even included a bear pit, which housed four brown bears. He stated that the zoo was intended as a means of offering his SS officers some 'distraction and amusement'. The area was accessible not only to the SS and their families but to privileged civilian workers employed in armaments factories adjoining the camp. Postcards were even printed and circulated, advertising the zoo's many features. The bears and the well-tended gardens were in full view of the starving prisoners who, by way of stark contrast, existed in abject misery, imprisoned in filthy conditions and treated as less than human. Surviving inmates told horrifying stories of Koch's sadistic pleasure in organising a number of 'spectator' days when SS guards were invited to watch, laugh and cheer as a terrified prisoner was thrust into the bear pit, where he would be quickly ripped to shreds and devoured by the ferocious animals. Over the years, much of the food allocated to the camp as prisoner rations was instead diverted to feed the zoo's animals.

By the beginning of the Second World War, the concentration camp was fully functional. Proudly mounted above the main gate to the camp was the Buchenwald motto, 'Recht oder unrecht – mein Vaterland', literally 'My country – right or wrong'. An electrically charged fence nearly four kilometres long surrounded the prisoners' enclosure.

Entrance to the main camp compound was made through an iron gate set within a narrow gatehouse, which was straddled by a two-storey brick and wooden guardhouse, surmounted in turn by a searchlight and clock tower. Fashioned into the gate was yet another motto, 'Jedem das Seine' (To each his own). On either side of the gatehouse were steel-doored punishment cells known to the inmates as bunkers, and beyond it lay the main rollcall or appell area, a dusty, rock-hard compound which was transformed into a cloying quagmire when the rains came. The wooden huts beyond the compound were roughly constructed and earthen-floored, without windows or sanitary facilities. The inmates were still forced to use the rough open pit.

The camp itself was set out in two sections – the Main Camp, with its brick buildings and wooden huts, and the Little Camp, in which conditions were indescribably wretched. Here the excess of prisoners were bunked in horse stables, originally intended to house twenty-eight beasts, but which were soon crowded with up to 2,000 men at any one time. Squashed together, with three or four men sharing a single thin blanket, and generally clad in putrid wet clothing, these exhausted and undernourished men slept on tiered wooden bunks. Washing facilities were primitive, personal hygiene was practically non-existent, and epidemics regularly coursed through these barracks.

Prior to the completion of a permanent crematorium at Buchenwald in 1941, a mobile unit was installed in order to dispose of those who had died. The combustion chamber in this unit was quite small, and the bodies literally had to be crammed in. Sometimes smaller body parts were not completely cremated. These gruesome remains were often scattered across the rollcall compound.

From October 1942, the shipment of Jewish prisoners to the death camps for annihilation became mandatory, and this policy remained in force until the summer of 1943. By then a severe lack of manpower resources meant that the surviving Jews found themselves being used as slave labour rather than being fed into the gas chambers and later cremated. Spared the immediate threat of extermination, they were worked at a gruelling schedule to the point of physical exhaustion.

The camp perimeter at Buchenwald was constantly patrolled, while machine-guns protruded from the guard towers, or miradors. At night, searchlights illuminated the electrified fences.

A five-kilometre asphalt road named Eicke Street (after the chief of the SS Death-Head unit) meandered away from the camp and was bordered by elite SS residences. It finally led to a cluster of luxuriously appointed villas belonging to the Kommandant and his senior officers, who delighted in the centrally heated comforts while enjoying sweeping views over the magnificent Thuringian Plains from the sheltered southerly slope of the Ettersburg. In a well-guarded stockade enclosure beyond the road stood the isolation huts, specially constructed as barracks for politically prominent inmates.

The Kommandant's wife, Ilse Koch, made special use of the riding academy hall at Buchenwald. This massive construction was nearly 100 metres long and 40 wide, with mirrored walls and a roof suspended more than 20 metres above the bark-chip ring. Frau Koch made frequent morning rides in the hall to the musical accompaniment of her own SS band. A former bar girl, the plump, red-haired and nymphomaniacal Ilse had accompanied her husband to the concentration camp in 1937, where she quickly became known to the inmates as 'The Bitch of Buchenwald'. With good reason, they feared her more than their sadistic guards.

Ilse was born in Dresden in 1907 and by the age of fourteen was working in a cigarette factory. Although never a great beauty, her glorious red hair and energetic sexual appetite attracted many young men to her bed, where she allowed them to indulge their fantasies and aberrations on her willing body. She later worked as a bar girl and then as an assistant for an elderly bookseller, whose business thrived due to his under-the-counter sales of pornographic literature. One of the store's best customers was a conceited young Gestapo officer by the name of Karl-Otto Koch.

Karl and Ilse quickly became lovers but both had strong sexual appetites and by mutual consent they actively pursued different bed partners. Ilse set about seducing many of the bedazzled young officers from Karl's regiment, giving her bemused lover a rating of each as a sex partner. When Himmler promoted Koch to colonel and appointed him Kommandant of Buchenwald, it came with a strong recommendation that he should marry and make his wife chatelaine of the camp. Karl and Ilse, with an eye to the future, readily complied.

The power of her non-accountable position soon turned Ilse into one of the most feared and sadistic creatures of the war. Accounts given at her post-war trial testified to her debauchery while at Buchenwald, and made for horrifying testimony, yet every incident was verified by witnesses eager to see justice brought to bear on this despised woman.

On many occasions, she would ride her horse through the prisoners' compound wearing nothing more than a brief swimsuit. The object of this exercise was to feign outrage if any inmate dared give her so much as a sideways glance, or to look for anyone whose sight displeased her. The penalty for such trivialities was a severe whipping or beating. On one such occasion, an unfortunate prisoner was caught furtively peering at her. On Ilse's order the man was held face-down in a muddy puddle until he drowned. Another time she was seen to take up a pistol and participate in a cold-blooded massacre of over twenty unfortunate inmates. She would order teams of terrified men to run around the compound dragging heavily-laden carts, singing at the tops of their voices, which gave the name 'singing horses' to this heinous activity.

Ilse's appetite for sexual perversion grew with her unchallenged power over life and death. Several times she was known to select a suitable prisoner for a night's orgy in company with her husband, whose bisexuality added to Ilse's enjoyment. In the morning the prisoner was taken away and executed lest he reveal any details of the night's activities. During her husband's five-year tenure at Buchenwald, Ilse gave birth to two sons and would often frolic in the nude with them on the lawn of their luxurious villa.

Eventually Ilse's carnal excesses even grew too much for her husband, who found more sedate pleasures sodomising young boys from the compound. But Ilse's perversions continued unchecked and soon a horrible rumour began to spread around the camp that she was having inmates killed and using their tanned skin to make gloves. Later evidence not only proved these rumours to be true, but far worse was to come.

At the time of the liberation of Buchenwald, a gruesome display of items was put together for official photographs, later to be used in evidence at Ilse's trial. According to witnesses, she would ride around the compound seeking out prisoners with what she considered attractive tattoos. She would have any such victim seized and taken to the camp dispensary, where he would be killed by means of a poison injection. The skin bearing the tattoo would then be carefully removed, cleaned, and tan-dried in the camp's pathology department. The resultant tattooed strips were then manufactured into lampshades and other household 'ornaments'. One man's tattoo which took Ilse's fancy bore the words 'Hansel and Gretel', while a favourite table lamp – a birthday present for Ilse – was manufactured from human bones with a shade made from skin.

An important witness at Ilse's post-war trial was a worker from the camp's pathology department, Joseph Akerman. He told of seeing hundreds of skin segments being stripped from the bodies of murdered inmates on her specific orders, and even recalled the birthday lamp. 'It was a complete lamp made of human skin and bone,' he testified. 'The light was switched on by pressure against the little toe of one of the three human feet which formed the stand.'

While Frau Koch used the camp and its inmates as her playthings, her husband began to grow wealthy by utilising the camp's labour force to his own advantage. Despite Himmler's doctrines of so-called honour and integrity within the SS, Karl Koch amassed a quick and considerable fortune by sending camp labour out to local private concerns who willingly lined his pockets in exchange for a cheap, expendable work force. However, Koch's greed proved his undoing when he came under the suspicious attention of local tax authorities who claimed that huge sums of money, around a million marks in all, had been misappropriated by the Kommandant.

SS leader Prince Waldeck-Pyrmont, the supreme legal authority in the district, had been made aware of corruption and other rumoured charges made against Standartenführer Koch and brought the matter to the attention of Heinrich Himmler, who refused to believe that such unsubstantiated charges could be laid against a trusted officer of the SS. Meanwhile, from September 1941 until August 1942, while the charges of corruption were being investigated by the SS, Koch was posted as the first commandant of KZ Majdanek, a concentration and extermination camp operated by the SS near the city of Lublin in occupied Poland. At the same time, many of Koch's actions at Buchenwald had caught the attention of his superiors. In one instance, Dr Walter Krämer, the head hospital orderly at Buchenwald, had been killed under questionable circumstances. An investigation revealed that Koch had ordered that both Krämer and hospital attendant Karl Peixof be executed as 'political prisoners'. They had treated him for syphilis and he feared they might reveal his secret, so he had them eliminated on a false pretext. Following investigations at Buchenwald which revealed overwhelming evidence of corruption, additional charges of embezzlement were raised against Koch, his wife Ilse, and other camp officials who had stolen vast amounts of valuables and money from murdered inmates, lining their own pockets instead of passing it on to Berlin to aid the war effort. Combined with the testimony of informants, it was sufficient for Karl Koch to be placed under arrest and gaoled in Weimar.

Himmler was said to be furious at his officer's now proven betrayal and demanded an example be made of him. Koch was subsequently tried by an SS tribunal, found guilty of profiteering and given the option of death by firing squad or serving on the Russian front. However, Prince Waldeck would have none of that. Mindful of Himmler's outrage, he overruled the judgement of the tribunal. Koch was removed from gaol and taken back to Buchenwald on 5 April 1945. Here, looking out over the scene of his many crimes, he was summarily executed by firing squad just days before the camp's liberation. Fittingly, his body was then disposed of in the camp crematorium.

With her husband's transfer to Lublin, Ilse remained for a time at Buchenwald, albeit in the reduced position of a domestic staff member under the new Kommandant, SS Colonel Hermann Pister. Frau Koch, her formerly unquestionable authority now greatly diminished, would stay with her two children (another had died in infancy) for another two years.

Following the liberation of Buchenwald by American forces on 11 April 1945, Ilse Koch managed to evade capture for a number of weeks until her luck ran out. As she was walking down a street in Ludwigsburg, north of Stuttgart, she was recognised by a Buchenwald survivor, arrested and gaoled.

At the Buchenwald trials, lasting from April to August 1947 within the walls of the former Dachau concentration camp and conducted by American military personnel whose legal authority had been conferred by the Judge Advocate General's Department within the US Third Army, twenty-two Nazi officials of Buchenwald concentration camp were sentenced to hang.

Ilse Koch, then aged 41 and eight months pregnant, was among those who received a life sentence. During the trial, she repeatedly denied any of the charges against her, to the clamorous hoots of derision from those assembled within the courtroom. She then resorted to a pretence of being mentally unbalanced, but this made no impression on the judges. A plea for clemency due to her imminent motherhood was put forward, but this was also rejected. The pregnancy, which occurred while she was in prison awaiting trial, was never officially explained, although the father was believed to have been a fellow prisoner. On 17 October the Americans struck a deal with the Bavarian Minister of Justice and 'released' Ilse Koch. She was immediately rearrested by the Germans and placed on trial for incitement to murder. On 29 October she gave birth to a baby boy – father never revealed – who was taken from her and sent off to a Bavarian orphanage. Four years later, on 15 January 1951, the German courts found her guilty and Frau Koch received her second life sentence.

Still holding hopes of an eventual release from Aichach prison, Ilse began learning English and took to writing poetry. She also corresponded with some poor misguided soul in Australia who had written to her in prison and even spoke of emigrating there to marry him on her release. But her lawyer's efforts to secure her release were all in vain. On 1 September 1967 Ilse Koch tied a strip of her bedsheet around her neck and hanged herself from the cell door. She left behind a suicide note saying, 'Death is a release for me. There is no other way.'

Ilse Koch was not the only person to take advantage of unlimited power over a helpless and wretched assemblage of humanity. Killings were commonplace in Buchenwald, and the methods employed were mostly barbarous.

By 1942, block number 46 had been constructed for use as a medical experiment centre. Here prisoners were used as human guinea pigs in a variety of sinister studies, which included injecting them with typhus and conducting experiments on how long a man could survive on a diet of sea water. Unskilled and discredited practitioners worked at discovering vaccines for a vast array of diseases including smallpox and cholera. They frequently indulged themselves in the practice of unnecessary surgical techniques attempting to cure, among other 'anti-social diseases', homosexuality.

Decompression and cold water survival tests also saw many of the victims suffer an early death. Men were immersed in freezing water for varying times then placed between two frightened sex workers from the camp brothel. If the men survived, the recovery time was noted. Many inmates destined for the crematorium ovens were sent via the experimental block where they received injections of phenol, milk, or sometimes just air. At the Nuremberg trials in 1946, Eugen Kogon gave the following testimony:

> In Block 50 I saw photographs of phosphor burns taken at Block 46. One need not be a specialist to imagine the suffering of people whose flesh was burnt down to the bones. When the experiment was completed after three months, all those who survived were liquidated.

Kogon, who served as a medical clerk at Buchenwald, also spoke of a fearful torture perpetrated on some poor unfortunates:

> Dreaded even worse than whipping was the punishment that involved being trussed up against a tree. Like all other penalties,

> it was imposed in entirely arbitrary fashion. It was executed in the following way: the hands were tightly tied on the back and then the body was hoisted up by [the guards] and suspended some six feet high from a tree or post, the feet hanging free and the entire weight resting on the twisted shoulder joints. The result was extremely painful shoulder dislocations. The victims screamed and moaned frightfully. Often they received beatings on their face, feet or sexual organs to boot. The helpless sufferers cried for water, for their wives and children, for a bullet to end their torment. Those who lost consciousness were revived by being drenched with cold water. This punishment lasted from half an hour to four hours. Those who survived it almost invariably sustained permanent injuries.

The camp's crematorium and mortuary block was a single-storey building with a basement below ground level. A stone staircase led down into the dank basement – the last steep steps for many prisoners. Those not escorted down the steps were simply shoved through a trapdoor in the floor above.

Embedded in the stone walls of the basement were 48 open steel hooks, set about two-and-a-half metres above the floor. The doomed prisoners would be tied back to back, then loose nooses made of high tensile piano wire were placed around their necks. Then, in pairs, they were hoisted up by the guards until the nooses dropped over the hooks, at which time the guards moved away. It was a cruel death. One unnamed former inmate, who looked into the basement after the liberation of the camp, recalls seeing scratch marks low down on the stone walls where the men had frantically kicked out in their brief death throes. After five minutes had elapsed, the bodies were lifted down. A 'coup de grace' was administered by means of a heavy wooden club, crushing the men's skulls. The bodies were then despatched in a large electric lift to the ground-floor crematorium, which had the capacity for disposing of almost 400 bodies a day.

In order to corrupt the more powerful of their political prisoners, the SS had even established a brothel at Buchenwald, bringing in women from another death camp at Ravensbrück who had been falsely promised they would be discharged after six months' 'service'. After serving their time, the women were simply shipped back to Ravensbrück and a fresh consignment sent in. The SS hoped that the senior inmates at Buchenwald would be more responsive to their commands if they were given the luxury of spending twenty minutes at a time with some of these women. All this really did, however, was cause a further corruption of power within the camp hierarchy, with the more-feared German Communists exerting their power over the subordinates in order to obtain extra gifts for the women, which in turn gave them lengthier sojourns in their beds. The majority of the camp's senior men avoided the brothel and its temptations, whereas higher-ranking members of the SS also took advantage of the brothel, and they could be found behind its doors at all hours of the evening.

Thousands of Buchenwald prisoners were used as forced labour in Germany's war factories, which were built underground to protect these facilities from Allied air attacks. Assignment to these armament factories was a virtual death sentence; the Germans could never relinquish a prisoner who had been engaged in such highly secret work, and once they had outlived their productive usefulness, they were killed. Some natural caves within the Kohnstein mountain near Nordhausen were converted into an underground concentration camp, a Buchenwald subsidiary known as Mittlebau-Dora.

Squadron Leader Phillip J. Lamason, DFC and Bar, RNZAF. He assumed leadership of the 168 airmen illegally sent to Buchenwald concentration camp
(Photo: Australian War Memorial PO2988.001)

Warrant Officer Raymond W. Perry, RAAF (Photo: Australian War Memorial PO2980.001)

Warrant Officer Thomas A. Malcolm, RAAF (Photo: Australian War Memorial PO3072.001)

Warrant Officer Keith C. Mills, RAAF (Photo: Australian War Memorial PO2962.001)

Flying Officer Robert N. Mills, RAAF (Photo: Frank Signorile/French National Archives)

Warrant Officer Eric L. Johnston, RAAF (left) and Warrant Officer James P. Gwilliam, RAAF (Photo: Australian War Memorial PO2961.002)

Flight Lieutenant Kevin Light, DFM, RAAF (Photo: K. Light)

Warrant Officer Mervyn J. Fairclough, RAAF (Photo: Australian War Memorial PO2965.001)

Warrant Officer Les K. Whellum, RAAF (Photo: L. K. Whellum)

Flight Lieutenant Malcolm F. Cullen, RNZAF (Photo: Australian War Memorial PO2974.001)

Phil Lamason's crew at No. 15 Squadron, RAF Mildenhall. From left: Flying Officer Ken Chapman, Pilot Officer Gerry Musgrove, Flying Officer Lionel George, Flight Lieutenant John Marpole, Squadron Leader Phil Lamason, Pilot Officer Tommy Dunk and Flight Sergeant Robbie Aitken (Photo: P. Lamason)

On the run across France: Local helper Colette Kalmanson with evading airmen Phil Lamason and Ken Chapman (Photo: Australian War Memorial P03072.002)

Prior to capture, three airmen destined for Buchenwald pose with their French benefactors, the Wyatts, Bastille Day, 1944. Eric Davis (second from left, at rear), Frank Salt (centre, with tie) and Ray Perry (on the right) (Photo: Australian War Memorial PO2980.003)

Pre-war postcard of the village of Coivrel (Photo: Jim Gwilliam)

Four Australian crewmembers and some of their helpers in Coivrel. The disguised airmen (arrested later that same day) are Keith Mills, Eric Johnston, Bob Mills (pilot) and Jim Gwilliam (Photo: Frank Signorile/French National Archives)

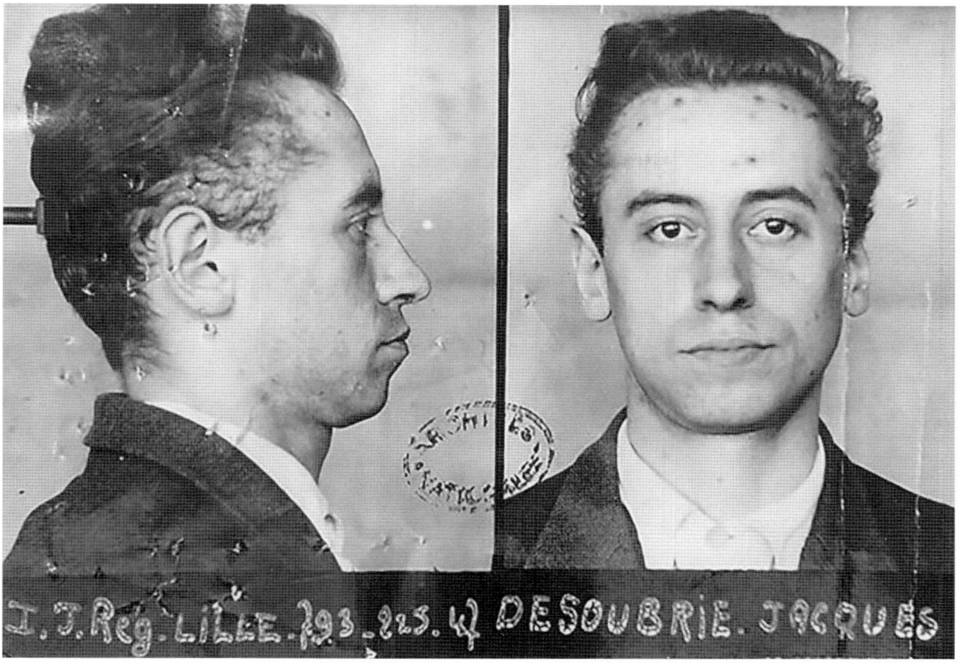

The Belgian traitor Jacques 'Captain Jacques' Desoubrie, responsible for handing many evading airmen over to the Gestapo (Photo: Frank Signorile/French National Archives)

Not dissimilar in appearance to Desoubrie, Guy de Marcheret was the other traitorous 'Captain Jacques' operating within the French Resistance in Paris on behalf of his German masters (Photo: Frank Signorile/French National Archives)

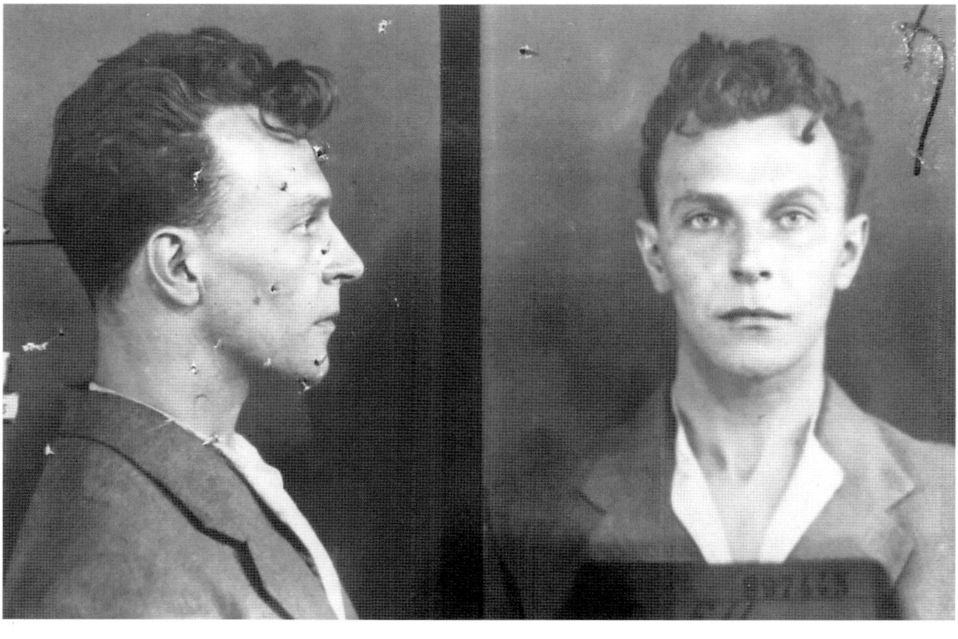

An overall view of Fresnes prison in Paris (Photo: Frank Falla Archive)

The Pantin rail yards, Paris, embarkation point for the nightmare journey to Buchenwald

Concentration camp Buchenwald (KLB) was located on the northern slopes of the Ettersburg, a hill north of the city of Weimar (Photo: United States Holocaust Memorial Museum, courtesy of Robert Michael Merritt)

The luxurious Villa Koch on the south side of the Ettersburg hill at Buchenwald (Photo: Buchenwald Memorial Museum)

The feared stone quarry at Buchenwald, where the hours were long and the workload brutal. Death was a common occurrence (Photo: United States Holocaust Memorial Museum, courtesy of Gedenkstaette Buchenwald)

Prisoners mixing concrete in the Buchenwald quarry (Photo: United States Holocaust Memorial Museum, courtesy of National Archives and Records Administration, College Park)

Sleeping conditions in the overcrowded and verminous, disease-riddled huts were appalling
(Photo: Yad Vashem Photo Archive, Jerusalem. 1495/9)

Karl and Ilse at Villa Koch with their children Artwin and Gisela (Photo: Buchenwald Memorial Museum, courtesy of National Archives, Washington)

The cruel legend above the camp's main gate, which translates as 'To each his own' (Photo: United States Holocaust Memorial Museum, courtesy of David Cohen)

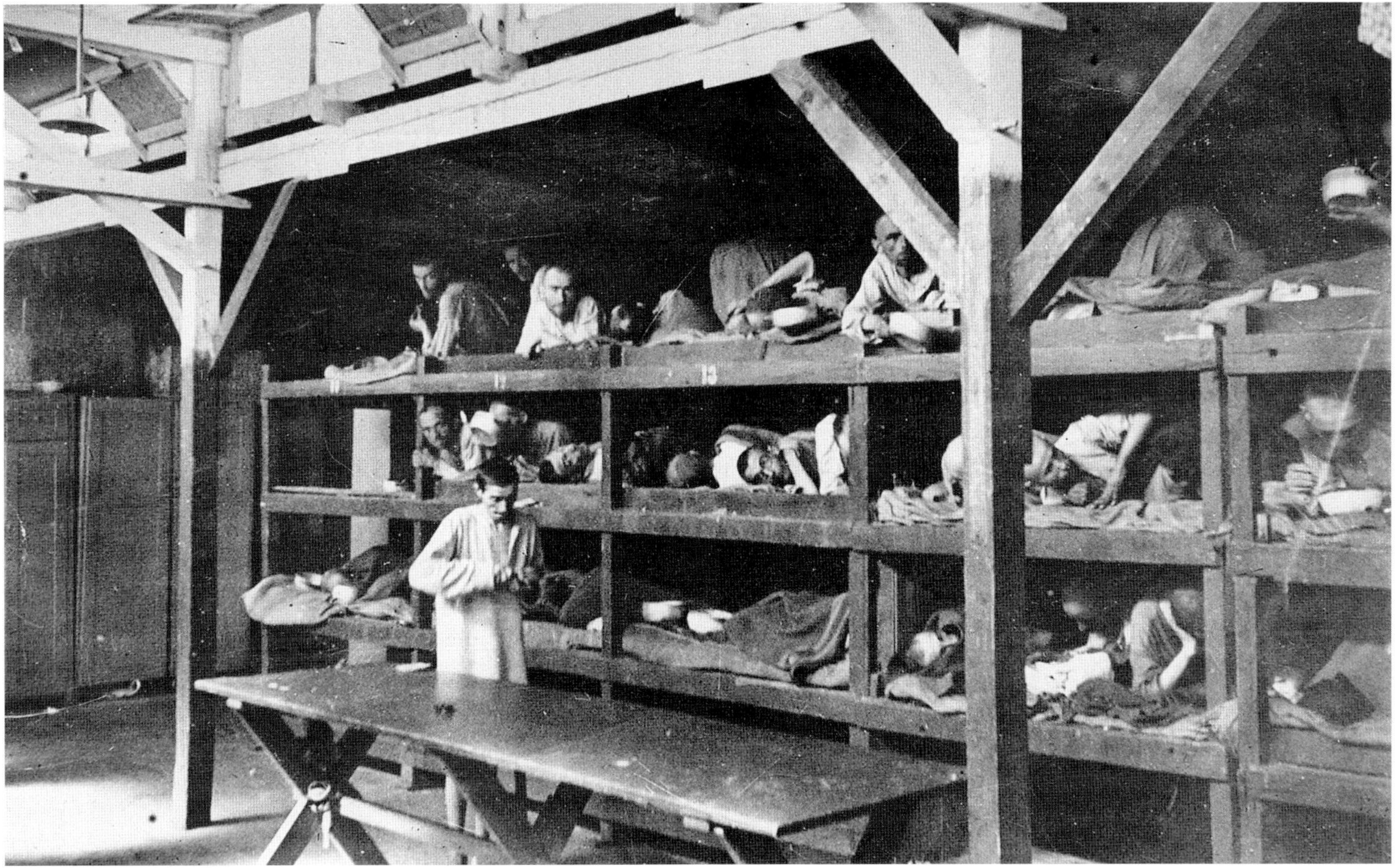

The so-called 'hospital' at Buchenwald, where any treatment was cursory at best (Photo: National Archives, Washington)

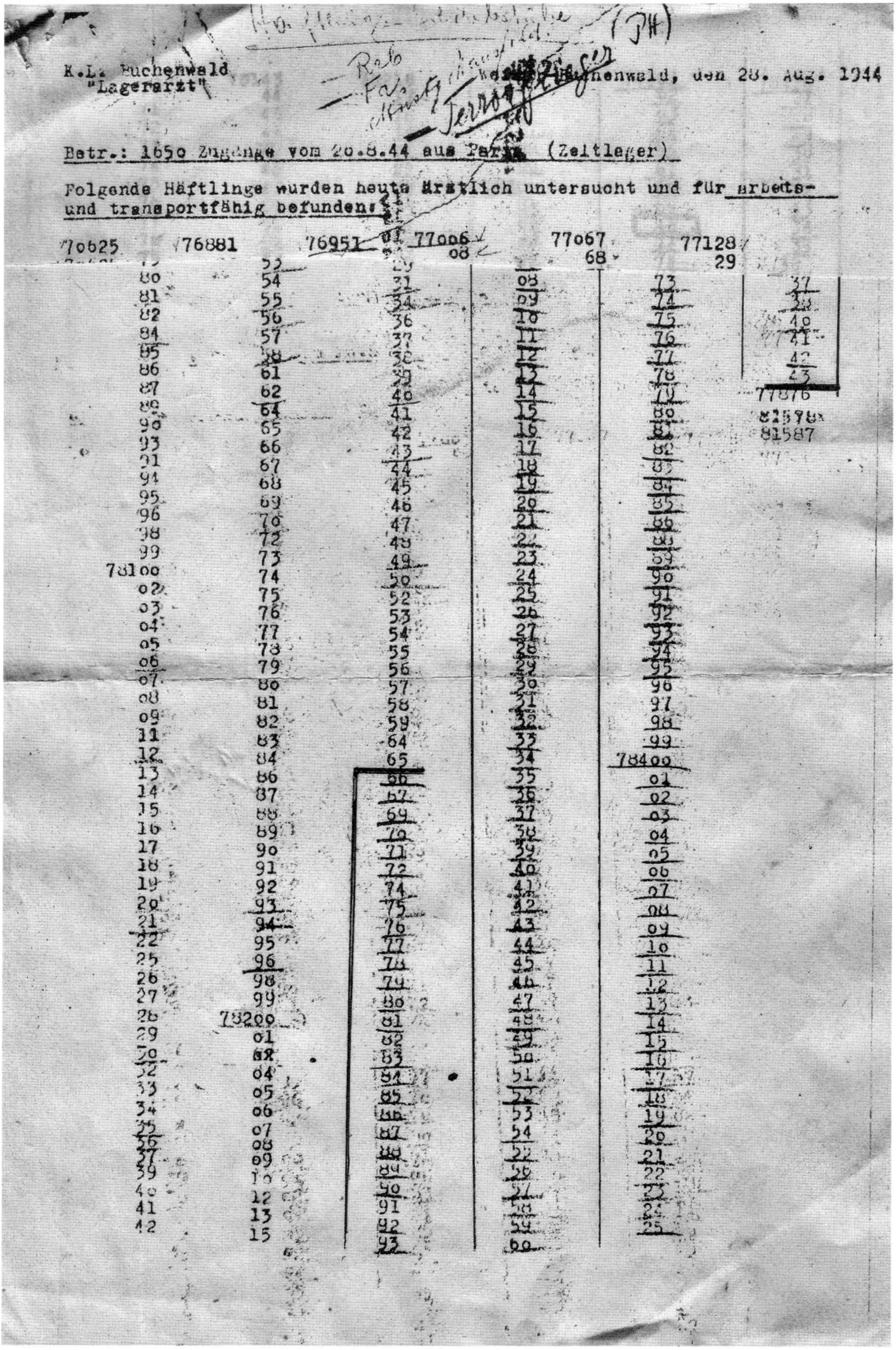

K.L. Buchenwald
"Lagerarzt"

Weimar-Buchenwald, den 28. Aug. 1944

Betr.: 1650 Zugänge vom 20.8.44 aus Paris (Zeltlager)

Folgende Häftlinge wurden heute ärztlich untersucht und für arbeits- und transportfähig befunden:

70625 79 80 81 82 84 85 86 87 89 90 93 91 94 95 96 98 99 78100 02 03 04 05 06 07 08 09 11 12 13 14 15 16 17 18 19 20 21 22 25 26 27 28 29 30 32 33 34 35 36 37 39 40 41 42

76881 53 54 55 56 57 58 61 62 64 65 66 67 68 69 70 72 73 74 75 76 77 78 79 80 81 82 83 84 86 87 88 89 90 91 92 93 94 95 96 98 99 78200 01 02 04 05 06 07 08 09 10 12 13 15

76951 29 31 34 36 37 38 39 40 41 42 43 44 45 46 47 48 49 50 52 53 54 55 56 57 58 59 64 65 66 67 69 70 71 72 74 75 76 77 78 79 80 81 82 83 84 85 86 87 88 89 90 91 92 93

77006 08 09 10 11 12 13 14 15 16 17 18 19 20 21 22 23 24 25 26 27 28 29 30 31 32 33 34 35 36 37 38 39 40 41 42 43 44 45 46 47 48 49 50 51 52 53 54 55 56 57 58 59 60

77067 68 73 74 75 76 77 78 79 80 81 82 83 84 85 86 88 89 90 91 92 93 94 95 96 97 98 99 78400 01 02 03 04 05 06 07 08 09 10 11 12 13 14 15 16 17 18 19 20 21 22 23 24 25

77128 29 37 38 40 41 42 43 77876 81578 81587

The transportation orders for the 168 'Terrorfliegers' included the handwritten notation 'DIKAL: Darf in kein anderes Lager' (Not to be transferred to another camp) – in other words, they were destined for elimination. The airmen's KLB numbers are within the bracketed area (Photo: Art Kinnis)

The crematorium at Buchenwald (Photo: United States Holocaust Memorial Museum, courtesy of David Cohen)

The ovens within the crematorium (Photo: National Archives, Washington)

The Kleinelager (Little Camp) was a quarantine area within Buchenwald that housed the contingent of airmen (Photo: Buchenwald Memorial Museum)

Goethe's tree in the camp compound. It was believed that when the tree fell, so too would Hitler's Third Reich (Photo: Musée de la Résistance et de la Déportation, Besançon)

During the latter war years, prisoners at Dora were forced to live in filthy conditions and work twelve-hour shifts on the production of Hitler's deadly V-weapons. They would not see daylight for weeks on end.

Dozens of louse-infected, pathetically thin corpses were transported from Dora to Buchenwald every second day, and the mortality rate never fell below 1,500 per month. These bodies were intertwined in death, and the first gruesome task on arrival at Buchenwald was to wrench each pathetic body from the pile of corpses for cremation.

Two armaments factories operated on the outskirts of the prisoners' compound at Buchenwald, obviously positioned to deter area bombing by the Allies. The Gustloff-Werke II (Gustloff Armaments Works, or GAW) was a factory funded by Jewish property and possessions appropriated by the regional Nazi leader in Thuringia. The Deutsche Ausrüstungswerke (German Equipment Works, or DAW) was a general armaments and radio factory owned by the SS, under trusteeship of the camp Kommandant Hermann Pister, which turned over an annual profit of half a million marks destined for Himmler's war coffers.

The prisoners who worked in both factories not only took to carrying out covert acts of sabotage, but succeeded in smuggling out weapons such as rifles and hand grenades. These arms went to a secret military resistance group within the camp, and were eventually used in the successful uprising which saw the camp liberated.

Prisoners arriving in Buchenwald were designated a camp number, and it was by this number that they were identified and answerable from that time on. After passing through the Effektenkammer (effects store – these days the camp museum) they were stripped of all their money and possessions prior to undergoing the removal of all their body hair and showering in an adjoining block. All of these new arrivals were then placed in the Little Camp quarantine area awaiting work orders from such places as the outside armaments factories. They were then subjected to a cursory medical examination, following which they were graded for duties according to their physical fitness levels. Their next move was into the Main Camp, where the Arbeitsstatistik (labour statistics office) raised a personal working card for each prisoner and allocated them to specially constituted working parties, known as Kommandos. These Kommandos were still functioning when the group of airmen arrived in Buchenwald in August 1944, and former KLB prisoner Stanley Booker explained what would befall the unfortunate prisoners on these work details.

> These Kommandos, known as Transports, gave cause to the greatest terror and apprehension, for they were used solely to dispose of inmates on expendable working parties. The Transports left the camp daily, marched out behind a magnificent military band in circus-type uniforms of gold lace and red velvet, which had originated in a Hungarian State Opera. After varying periods as slave labourers in the various outcamps and factories, the telling twelve-hour working days resulted in the prisoners becoming exhausted and burned out. At this stage they were returned to the Main Camp for extermination in the camp crematorium.
>
> Within the camp itself, those inmates fortunate enough not to be allocated to external working Transports were detailed daily to various internal tasks, such as the dreaded quarry or camp sewage pit, ditch digging, railway and road maintenance, camp administration, kitchen details or miscellaneous duties in the medical block.

The camp was divided into two components – the Main Camp, which comprised the pre-war accommodation surrounding the main Appellplatz, and the Little Camp, used as the quarantine area. It was accepted that conditions in the Little Camp were exceptionally bad, and that any long-term prisoners kept there and not allocated to an outside Kommando within the first few days were considered expendable. One of the most feared Kommandos was to be detailed to work in the camp quarry, located on the extremity of the Little Camp, from where most of the labour was obtained. This was where the greatest number of deaths were recorded every day. The prisoners were forced to break stones with the most basic of tools, load them with their bare hands into rail tipper trucks, and push them up a steep incline to the surface level. Inmates were liquidated by being driven to sheer exhaustion, and that's when they were shot by the guards or simply beaten to death.

Another of the unsavoury characters inhabiting the camp in the early war years was the notorious hangman of Buchenwald, SS Scharführer (Master Sergeant) Walter Gerhard Martin Sommer, whose dominion was the isolation cells or bunker, located in one wing of the gatehouse. The bunker was comprised of a series of compact concrete cells, each with a small window embrasure and radiator high on the wall, and a raised concrete platform that served as a bed. A magnifying peephole was set into each door so the prisoners could be monitored, and any transgressions, however minor, were rewarded with twenty-five lashes of a whip.

The bunker was used for the interrogation and torture of prisoners, and Martin Sommer was adept at both. One of his favourite methods of interrogation was to have the prisoner stripped naked and then alternately immerse his victim's testicles in ice-cold and boiling water. After a while the skin would begin to strip from the man's scrotum, at which Sommer would splash on a 'treatment' of iodine, causing the prisoner extreme pain.

According to evidence given by him during the trial of Kommandant Koch, Sommer was personally responsible for the torture and death of over 150 prisoners in one six-month period. He flogged, stamped on, hanged or deliberately poisoned any prisoner brought to the bunker. As a confidant of the Kommandant, even the SS at Buchenwald feared Sommer and they soon became aware that he held sufficient power to have any of them transferred or even eliminated if they displeased him.

On arrival at the bunker, each prisoner was stripped and searched, then tied to the radiator in his cell to await the attention of Sommer. Should the prisoner be found asleep during this time he was thrashed mercilessly by a guard. The killings were administered in a variety of ways. Sometimes Sommer would simply hang the man from the window or radiator of his cell; at other times he would beat them to death with an iron bar. In one instance he placed a prisoner's head in an iron clamp, which he screwed tight until the man's head was crushed.

There were many verified examples of his barbarism. In 1940, seven Jews were being held in a single cell when Sommer entered carrying a tin water pail. He proceeded to beat two of the men to death with the pail, following which he tore a piece of iron from the radiator and in a frenzy of unbridled rage used it to kill the other occupants.

Sommer harboured a particular hatred for men of the cloth; on one occasion he ordered that two Austrian priests, Otto Neururer and Mathias Spannlang, be crucified upside-down. He also beat a Catholic priest to death who had enraged him by performing the Sacrament of Penance for a fellow prisoner. He inflicted yet another beating on a German pastor before having the man taken outside and tied naked to a post in the middle of winter. Every so often he would throw a bucket of water over the clergyman until the man literally froze to death.

In his 1950 book, *The Theory and Practice of Hell*, former prisoner Eugen Kogon relates many of the inhumanities practised by Martin Sommer during his reign of terror in Buchenwald's bunker.

> It was . . . customary to feed the prisoners cathartics in their food, until they fell ill with bloody stools. Of course there were no antidotes. There were two toilets in the bunker; one for the prisoners, the other for the SS. Whenever a prisoner received his twenty-five lashes, he had to bend over and immerse his head in the excrement-filled toilet bowl. When the punishment had been administered, he was not permitted to wipe the excrement from his face.
>
> On one occasion Sommer shackled seven young Polish prisoners to their cots. Their diet was reduced to salt water and pickles until they perished. Bunker orderly Gritz described how their fearful screams, and finally moans, pierced his eardrums.
>
> Some of the tortures inflicted by Sommer were nightmares of sadism. He liked to strangle prisoners with his bare hands. His greatest sport was to herd all his prisoners into the corridor, about four feet wide, where he had them do knee bends and hop

about until they dropped from exhaustion. He would then trample them with his heels, until the blood spurted from their ears and nose and at least a few were left dead. On one occasion he crowded fifteen prisoners into a single cell, giving them only a children's chamber pot which they were not permitted to empty for some ten days by which time the floor of the cell was ankle-deep in excrement. Subsequently Sommer murdered all fifteen men.

His own quarters were decorated with an illuminated skull. At night he would sometimes summon a victim from one of the cells and leisurely do away with him in his room. He would then place the body under his bed and fall asleep peacefully, his work well done.

Such was the place to which the airmen arrived on 20 August 1944. By that time such evil protagonists as Martin Sommer and Karl Koch had been removed from power by Himmler, and the influence of Ilse Koch was greatly diluted. In 1943, an investigation was held into overt cruelty and corruption at Buchenwald. As a result, Sommer was reduced in rank and sent in disgrace to a penal battalion on the Eastern front, where he lost his right leg and permanent use of his badly damaged left arm in a tank explosion. Taken prisoner by the Soviet army, he was held as a POW until 1950, when he was charged and imprisoned as a war criminal. Five years later he was released back into German hands as part of a prisoner exchange negotiated by Chancellor Konrad Adenauer. Now living in West Germany, he married his nurse and they had a child. In 1957, he was finally indicted for complicity in the death of 101 concentration camp inmates, and the following year was deemed healthy enough to stand trial. Convicted of 25 of those deaths, he was given a life sentence which he appealed, using his disabilities as a defence for not being returned to prison. In May 1959, his conviction was upheld by the West German Federal Court. Sommer would remain in gaol until 1971, when he could no longer receive custodial treatment for his severe war injuries. He was subsequently transferred to a prison hospital in Schwarzenbruck for full-time care, where he lingered until his death on 7 June 1988, aged 74.

Despite the removal of Koch and Sommer, the industry of mass extermination continued at Buchenwald. By late 1944 physical conditions had deteriorated even further as the number of prisoners increased due to Hitler's unchecked policy of eliminating those he regarded as subhuman.

According to the official statistics, a total of 238,980 prisoners were admitted to Buchenwald between July 1937 and March 1945, of whom 56,545 died. Approximately 161,000 prisoners left the camp for work at armaments or munitions factories, or were transferred to other death camps.

For several hours after their arrival at Buchenwald, the airmen stood under the heat of the afternoon sun. However, they were more concerned for the safety of the French prisoners who had shared their nightmare train journey across France and Germany. On arrival at the camp, these men and boys had been forced to enter a large brick hut, and they had not emerged.

As the airmen waited for something to happen, Phil Lamason walked up and down, instructing the men that they were to conduct themselves as a military body, and accordingly would march correctly whenever they were moving around the camp. He reiterated that they were rightfully prisoners of war, and not political or criminal prisoners. Military decorum was to be maintained at all times and the orders of superior officers obeyed, come what may, until representation could be made through the proper channels. His words encouraged the men, who respected the stocky New Zealander, and they bore their circumstances with markedly more dignity. Nevertheless, as Tommy Blackham recalled, it was difficult for the airmen to maintain their discipline and silence at times. 'Every time an SS man came along we had to stand to attention . . . All our personal belonging had been confiscated – these included military identity discs which, the Germans said, could be bought in France for a few francs.'

When it came time for the airmen to strip and enter the brick building, Lamason directed the Dutch translator Spierenburg to object to this treatment on behalf of his men, claiming the rights of prisoners of war. These appeals were ignored and the first of the men were shoved into an anteroom in the building. Here, any remaining contents of their pockets were placed in an envelope while all their clothing was checked into a bag which was then tagged with their names. Canadian airman Ed Carter-Edwards vividly remembers their following painful welcome to Buchenwald.

> They cut off all our hair, every strand from every part of our bodies. The guys who sheared us were Russian prisoners from the camp, which at that time held around 40,000 people. There were Russians, Poles, Czechs, French, every nationality imaginable; political prisoners, soldiers, black market agents, and everything else. The fellows who clipped us were most unkind. They used old-style clippers, cutting underneath our arms and between our legs. They were so rough they nicked pretty badly; we were bleeding all

> over, and to finish off their pleasure they used a swab and stuck it in a pail of fluid and dipped it under our arms and between our legs. It was some kind of lye and oh, did it burn! Imagine nearly 170 airmen dancing around like stripped chickens. It was funny but painful at the same time.

Totally devoid of hair and clothing, the men were told they had to have showers and were ushered into a large adjoining shower block. They entered with great trepidation, for the word had gone around that the Germans frequently killed prisoners by placing them into a so-called shower room which was in reality a gas chamber.

Fortunately, Buchenwald was one of several Nazi concentration camps that did not have gas chambers and the men's relief when sprays of steaming hot water spluttered out of the ceiling fixtures was profound. After their shower, they were issued half-metre-square rags, each of which was to be used as a towel by two men. Having dried themselves as best they could, they were moved on and into a clothing store. Here they were confronted by a pile of clothing on the floor, with instructions to find something that fitted them. The clothes were mostly the standard prison garb of cotton shirt and trousers – all of which had seen better days, and were hand-me-downs from previous inmates, although there were no belts or string to hold up their trousers. Prior to their reissue, the clothes had been baked at high temperatures to kill off any lice lurking in the seams. No shoes were issued and the men had to go barefoot. Some did not even receive decent clothing items and had to do with what they were given. As American radio operator Sergeant Chasten 'Chat' Bowen later recalled, 'They gave me a woman's silk blouse and women's slacks. I had no shoes, no socks.'

Once dressed, the airmen were taken back through the gateway to a large office for registration, where a battery of scriveners – prisoners like themselves, but wearing black armbands and berets – ordered them to give personal details for their camp registration forms. These forms required information the airmen were not prepared to reveal, so they only gave their name, rank and service number. Stratton Appleman from the USAAF recalled that events surrounding this mass obstinacy contained a little serendipity.

> After a lot of pushing and shoving, it soon became apparent that we were expected to form into a single line for moving through still another building. Apparently I was the first military person in line, and because all communication was in German or French, I had no idea of what was going on. Once I got toward the head of the line, however, I thought it was just another interrogation.
>
> An elderly gentleman addressed a question at me, first in German, then French, then Spanish. When I responded 'I am an American Air Corps officer; I speak English only and I demand recognition as a prisoner of war', the interrogator asked in English, 'What part of Texas are you from?' He explained that like most of the other authorities in the camp other than those in uniform, he was also a prisoner. In fact he had been a political detainee for some twelve years following a career in the German consular service. His language skills had caused him to get the chore of interviewing prisoners for assignments, either in the armaments plant at Buchenwald or on work details elsewhere. Despite the fact that I had inadvertently confirmed his guess about my geographic origins, I told him that I must follow my military orders to furnish only my name, rank and serial number. After a half-hearted attempt to convince me that

he wanted only information pertaining to my personal skills and abilities – absolutely no military information – he conferred with his colleagues then asked me to step aside.

I felt once again that my adherence to military orders had paid off. Seeing a few Americans I recognised in the line behind me, I explained what had happened and urged them to pass it on. As each of the downed airmen reached the interrogator, they explained their status and asked for POW status. Each was asked to step aside.

Then we created a bureaucratic problem for the camp authorities which had the effect of uniting us. It was only then we got a comprehensive picture of how many of us were in the same predicament, and it was only then that we came to be dealt with as an entity.

This mass defiance by the airmen soon attracted the attention of the foremen prisoners, known in concentration camps as Kapos ('prisoner functionary'). They threatened the airmen and banged their fists on the desks, but to no avail. In the face of this small storm of rebellion, the senior Kapo finally ordered his clerks to take the minimum details available and issue each man with a small white cloth tag bearing his prison number. He was furious but fortunately kept himself in check. The men were then individually photographed, holding a slate on which had been chalked their five-figure camp number. They felt they had won a small victory as they assembled outside the office in the heavy night air, but their smiles faded when they were surrounded by a squad of SS guards armed with lumps of wood. The Germans began shouting, and clubbed into the group of airmen, urging them to run back through the gateway and along the stony path. Heavy blows rained down on them as they ran and staggered barefoot along the path and through the gate, finally assembling with the French prisoners once again in the parade area under the watchful eyes of the guards.

Following another count, they were lined up in columns of five and marched towards the wired-off area known as the 'Kleine Lager' or Little Camp, an already overcrowded space for new arrivals. As they entered the first entrance to Little Camp, other prisoners lined the bordering wire fence and asked the new men for their nationalities. When these inmates realised that many of the new arrivals were Anglo-American, they were both surprised and elated. In a multitude of tongues, they pleaded for news of the war as the airmen passed by. Frenchmen wept and cried out to their countrymen that the war would soon end. For some of the British airmen it was a surprise to hear an occasional shout in English; they later learned that these prisoners were a small number of Channel Island dissenters, imprisoned after the Germans occupied the islands in July 1940.

The new arrivals trudged on past row upon row of dark-green wooden huts of one or two storeys. They turned a corner and moved down a slight incline, at the foot of which they were counted through a gate and then again at another gate a hundred metres on. Barbed wire surrounded them at all times. By now it was nine o'clock and darkness had closed in as they finally entered the Little Camp.

As the last gate closed behind them they all looked around their cobblestoned pen in dismay. It held no building other than a small stone construction five by three metres in size, housing the Lager Ältester (Camp Senior) and his assistants. The only form of cover apart from two large trees was provided by five crowded marquee-style tents, which housed only the very sick.

Their position was quite evident – they would have to sleep out in the open. Some thin blankets had been issued to the exhausted men, but not enough for all. Nevertheless, they cleared the area and made themselves as comfortable as possible before stretching out on the cold, hard cobblestones to try to sleep. Surprisingly, an urn of lukewarm soup was delivered to them, which was quickly consumed using some communal bowls and spoons. For many it was their first decent meal since leaving Fresnes.

The following morning at four o'clock, the prisoners in the Little Camp were roused for rollcall, a slow and tedious process after which a third of a litre of cold ersatz 'coffee' – a bitter brew made from acorns – was issued to each prisoner. The newest inmates of the Little Camp were then free to wander about, talk to each other and get the lie of the land.

There were almost 3,000 people in this section of the camp, including Russians, Poles, Jews and Frenchmen – some of whom were well known to them. Phil Lamason recognised with dismay his former helper Georges Prevot and managed to talk to the distraught man at length. Prevot, he noticed, had shed a lot of weight.

The brick building they had noticed the previous night housed a latrine at one end, which was in constant use, while in a room at the far end, the bodies of those who had died during the night had been stacked prior to transportation to the crematorium. Jim Hastin recalled peering through the window one day and counting seventeen corpses.

In the rectangular area between the tents and the stone hut was a large cobbled mound known as the Rock Pile, and this was to become the airmen's 'quarters'. Elsewhere, the ground was a clay-like black soil. Through other prisoners, they soon came to know something of the organisation of the camp.

Each block had its own ältester, all of whom were long-term political or criminal prisoners who had succumbed to treachery with the promise of extra food rations, other privileges, and less work. These masters among the underlings were placed in a position of authority over the prisoners of all nationalities.

The regular prisoners' garb was the standard blue-and-grey-striped pyjama-style clothing, while the Germans in authority wore black berets and armbands lettered 'Kapo', 'Vorarbeiter' (work foreman) or 'Lagerschutz' (camp policeman).

Each prisoner category wore a different-coloured triangle on their jacket and trousers to denote their race, allegiance or crime, with an individual camp number on a white cloth patch below the triangle. In the case of 'other nationalities' a black letter indicating their origin was embroidered on a red triangle. F stood for French, T for Czechs, R for Russians, P for Poles and so on. The colours of the triangles indicated the class of prisoner as follows:

Red without letters – German political prisoner

Red with black letters – Other nationalities

Green – Common law offenders

Yellow – Jews

Pink – Homosexuals

Violet – Jehovah's Witnesses or others imprisoned for religious beliefs

Black – Gypsies, 'shiftless elements' and work dodgers

A parade or appell was held every evening, when prisoners were meticulously counted, first by the block-führers and then by SS guards. Appell for the Main Camp was held on the large compound, where a floating population of prisoners, numbering in their tens of thousands, were counted. If German guards needed to be addressed at these rollcalls, it had to be from a distance of at least three metres.

Working parties were marched out of the camp every day after the 4 am appell in all types of conditions. The majority of these prisoners would either hew stones in the quarry, drag logs, or work on roads or other nearby utilities.

Food consisted of a small daily ration of the tough black knäckebröd, a third of a litre of soup, and acorn coffee, which was always lukewarm or cold by the time it was delivered to the Little Camp. If so much as a drop was spilt or splashed out of the urn, the entire carrying detail was beaten by the guards. The soup and bread also came in urns and were issued at eleven o'clock. The so-called 'soup' was generally little more than grass or nettles soaked in hot water, often containing bugs and maggots and sometimes a cube or two of meat from an unspecified source. The unleavened black bread was topped by a cursory wipe of a margarine substitute.

The airmen were appalled at the sight of the other prisoners fighting and scratching to scrape the bottoms of the food urns once the issue had been fully handed out. The stronger ones beat the weak underfoot and the weak sometimes died. But survival was the grim game, and those who have never known the desperation of true starvation could have no appreciation of the effect it can have on otherwise rational human beings.

Apart from the soup they'd been given on arrival, the first food the airmen received were small individual portions of dark grey bread, which smelt vile and tasted even worse. Several men unthinkingly threw it away in disgust, and were shocked at the ensuing panic as dozens of starving inmates rushed at it, fighting for the pathetic scraps like wild animals, scratching, punching and elbowing each other. With a mixture of pity and disgust, the other airmen tossed their bread into the rapidly growing melee. The following day, they once again tossed their bread to a group who had been patiently waiting nearby, but this practice was quickly brought to an end by Lamason. He did not want his men to be responsible for any injuries or death. Furthermore, he reminded them that the bread was their chief source of sustenance, as there was little nourishment to be had in the evil-smelling soup, which could be used to soften the bread a little. This meagre meal was then washed down with their half-cup of lukewarm coffee.

Dysentery was rife in the camp, so some of the men began toasting their bread over small fires, hoping that by burning it the resultant carbon might prevent or alleviate the disease.

As senior officer, Lamason chose seventeen officers to help him maintain discipline among the men. Each of these officers then became responsible for his own unit of nine or ten men. This served to not only better organise soup and food distribution, but enabled the leaders to quickly get to know at least a few of the men under their supervision. One of the first assignments Lamason gave these leaders was to mount a guard detail both day and night to prevent pilfering by other prisoners, which had begun their first night in the Little Camp.

Buchenwald was an extremely large camp and most nationalities were represented in the prisoner population. There was considerable political friction amongst the prisoners, although by this time an International Camp Committee had been formed to prepare a united front against the SS. As the airmen would soon come to learn, the most powerful of the factions were the German and French Communists, Polish and Russian nationalists and Czechoslovakians.

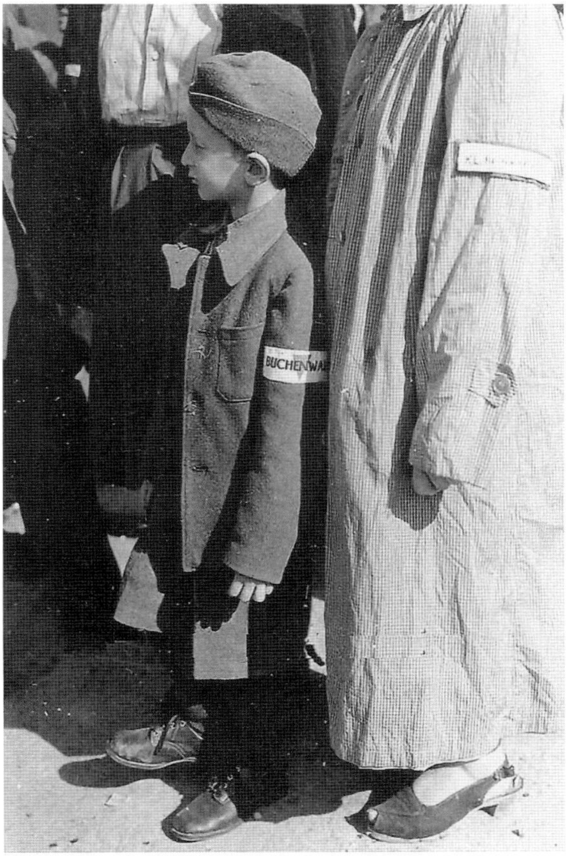

Joseph Schleifstein was just three years old when he was sent to Buchenwald with his parents. His father managed to hide the boy until the camp was liberated, saving him from certain death. Joseph and his parents survived the war (Photo: National Archives, Washington)

(Photo: United States Holocaust Memorial Museum, courtesy of Aviva Kempner)

Prisoners at forced labour on the assembly line of the Gustloff Werke II munitions plant in the Buchenwald concentration camp (Photo: United States Holocaust Memorial Museum, courtesy of Gedenkstaette Buchenwald)

A reconnaissance photo taken of Buchenwald. 1. Gustloff Armament Works (GAW) 2. SS Officers' and Troop Area 3. German Barracks 4. Riding Academy 5. German Armament Works (DAW) 6. Gatehouse and Main Tower 7. Appell Platz (Rollcall Compound) 8. Crematorium 9. Headquarters Area 10. Prisoners' Barracks 11. Camp Zoo 12. Goethe's Oak 13. SS Garages 14. Kommandant's Villa (Photo: USAF Photographic Collection, National Air & Space Museum, Smithsonian Institution)

With incredible accuracy, American bombers destroyed two armaments plants huddled against the concentration camp just prior to the bombing raid of August 1944. The quarantine area known as the Little Camp is out of photo, to the rear of the prisoners' barracks (Photo: USAF Photographic Collection, National Air & Space Museum, Smithsonian Institution)

Low altitude flight photo of the Gustloff plant following the bombing raid (Photo: Buchenwald Memorial Museum, courtesy of National Archives, Washington)

After the air raid came the massive task of clearing up the devastation (Photo: United States Holocaust Memorial Museum, courtesy of Gedenkstaette Buchenwald)

Luftwaffe Oberst Johannes Tautloft, believed to have been instrumental in transferring the airmen out of Buchenwald

New Zealand airman Malcolm Cullen on arrival at Stalag Luft III

A group of Buchenwald airmen POWs following their transfer to Stalag Luft III
(Photo: P. Lamason)

(Above and left): As liberating American troops watch on, former slave prisoners of the Germans file out of the gates of Buchenwald and into freedom (Photos: United States Holocaust Memorial Museum, courtesy of National Archives and Records Administration, College Park)

Wing Commander F. F. E. Yeo-Thomas, the famed 'White Rabbit' (Photo: Barbara Yeo-Thomas)

Flight Lieutenant Levitt C. Beck, Jr., USAAF, who died of illness in Buchenwald (Photo: National Archives, Washington)

Flying Officer Philip Hemmens, RAF, who passed away in the camp hospital

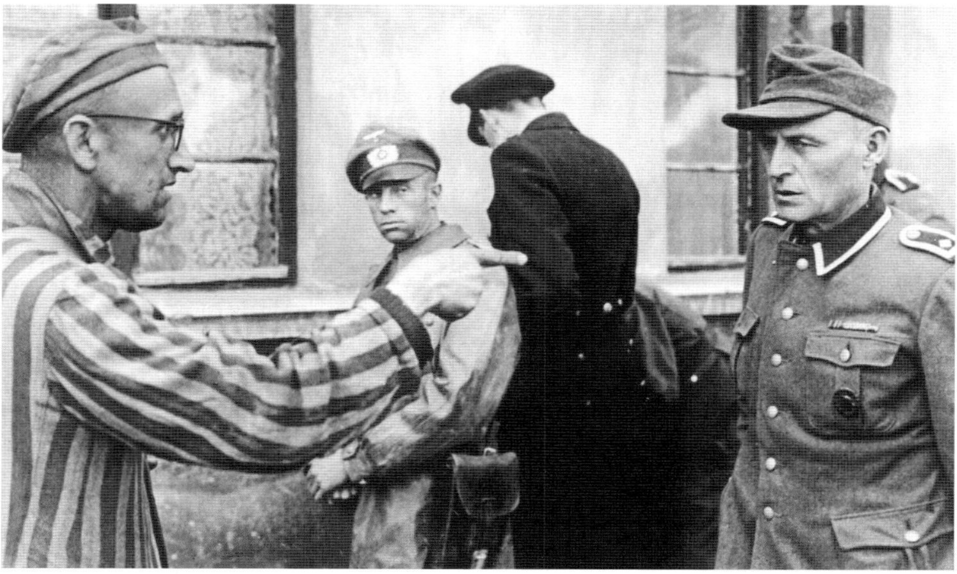

Following the liberation of Buchenwald, the former prisoners turned on their tormentors (Photo: National Archives, Washington)

Following the camp's liberation, American soldiers forced the citizens of Weimar to enter the camp to see the horrors that had occurred while they remained oblivious and uncaring (Photo: National Archives, Washington)

Faced with the appalling sight of hundreds of dead bodies and evidence of the atrocities committed by their countrymen, many citizens broke down (Photos: United States Holocaust Memorial Museum)

Kentucky Senator Alben W. Barkley views a pile of emaciated bodies while visiting the camp (Photo: United States Holocaust Memorial Museum, courtesy of National Archives)

A group of American soldiers talk with some of the newly liberated inmates, learning what they had endured in the camp (Photo: National Archives, Washington)

A political sign was painted on the wall of a barracks hut following the camp's liberation and an American soldier stands in front of an effigy of Hitler. It reads: 'Hitler must die for Germany to live' (Photo: United States Holocaust Memorial Museum, courtesy of Rebecca Tran)

U.S. Congressmen on a tour of the Buchenwald crematorium mortuary on 24 April 1945 are shown how the SOE agents were hung from wall-mounted hooks using piano wire (Photo: National Archives, Washington)

The Congressmen are shown a mallet used to dispatch victims if they did not die quickly enough (Photo: National Archives, Washington)

A trainload of liberated Jewish youths prior to transportation from Buchenwald to an aid centre in France (Photo: United States Holocaust Memorial Museum, courtesy of Robert Waisman)

Later camp Kommandant Hermann Pister following his arrest (Photo: National Archives, Washington)

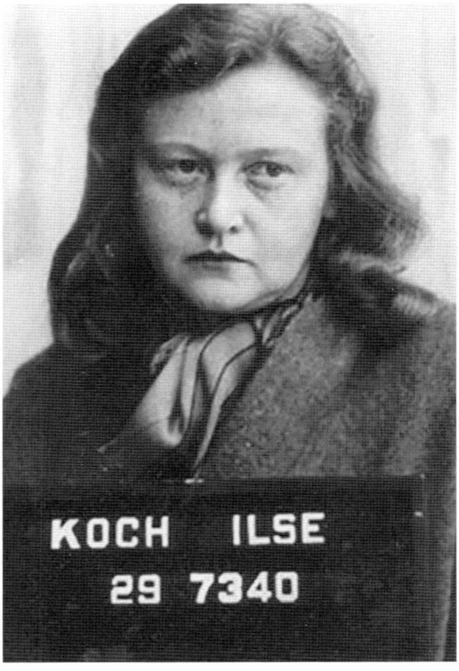

Ilse Koch was also arrested and would face trial for her crimes against humanity (Photo: National Archives, Washington)

Koch, along with other war criminals, finally faces justice at the Dachau trials
(Photos: United States Holocaust Memorial Museum, courtesy of National Archives)

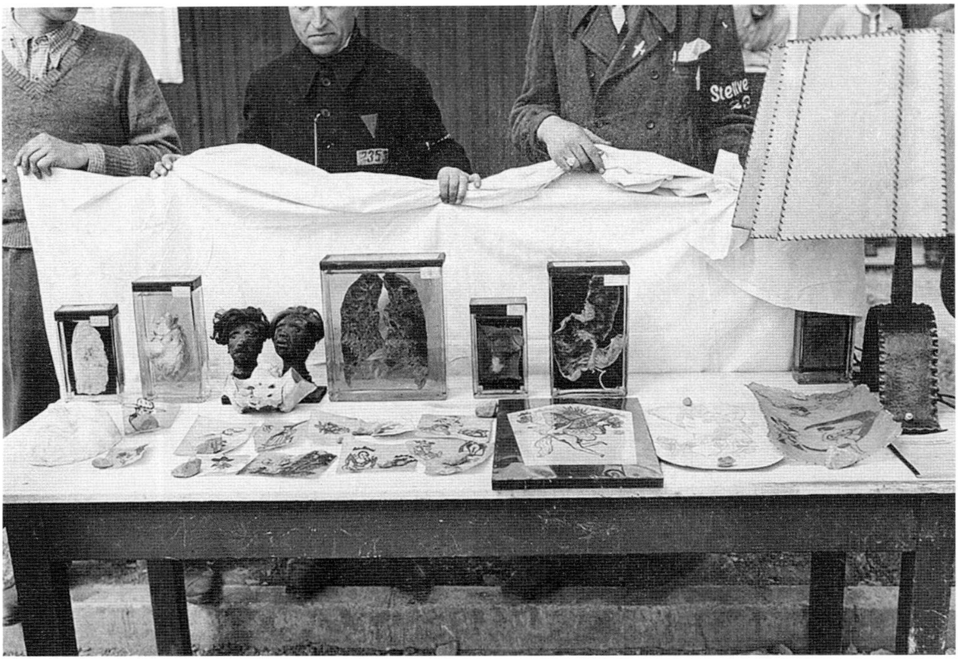

Some of Ilse Koch's depravity on display after the liberation of Buchenwald. Exhibits include sections of tattooed skin, shrunken heads and table lamps. Also on display is a massive collection of seized gold wedding rings (Photo: United States Holocaust Memorial Museum, courtesy of National Archives)

Ilse Koch's shrunken heads (Photo: International Tracing Service Arolsen)

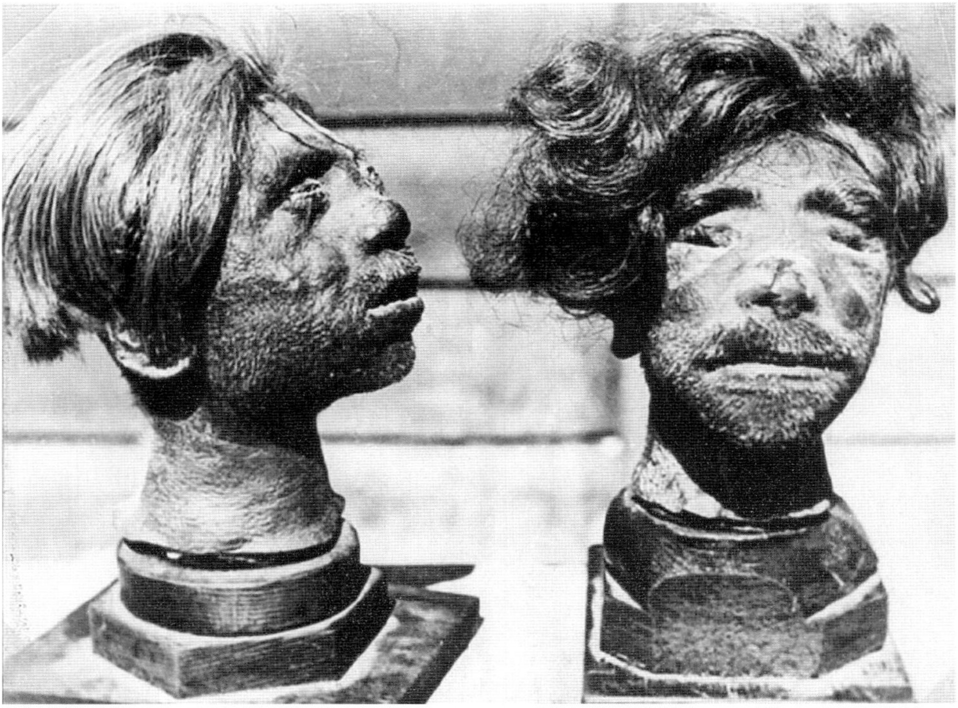

The surviving Australian KLB airmen at a celebratory function at Canberra's National Press Centre on 24 June 1988. From left: Ian Innes (Bob Mills' crew, managed to evade capture), Tom Malcolm, Major-General Alan Morrison (representing the Minister for Veterans' Affairs), Kevin Light, Eric Johnston, Jim Gwilliam, Keith Mills, Bob Mills and author Colin Burgess. Ray Perry and Les Whellum were unable to attend (Photo: Colin Burgess)

The surviving members of Bob Mills' crew: Bob Mills, Jim Gwilliam, Keith Mills, Ian Innes and Eric Johnston (Photo: Colin Burgess)

At a function held in 1996, Phil Lamason (centre) is reunited with Eric Johnston, Ian Innes, Jim Gwilliam and Keith Mills (Photo: Pam Gwilliam)

Art Kinnis, conservator of the KLB Club (Photo: Karen & Jack Kinnis)

A young Art Kinnis in his RCAF uniform (Photo: Karen & Jack Kinnis)

One of the international KLB airmen, American Joe Moser, a P-38 pilot with the USAAC. He later released his book, *A Fighter Pilot in Buchenwald* (Photo: Joe Moser)

At the age of 98, RAF Halifax bomber navigator Stanley Booker, MBE, a KLB airman from Berkshire, was awarded the Legion D'Honneur by the French government for his post-war work with British Intelligence (Photo: Stanley Booker)

The main entrance to Buchenwald photographed by the author in 1996
(Photo: Colin Burgess)

The Buchenwald memorial plaque dedicated to the KLB airmen (Photo: Colin Burgess)

On the same visit, a photograph of the area once known as the Little Camp
(Photo: Colin Burgess)

Early on in the life of the camp, the anti-Fascist prisoners found that the best way to protect and assert their interests was to place their own men into positions of importance. Later, when the SS tried to displace these power-holders with their own men, the outsiders found themselves without any effectual authority due to the organisational structure already in place, and were soon withdrawn. Eventually the SS came to realise that better discipline was achieved within the camp if the prisoners were permitted to organise and administer the camp routine. There were no further attempts to counter the hegemony set up by the political inmates at Buchenwald. According to former political prisoner Eugen Kogon, the German Communists brought the best qualifications to the accomplishment of this task.

> In contrast to men of liberal views, they had always been inured to absolute party discipline, and in methods and means they were almost the only ones who were the enemy's match. In addition they had the most extensive camp experience. It is to be regretted – and was actually the cause of certain setbacks – that especially in the early years, the Communists excluded anti-Fascists of persuasion other than their own, but in practice it could not be helped.
>
> Within their own ranks the Communists were by no means unanimous, though they suppressed dissent with an iron hand, occasionally even by the murder of dissenters. Distrustful of anyone not of like mind, they were out to support only unconditional followers of the prevailing Communist party line. Only occasionally did they come to accept selective collaboration with others.
>
> The positive achievement of the Communists on behalf of the concentration-camp prisoners can hardly be overrated. In many

> cases the whole camp literally owed them its life, even though their motives seldom sprang from pure altruism but rather from the collective instinct for self-preservation in which the whole camp joined because of its positive results.

In the last year of the war, self-government by the inmates in Buchenwald was so inculcated into the day-to-day activities of the camp that the SS had no real idea of the internal situation – nor did they really care. They were exhausted by the years of bitter warfare and the realisation that defeat had become increasingly inevitable, so as long as the camps still ran to expectations they were happy to allow the Communists to mostly have their way in its administration.

The virtual abrogation of camp authority by the SS allowed the Communists to secretly organise a common front of all prisoners prepared to fight against their captors, and resistance activities were created both within and outside of the camp. Inmates employed in the camp office and the labour statistics department falsified information so that unskilled workers were transported to factories requiring highly skilled personnel, and they were able to preclude the sick and weak from assignment to hard labour details. Others helped sabotage the German war effort by ensuring that materials destined for armaments factories went astray or were the wrong type, technical drawings were subtly altered, and valuable resources were wrongly stored or wasted. Elsewhere, inmates working as a doctors or medical attendants protected fellow prisoners slated for execution by altering their names to those of others already deceased.

As they came to meet and know prisoners of other nationalities in the Little Camp, so the airmen became aware of the horrors perpetrated at Buchenwald. They also learned basic but valuable survival techniques, such as boiling water when making a 'brew' to prevent the onset of dysentery. This water was obtained from the latrine building at certain hours of the day, and though attempts were made to keep the water pure, it still stank even after boiling.

Due to their unique situation, and because of the non-transfer 'DIKAL' endorsement on their papers, the camp administrators chose not to allocate any of the airmen to outside Kommandos, even though the SS doctor had passed all of them as fit for work. They knew the airmen were in Buchenwald illegally and could not be presented with an opportunity to escape. Quite simply, no one beyond the camp perimeter could ever know they were there. For the airmen, this at least meant they were assigned to such minor domestic tasks as cleaning, carrying, and road maintenance within the camp.

Although the five tents served as hospitals, no place of healing was ever filthier, and it was common to see corpses being daily removed by the stretcher bearers. Other prisoners would momentarily pause to doff their caps or place a hand over their hearts as a mark of respect as a body was carried by. Everyday life then resumed. In these 'hospitals', paper bandages were used many times over on gaping, putrid wounds. No medicines were available, apart from the occasional aspirin. Medical personnel would pass from one patient to another, cutting decaying matter from open sores without any form of anaesthetic, using the same, unsterilised pocket knives.

Even standing at attention on appell was no guarantee of being left alone by the guards. On the airmen's second day, during the evening count, Bob Mills was standing at the front of the ranks in the accustomed air force manner – hands tightly clenched, thumbs pointing along where the seams of his trousers would normally be.

Suddenly an SS guard roared up, yelling at the top of his voice and indicating a problem with Mills' hands, but the South Australian did not understand what he was doing wrong. The guard swiped his Luger across Mills' face, drawing blood, then strode off yelling and waving his gun. A bewildered Bob Mills was later told that prisoners were required to stand with their hands flat by their sides to indicate they were not holding any sort of weapon in them. The same thing happened to Ron Leverington from Hampshire the following day. Malcolm Cullen recalls that the men came to know their 'lager ältester' Hoffman quite well at appells.

> He was a long term prisoner and was as mad as a hatter. He carried with him a heavy stick and had no compunction whatever in using it. It was common to be held to attention for three hours waiting to be counted, and if there had to be a recount the hours dragged on almost indefinitely. The madman rounded up all with the aid of voice and stick, and strode up and down in front of the ranks, with eyes blazing and jaws clamping. His mouth never seemed to be still and he drooled horribly. Dysentery was common among those who had been in the lager for some time, and if these poor unfortunates were caught in the aborts [toilets] during appell they were chased and beaten unmercifully until their crazy overlord was out of breath.
>
> Our group toed the line very strictly and seemed to impress this monstrosity by its military bearing and ability to understand and comply promptly to orders given by its Senior Officer. Apart from roaring at us frequently, he did not trouble us very much.

5

TERROR FROM THE SKIES

On the morning of 24 August 1944, a special appell was called on the concrete area in the Little Camp. The 'Terrorflieger' contingent was separated from the other prisoners and each man was given two very painful injections of a green fluid in the chest. Being aware of the potential significance of some injections through prisoners working in the medical block, this was not a very happy parade.

Then, at 11:45 am, the day seemed to improve considerably for all the prisoners as they looked expectantly into the sky after the camp's air raid sirens began wailing out a warning. The dull thudding sounds of bombing in the direction of Leipzig to the north-east of the camp filled their hearts with a sense of satisfaction. Vapour trails began to cross the clear sky as most of the main camp inmates were rapidly shunted into their barracks. Many of the airmen elected to remain outside, watching with interest and then mounting trepidation as two large formations of Flying Fortress bombers from the US Army Air Force swept in – 129 aircraft in all – and headed straight for the camp. Despite their understandable anxiety, the men were gladdened by the sight of so many gleaming aircraft flying in unimpeded formation over enemy territory.

Suddenly a Very pistol was fired from a window in the leading aircraft, and a white bombing marker hurtled to the ground – the signal to commence an attack. 'Jesus Christ – look out!' one of the airmen yelled. At the same time the terrified SS guards barked out orders for everyone to lie flat on the ground, then covered them with machine-guns, all the time eyeing the skies with apprehension.

The targets of the American bombers this day were the Gustloff and DAW factories outside the camp, where the essential gyro components for Hitler's V-1 buzz bombs were being assembled, using slave labour from the camp.

The men heard the first bombs descending; a high whining sound that grew in volume until culminating in a series of earth-shattering explosions. The bombs landed a little over 200 metres from the prone airmen, who watched and felt the explosions with mixed feelings, and not a little admiration for the unexpected accuracy of the bombing as the nearby factories were destroyed, bomb after bomb exploding within their walls. Sadly, many prisoners would have died as the bombs rained down on the factories. Streams of terrified workers began pouring out of the factories, but as they fled from one death they ran headlong into another, as outraged guards shot them down in their scores. Political prisoners, Russian slaves and Jewish children alike were torn apart by machine-gun fire and fell in heaps outside the blazing factories. The explosives within these buildings then began to detonate, compounding the fearful destruction.

As Art Kinnis later recalled: 'It was not over, for we soon spotted the main force, and this time, to our horror, the signal went down before they were directly above. Knowing how a bomb falls, we all knew that these were for us. Each chap endeavoured to get lower than his mate and, outside of keeping our heads down, ostrich fashion, no cover was obtainable. I sincerely hope that I never hear the screech, thud, and rumble of dropping bombs again. It was far too close for comfort.'

Very few bombs actually landed within the concentration camp itself. The bomb aimers above seemed to have used exemplary skill in destroying their main targets and avoiding the populated camp area. Nevertheless, there was panic and chaos within the main camp. Incendiary bombs had started fires in several blocks, and the Germans were screaming panic-stricken orders, trying to direct the berserk hordes of prisoners. A group of 37 Allied secret agents being held in Buchenwald, who had remained outside their Block 17 quarters, cheered and hurrahed as the bombs wrought the destruction of the hated factories.

Several of the airmen sustained minor injuries, but no one was seriously hurt by the shrapnel which flew in all directions. Canadian Bill Gibson recalled lying flat on the ground in the Little Camp as the bombs rained down. 'The fellow lying next to me [fellow Canadian Frank Salt] said he was hit. I looked, and he had a piece of shrapnel sticking out of his shoulder about an inch and one-half.' Gibson managed to grasp the piece of shrapnel and pull it out. 'But I forgot it was red hot, and my fingers got burnt.'

As the aircraft turned for home and the skies above the camp cleared, the relief everyone felt was short-lived, as some panicked guards armed with Schmeisser firearms rushed into the Little Camp shouting, 'Alle Americanner und Englander – Aus!'

Many of the airmen feared they were about to be executed in reprisal for the bombing of the camp and factories as the guards herded them through the gate into the main camp. Everywhere there was pandemonium, and their anxiety grew as they were instructed to line up in front of a manned MG 42 machine-gun. Around them on the parade ground lay the dead and wounded; men with shattered arms, missing legs, charred faces and bodies, many screaming incessantly in unimaginable pain.

As a badly flustered, red-faced German officer moved in to address the airmen, several of them began to mutter quiet prayers and shake hands to farewell friends. American pilot Joe Moser from Washington State was among those who thought they might have reached the end of their road.

> The officer who stood in front and spoke to us was clearly furious. But instead of receiving the bullets from the machine-gun, we were given orders to go into the factory building and help fight the fires. We were told to find anything that could be salvaged and take it out of the burning buildings. I felt immense relief – at first. Then I thought, how can I fight a fire with bare feet? We were not given any tools, or hoses, or any equipment.

While loath to assist, the men thought it prudent to comply, as the guards were extremely jittery and seemed ready to open fire at the slightest sign of rebellion. Barefoot, and dressed only in thin trousers, the men began to beat out several of the smaller fires and clear some of the wood and brick rubble. Numerous unexploded incendiaries lay amongst the debris. The guards, standing at a cautious distance, ordered these removed as well.

It was hot, dirty and dangerous work, and the men sustained many painful blisters to their feet and bodies as cinders fell all around. Eventually the incendiaries had been cleared from the vicinity and bucket brigades had quenched the worst of the fires.

Several of the airmen assigned to moving food and clothing stores were able to purloin some welcome supplies, but a few went a little overboard. Phil Lamason, much to his horror, came across one of his men wearing a highly polished pair of boots he had yanked off a dead German guard. 'You bloody fool!' he hissed. 'Get those off and get rid of them before another guard notices and shoots you on the spot!' The man, suitably chastised, discarded the offending footwear.

Meanwhile, the dead and injured were taken away on stretchers and planks of wood. Blackened, rigid corpses were strewn everywhere in and around the blazing huts, and the stench of burning flesh – a smell now well known to those within the camp – hung heavily in the air.

In the centre of the camp, many of the longer-term inmates stared in amazement at an incredible sight that now confronted them. Goethe's tree had been hit by an explosive incendiary and was now a blackened and shattered stump pointing to the sky. The despised symbol of the Third Reich's strength and supremacy had fallen.

In the Gustloff armaments works, seven of the ten main workshops had been totally destroyed, the boiler house was gutted, and other smaller buildings damaged. Within the garage and storage areas, fourteen buildings were destroyed, nine severely damaged, and a large number of trucks torn to pieces. In the DAW enclosure, thirteen buildings had been blown apart and another two gutted by fire. Gestapo headquarters had also been devastated in the raid, with eleven buildings flattened and set alight.

Seven buildings in the concentration camp had been destroyed. In all, 175 thousand-pound bombs had been dropped during the raid, as well as 583 five-hundred-pound bombs and 279 five-hundred-pound incendiaries – a total of 300 tons of explosives.

When the final death tally came to be known, it was revealed that nearly 80 Germans had been killed and around 300 wounded. The toll amongst the prisoners was appreciably higher, with almost 2,000 casualties, including 400 dead.

The 129 Boeing B-17 Flying Fortresses involved in the raid were from the 613th Bomb Squadron, 401st Bombardment Group. The operation that day was coded Mission 132, and their objective was the total destruction of the Gustloff-Werke armament factory.

As the group's operations officer, Lieutenant Colonel Allison Brooks, later revealed: 'In the briefing on the Weimar mission, the intelligence officer stressed that there was presumed to be a concentration camp next to the factory and that we were to make every effort for precision bombing, right on the target and the confines of the target only.'

Despite this, the group's official records make no mention of a concentration camp in the vicinity of the targeted factory. One crewman, Joseph Geraldi, remains certain there was no mention of the Buchenwald camp and its inmates in their briefing. 'We were never told a concentration camp was there,' he recalled. 'Hitler was sending V1 and V2 rockets to England, so we were well aware of the rockets, and that was our target for the day. What we were told at briefing was, "Today we are going to hit a V2 factory at Weimar."'

It seems fortunate, therefore, that there was enough distance between the factory and the camp, and it was only this fact – not orders to prevent dropping bombs over the camp – that saved many more lives, including those of the airmen.

Frank Salt, who had been hit and wounded by flying shrapnel, was taken to the Main Camp hospital for treatment. Canadian Art Kinnis later recorded his aircrew colleague's impressions in his diary.

> Karl, second in charge of the Little Camp, rushed [Salt] away to hospital. Out on the main road past the cinema they came to grips with a stream of wounded and dying prisoners, all on their way for what scant attention might be obtained. Once inside the hospital grounds it became apparent that the situation was far beyond control. Wounded were standing, sitting and lying everywhere. Hospital attendants were making crude attempts to aid the seriously injured, but if a man appeared well-bandaged he received no further treatment.
>
> Utter chaos was the scene that would greet everyone. Wounded were being carried on stretchers, planks, doors, any object that would serve, in a continuous moving body to join this milling, suffering mass of humanity.
>
> Cases requiring operations were rapidly put to one side, but it was readily seen that the few doctors could not cope. Many were those that died on the lawns. They were stripped, roughly slung onto carts, and then hauled away when the load was sufficient for the human horses to pull. Efforts for comfort were few, medical supplies were quickly used up, but the suffering went on and on. Late afternoon coffee was served which, in its small way, was a blessing. The ambulance vans from Weimar arrived with medical supplies. As soon as these were unloaded they took off and returned to Weimar, loaded more supplies and returned to the camp.
>
> The doctors by this time had sorted all into the serious and not serious; the latter (Salt included) being sent back to their barracks.

> Legless, armless, and badly mauled were still on the ground when Frank left, thankful to leave what will always remain a horrible afternoon.

Among those seriously injured in the raid was Princess Mafalda, one of the daughters of King Emmanuel III of Italy. She was married to a German official, but had been outspoken and came to notice for her hatred of Adolf Hitler, causing her to be arrested and thrown into Buchenwald. The isolation barracks where she was held had been hit and gutted by fire, and she received severe wounds to her legs. As there was no women's hospital within the camp, she was taken on a stretcher to the brothel where, held in the comforting arms of a weeping, distraught woman, she lapsed into a coma. Doctor Schiedlansky, the camp Medical Officer, was summoned to tend the princess. Immediately on seeing her shattered legs he commenced a double amputation. The princess, clutched tightly in the girl's embrace, moaned and gripped her arms as the operation began, but the severe trauma and loss of blood proved too much, and she quickly succumbed. Her body was ignominiously tossed on top of a heap of twisted corpses and later burnt.

The Germans were furious at the damage caused to the camp, and to their beloved Goethe's tree. Many of the guards screamed and spat at the airmen, calling them 'Verdammt Terror-fliegers!' over and over.

That same day the men were ordered to report en masse to the SS headquarters where, amid the devastation, Kommandant Pister took the opportunity to vent his personal hostility on the airmen. Parading up and down in front of the charcoal-covered men, he gave them a tormented lecture through an equally excited interpreter on bombing and destruction and then, shaking his clenched and gloved fists, said he expected them to pay the cost of the damage! At this many of the men relaxed enough to actually smile, but the situation was far too volatile to make any comment.

At the end of his tirade, Pister's attitude suddenly softened. 'I am grateful for your cooperation in helping to clear the damage this morning. Your position here is under review.' The airmen were amazed. This was the first positive statement they'd had on their situation since arriving at the camp.

Later a German officer told some of the men that the SS had called upon their services to help clear up because it was realised they could rely on the airmen's integrity under pressure, and they would keep their heads under adverse conditions. They were further informed the SS had anticipated that such a raid on the camp might break the electrical circuit in the boundary fence. Accordingly, the perimeter was surrounded by guards armed with flame-throwers, under orders to deal with any signs of a mass break-out.

Disease, in particular dysentery, began to strike at the airmen. The long appells became a torment of pain and shame, as they were not permitted to go to the toilets and had to suffer the indignity of foul-smelling excreta running down the back of their legs. To make matters even worse, the sky was beginning to pale to a watery grey, and billows of cumulus cloud started piling up in the west. If the rains came, as seemed inevitable, the men feared the worst.

Some days after the bombing raid, the sky turned black and a light drizzle began to fall. Thunder rumbled ominously in the distance as the men's thin blankets soon became soaked, and the cobblestones on which they lay grew wet and slippery. Thankfully the rain stopped mid-morning, but the sky was still overcast and the wind had risen to a stiff breeze. Then the skies opened up again with a vengeance and heavy rain belted down.

Over the next two days, the airmen fought against the elements until, when it seemed they would all die from exposure, they were moved to a wooden barracks block in the next compound up the hill. As they marched up in driving rain with blankets over their heads, some took off their shirts and tried to keep them dry by holding them under their arms. Finally they made their way into the crowded block and found places for themselves on the wooden floor.

Block 58 was a windowless hut thirty metres long and eight metres wide. There were no bunks as such, but four tiers of wooden shelves divided into compartments in which three men had to sleep under conditions barely suitable for one. In fact they were more like wide bookcases than beds. These shelves were packed with sleeping bodies when the airmen arrived, amongst them 500 German gypsy boys, aged from around six to sixteen. There was no room for the newcomers, but they were at least grateful that they now had a roof over their heads. They wrapped themselves in their damp blankets and dropped off to sleep.

The rain continued for several days and the airmen seldom left the barracks except for the compulsory appells, although the work continued as usual for the other prisoners. There was much to be horrified about in their new quarters, but the airmen were especially appalled at the age of some of the children in Block 58 and the work they were expected to carry out in the dreaded quarry and elsewhere. In talking to other prisoners they discovered that a special block had been set up in the main camp specifically for children other than the gypsies. This children's barracks, in Block 8, was crammed at that time with nearly 2,000 youngsters from a number of countries. Almost all were of Jewish extraction, children of executed partisans and Soviet and state officials. They had been callously wrenched from their parents' arms for transportation to Buchenwald, and most would eventually go to other camps such as Auschwitz, where their young lives would tragically end in the gas chambers. The first contingent of children arrived in Buchenwald in 1939, together with the Polish prisoners, and were given chores within the grounds such as cleaning the officers' barracks and helping in the kitchens.

A group of anti-Fascists had demanded that for safety and security, the children should be accommodated in their own block, and the SS camp administrator had reluctantly agreed. This solidarity amongst the adult prisoners protected the children against some of the more brutal treatment by the SS. The inmates were even able to set up an education system using the talents of Soviet and German teachers, in particular a gentile Czech who not only taught the children but was appointed to supervise their barracks. These anti-Fascist prisoners fought their hardest battles in trying to keep the children in Buchenwald when they were scheduled for transportation, which would ultimately carry them to their death elsewhere. Through their efforts, a total of 904 children were able to survive the war.

The youngest child ever to inhabit Block 8, registered on arrival as a 'partisan', was just three years old. His name was Stefan Jerzy Zweig. While Stefan and his father Zacharias had been transported to Buchenwald, his mother and sister were sent to Auschwitz, where they perished soon after in a gas chamber. Guards separated the boy and his father once they had passed through the gates of Buchenwald, but salvation came in the form of a prisoner named Willie Bleicher, who – risking certain death for his act of kindness – managed to hide and feed the child. He was helped in this selfless succour by members of the Socialist and Communist underground resistance movement within the camp. Bleicher was aware that the camp Kapos would eventually have Stefan killed as someone far too young to work, and therefore a waste of food. Stefan was still registered as a child within the camp, so when orders came in the fall of 1944 for all remaining children in the camp to be sent to Auschwitz (and certain death), Bleicher managed to bribe the camp doctor into certifying that the young boy was suffering from infectious typhus, thus avoiding the transportation order. Both Stefan and his father managed to survive until the camp was liberated and they were finally able to be reunited.

There were 765 prisoners crammed into Block 58 with the airmen, which meant that by night the air became exceedingly foul. The French, Jewish and gypsy inhabitants were running with lice, which swarmed all over the newcomers and nearly drove them mad. A few days after they moved into Block 58, a group of gypsies were evacuated to another camp – and possibly the gas chambers – leaving 450 in the block, which meant that the airmen were able to find space in the shelf-like beds around the walls. Life became slightly more tolerable for them, despite the fury of the lice and fleas. Each man had only about 45 centimetres of sleeping space, with no mattresses or pillows, and sometimes only one thin blanket between three or four, but it was certainly preferable to sleeping outside in the rain.

They were not permitted to write home, and there were no Red Cross parcels. The barrack lights went out at 10 pm and the area was patrolled by SS guards with ferocious dogs. Sport or recreation of any kind was forbidden. The different nationalities gave the airmen some camp money, known as lagermarks, and with this they were able to buy cigarettes from the canteen building at a rate of 25 per man per week.

In one corner of the hut stood a large earthenware washtub, where the men were able to wash their faces and hands but little else, and they were forced to use their own shirts as towels. There was a small, filthy toilet block positioned just outside their barracks. Inside, this consisted of a trench just over a metre wide, which tapered down to a third of that width a metre-and-a-half below. The sides and bottom of the trench were concreted, and some constantly-running fresh water carried most of the effluent away. Along each side of the trench was a single rail, supported at intervals by sturdier, rough-sawn rails over the trench. The men, most suffering from the effects of dysentery and dizzy from disease and a lack of nutrition, were forced to squat on those bridging rails. A little further away was the main latrine block, built in a similar fashion but on a far larger scale.

The Frenchmen in Block 58 were forced to work outside of the camp during the day, mostly in the quarry, returning exhausted late in the evening. Sometimes they managed to bring back some garlic, which they shared around. It was carefully cut up and placed onto stale slices of bread, which helped to make the bread a little more palatable. On odd occasions their watery soup contained suspicious shards of meat which the men stoically devoured while trying to think about something else.

Every morning a handcart pulled by prisoners from the Little Camp did the rounds, and the bodies of those who had died during the night were piled on top. In the final months of Buchenwald's operation there was a critical shortage of coal, and bodies waiting to be cremated were thrown onto piles of corpses situated all around the camp. Rats swarmed through these piles, greatly increasing the threat of a typhus epidemic, and something had to be done. Permission was finally received from Himmler to conduct mass burials, but this interment in vast graves was generally confined to German prisoners; even in death it was not deemed appropriate to bury Germans and Jews in the same grave.

On one occasion, Bob Mills was coerced into working on the cart. When all the bodies had been loaded they hauled the heavy cart into the main camp and over to the crematorium, where he actually witnessed emaciated corpses being fed into the ovens – a sight he would never forget. Otherwise, as he recalls, life went on in the Little Camp.

> We now had one appell per day. This was in the evening and, as before, lasted from two to three hours. We all received one blanket each and a clean shirt – another was issued about four weeks later. We also had a shower which everyone enjoyed immensely. Our hair was kept clipped short, much to our annoyance, but we found it easier to keep clean. We had to go to the kitchens and carry back all the food for the block as the Frenchmen who were our block-mates had to work from dawn until 6 pm. In wet weather this was quite a job as the ground became very slippery and muddy, but we either had to do it or starve. When the weather became colder we were given a topcoat each and this helped enormously for going out into the cold, as we had to get up at 4:30 am if we wished to have our morning coffee and collect our daily bread ration.

Life for the airmen had now settled into a monotonous pattern of rollcalls every night, the same meagre and insubstantial food ration, and each of the men became worried at their continual weight loss. Fleas and bed bugs still proved a constant source of irritation and the men itched incessantly, willing themselves not to scratch, for the smallest open sore invited infection. With no medicine or nutritious food these wounds would not heal and gave way to weeping, open sores. The men soon learned to stuff any such holes in their flesh with small wedges of paper to soak up the matter. Tom Blackham had a deep, suppurating cut five centimetres wide that needed constant attention.

Welshman Terry Gould from Caerphilly was shot down over France on 2 June 1944, just four days before D-Day. He shared some very vivid memories of his time in Buchenwald.

> It was like hell to us; we saw many atrocities. People were dying all the time through lack of nourishment and typhus. The cremation of the dead took place every Wednesday and Friday. We always knew the day because that day we had half-rations of soup as they took our fuel for the crematorium. One day a police officer who had collaborated with the Germans in Poland was brought into the camp. There were about thirty or forty Poles there and they recognised and lynched him. He was soon dead.

The men would spend all day sitting outside on the ground, filling in the long daylight hours with desultory conversation and an occasional doze in the sunshine. They knew the days were growing shorter and cooler and they would soon be spending most of the time on the wooden bunks in their barracks, which seemed to grow even harder as the flesh wilted from their bodies.

By this time, through the efforts of Christopher Burney, the airmen had managed to acquire a number of food bowls, known in the camp as gammels, although they mostly had to be shared around and carefully guarded. These were an absolute necessity if one was to receive a portion of the day's watery soup. No gammel, no food – it was a hard fact of life in the camp, and thieves were constantly on the lookout for untended bowls in order to obtain extra rations.

Every Thursday the men had to wash out their barracks and the shelves on which they slept while under the supervision of their block ältester, and cover the floor with quicklime. This gave off a pungent chlorine smell, but at least it provided some small means of maintaining hygiene. However, if there was no sunshine that day the bunks did not dry out and the damp would seep through thin blankets, striking at shoulders and hips.

Eric Johnston was suffering terrible pain, caused by a huge pus-filled whitlow on his right heel. It was inflamed and causing him so much agony that a medical orderly was called to the block. The men, especially Eric, did not expect much in the way of medical treatment – nor did he receive it. The grudging orderly who finally arrived treated the wound quickly and painfully by simply cutting into Eric's heel and digging out the whitlow without any thought of antiseptic. Eric winced and groaned, but at least he had received some form of treatment. The orderly casually bound the foot with toilet paper and left. There were certainly no bandages to be had, but the toilet paper dressing was changed periodically. At least it was clean and relatively sterile.

One day a party of 500 Jews who had been brought into Buchenwald were massed for despatch to Auschwitz. These men had been forced to work in a synthetic petrol factory near Leipzig, and some had been burned terribly when the factory was bombed by the Americans. These terrified individuals were marched to the railway station and crushed into four cattle trucks. Those close to death and unable to walk to the siding were piled onto carts drawn by other prisoners, who were forced to push them along Caracho Road at double time. The strongest in the carts struggled feebly to raise their heads from beneath the pile of dying and dead on the trip to the station. Their bodies were simply slung through the open doors of the cattle trucks. One Pole who attempted to escape was easily captured by the guards and hanged in front of the others – as an example. The hanging was a clumsy affair, and the Pole took a full five minutes to die.

In September, 1,700 Danes, mostly police officers, arrived at Buchenwald and were placed into huts near the airmen. They had not only refused to cooperate with the German occupation forces in Denmark, but supported the Resistance's acts of sabotage. They had proved to be something of an embarrassment while imprisoned in their homeland. According to Ray Perry, they were 'a fine looking body of men, but the rigours of life in a concentration camp would soon take their toll'.

While generally keeping to themselves and avoiding illegal undertakings against their captors, the Danes proved to be of immeasurable assistance to their fellow prisoners by providing some food items from the Red Cross parcels they were permitted to receive. Later a group of 350 Norwegian students found themselves cast into Buchenwald, and they too were appalled at the conditions and circumstances of the camp.

While acts of great perversity were committed daily throughout the camp, and shock soon gave way to a numbing inurement, there would be no more soul-searching experience for the airmen to witness than the day the SS, without any prior warning, hauled the remaining 250 gypsy children from Block 58, herded them into a group, and surrounded them with carbine-bearing guards.

These poor innocent children, many of whom had suffered castration at the hands of unfeeling butchers in the medical block, cried and called out for their frantic fathers or relatives, who were held at bay by blows from the guards' carbines or machine pistols. The heart-rending sobbing and screaming would haunt many an inmate who was witness to the events of that day. Those children without family members in the camp cried out for friends who had protected and tended them in camp, either for reasons of compassion or even sexual gratification, while the adults moaned and wept for the children they knew they would never see again.

The crying and screaming children were hustled into a long pantechnicon vehicle, and the back of the van was then closed. For the rest of that day an ominous silence hung over the camp, save for the distraught weeping of loved ones. It was a day of barbarism and tragedy no one who was there would ever want to remember . . . or could ever forget. It was later rumoured, but never confirmed, that the pantechnicon was in fact an elaborate gas chamber similar to those in use in Germany at that time, and that the gypsy children had suffocated, possibly from carbon monoxide poisoning, before the vehicle even left Buchenwald.

*

William Powell from Arizona, one of the USAAF airmen, was devastated to find in the camp hospital a young Belgian who had assisted him after he was shot down.

> The young man had been a contact for me in Brussels after a crew member and I had walked to there in an attempt to get back. I saw him at Buchenwald in a so-called hospital, shot with typhus and on the verge of death. Both legs had to be amputated and of course he died, leaving a wife and three children. I did not realise what war could do to a country until I was forced to parachute out of our plane and then evade capture for seven months with the aid of the Belgian people. Their lives were on the line every day, as well as not having any freedom.
>
> In a small town near Brugelette there was a farm run by a girl of about eighteen and her mother. I did not stay with them but was living on a farm next door. This woman and her mother, in spite of a German garrison which was quartered in a large house less than a mile from the farm, had up to seven Allied flyers hidden on the farm. They even held a church service for the crew of a downed B-17 that fell near the farm. After I left, the mother and daughter were picked up by the Gestapo and imprisoned and then sent on a train to a concentration camp. Fortunately the Americans broke through and liberated the train. The girl's father was already a prisoner of the Germans.
>
> I came to admire the Belgian people very much as they really resisted their country's occupation to the fullest extent. It must take a lot of dedication and courage to put your life on the line.

6

IN THE VALLEY OF THE SHADOW

For a nation so meticulously precise in the wartime documentation of its prisoners, the Germans somehow allowed a captured enemy agent of extraordinary talent to pull the wool over their collective eyes and eventually escape from their clutches.

The remarkable story of Wing Commander Forest Frederick Edward 'Tommy' Yeo-Thomas, RAFVR, GC, MC and Bar, Légion d'honneur and Croix de Guerre has been told before, most notably in Bruce Marshall's outstanding book *The White Rabbit*. Little is mentioned, however, of the prominent part he played in the lives and ultimate salvation of the airmen at Buchenwald, so it is worth recounting in brief this man's remarkable story prior to his arrival as a prisoner at the concentration camp.

Yeo-Thomas was born in London's Holborn area on 17 June 1901, but was educated for the most part in France. A determined and highly temperamental youth, his unorthodox behaviour saw him expelled from schools in both France and England. At age sixteen he managed to bluff his way into military service by claiming to be two years older, and served with the Allied armies until the end of the war of 1914–18.

His first experience of war came to what he later described as 'a premature end' with the signing of the Armistice, and in seeking out further action he sided with the Poles in their fight against the Russians over the following two years. He was taken by the Bolsheviks, but in the first of his many daring escapes, and displaying the boldness exemplified in his later adventures, he managed to flee from a daybreak appointment with a firing squad.

In 1930 he returned to Paris and worked at a variety of positions before joining the renowned dressmaking firm of Molyneux in 1932, where he eventually became one of the directors. However, the song of war still enticed Yeo-Thomas over the years, and once he even contemplated enlistment in the French Foreign Legion. Instead he offered his services to the Royal Air Force, who took him on as an interpreter. Following a period of relative inactivity, he became an intelligence officer, entering the RF (French Resistance) section of Special Operations Executive (SOE) under Captain Eric Piquet-Wicks. This section organised the supply and parachuting of arms and equipment to the various Resistance movements across France, and the transport of covert agents to and from that country.

On 23 February 1943, Yeo-Thomas was parachuted into France on his first operation for SOE under the code name 'White Rabbit', later returning to England with an American Air Force officer he had rescued. On his second mission into France on 17 September that year, he obtained valuable information for his bosses back in London, evading capture on no fewer than six occasions. He returned to England eight weeks later.

By this time Yeo-Thomas was starting to gamble against the odds, but his renowned audacity drove him on. On his next assignment in enemy territory he was betrayed to the Gestapo, who captured the British agent and gave him a savage beating. He then underwent four days of continuous interrogation, interspersed with floggings and sessions of torture. The vicious treatment included immersing him head-downwards in ice-cold water with his arms and legs chained. These interrogations went on for two months, but he stuck to his cover story that he was simply a downed airman by the name of Kenneth Dodkin. The real Squadron Leader Dodkin had worked with Yeo-Thomas back in England, coaching him at length on his life and service history. The Germans were not entirely convinced with Yeo-Thomas's story and offered him his freedom in exchange for information on the head of a Resistance group, but he kept reiterating that he was Squadron Leader Dodkin. Eventually he contracted blood poisoning from the chains which cut into his wrists and came close to losing his left arm.

After two daring but ultimately unsuccessful attempts to escape, Yeo-Thomas was transported to Fresnes prison, where he spent four months in Cell 293 in the 2nd Division, receiving further interrogation and very little food. Throughout those months of almost incessant maltreatment he refused to give any information beyond Dodkin's name, rank and service number. Any snippets that he deliberately let slip related to Dodkin's past. He knew full well that the German intelligence people would have checked these details and found them correct.

Whatever their doubts, the Germans still felt sure their prisoner was an enemy agent, but they seemed to decide that 'Dodkin' was small fry in the order of things. Along with a group of captured

SOE operatives, he was eventually transferred to the Camp de Royallieu internment and deportation centre in the city of Compiègne near Paris. Once there he made two escape attempts before he and thirty-six other prisoners were called out and sent under heavy guard to Germany. There was a three-day stopover at the town of Saarbrücken, where he and the other operatives were beaten yet again and confined to a small hut. Their final destination was Buchenwald concentration camp, which they reached on 17 August – just three days before the train arrived carrying the large group of captured airmen.

After registration, the thirty-seven agents were placed into Block 17, an isolated hut surrounded by barbed wire which contained 380 prisoners. As soon as they were settled into their quarters Yeo-Thomas held a council to coordinate their future escape activities. In the afternoon he met with two fellow SOE operatives already in the camp, Maurice Pertschuk and Christopher Burney, both of whom he knew well. He also made contact with two Russian colonels through one of his British officers who spoke Bulgarian, and talked with them at length about the need to smuggle in arms to back up an escape attempt. Yeo-Thomas knew his group was there under imminent sentence of execution, and speed in arranging such matters was imperative. On 20 August came the welcome news that a large contingent of British, Canadian and American airmen had arrived at the camp and were undergoing arrival formalities at the administration area. Yeo-Thomas set about talking with the senior officer of these men at the earliest opportunity.

When Yeo-Thomas eventually met with Phil Lamason he introduced himself by his assumed identity of Squadron Leader Kenneth Dodkin. From then on, to his complete bewilderment, things did not seem to go at all well; the New Zealander instantly became withdrawn and noncommittal. As it turned out, Lamason knew the real Dodkin quite well, having carried him on two missions before the fellow became non-operational, but he was not about to let on. Lamason was then introduced to Christopher Burney, in whom he felt he could confide. When they were alone he informed the SOE agent that the prisoner pretending to be Dodkin was in fact an impostor. Burney was surprised that Lamason knew the real Dodkin, and quickly assured him that things were in order, saying there was a very valid reason for the use of the alias. Thereafter Lamason always referred to Yeo- Thomas as Dodkin, but was one of the very few men who knew the brash Englishman's true identity.

According to his biographer Bruce Marshall, Yeo-Thomas was able to establish a firm friendship and close working relationship with Lamason. It was essential for the common good of the men under their command.

> To Yeo-Thomas the arrival of these new recruits for his army seemed providential. Not only with a potential of more than 200 men at his disposal was he now in a better position to bargain with the Russians, but the fact that the majority were trained flyers appeared little short of miraculous.
>
> About 12 kilometres from Buchenwald, he had learned, was a small and poorly guarded airfield called Nohra. Provided they could fight their way out of Buchenwald, he was soon persuading Lamason, there would be little to prevent their attacking the airfield, seizing the bombers and flying back to the Allied lines. The combined forces of themselves and the Russians would be divided up into units of ten, this time not according to nationality, but with

> a pilot, navigator, air gunner, engineer and radio operator in each team. Lamason, as hot-headed as Tommy, readily agreed.
>
> There seemed to be only two stumbling-blocks; one was the presence in Lamason's group of a so-called American flyer suspected to have been planted there as a stool pigeon, and who would require to be kept in ignorance of their plan and watched; and the other was the lack of arms. But even the latter was not insuperable: there were, Yeo-Thomas had discovered, arms in the camp, but only the Communist leaders knew where they were concealed, and so far all his attempts to make them divulge this secret had failed.

Wanting to set the record straight, Lamason revealed to the author that the unsubstantiated reference to the 'American flyer' should have been deleted from Marshall's book to forestall undeserved post-war suspicion falling on any of the American KLB airmen contingent. The flyer in question was not an American but their Dutch interpreter Spierenburg, who had been seen talking privately to some of the German guards. This man, as with all the KLB airmen of all nationalities, proved to be completely trustworthy and beyond suspicion.

Then a profound tragedy struck. On 9 September 1944, an announcement blared out over the camp's tannoy systems, ordering sixteen of Yeo-Thomas's men to report to the bunker in the watchtower. The men named were assembled and taken away, fully expecting to return after some type of formality or further interrogation. One of the men, a Canadian by the name of Frank Pickersgill, led the men in singing 'It's a Long Way to Tipperary' as they were led away. On arrival at the tower they were callously informed that their execution had been ordered. They were then thrown into the bunker for the night. A priest, attempting to give the Roman Catholics among them extreme unction, was denied access to the condemned men. He could hear the sounds of the men being savagely beaten, but there was nothing he could do. The following day they were removed from the bunker for a few minutes, only to be thrust back in again.

A short time later, the sixteen were taken across to the wooden mortuary block. Once inside they were tied in pairs by the hands, standing back to back. Nooses made from piano wire were then placed around their necks, and each pair of men was hoisted aloft by guards until the nooses engaged over steel hooks protruding from the walls, after which they were left to hang. They died a violent, agonising death, thrashing about as the wire nooses bit deeply into their necks. Once their struggles had ceased, they were lifted down and their death verified. The bodies were then sent upstairs for incineration in the crematorium's ovens.

Once news of the murder of his men had been verified, Yeo-Thomas initiated a desperate scheme to save as many of the remaining agents as possible. He had earlier been approached by political prisoner Eugen Kogon, who had been in Buchenwald since September 1939, and Professor Alfred Balachowsky of the Pasteur Institute in Paris, whose assigned tasks at the camp included an attempt to produce an anti-typhus vaccine. Both men worked together in Block 50 on medical experiments. They had persuaded Sturmbannführer Ding-Schuler, the head of Block 46, that an Allied victory was imminent and he should try to save the lives of some of the British agents. Ding-Schuler had been injecting deadly viruses into prisoners with impunity and knew he would be called to account for his heinous crimes after the war. He finally gave in. The plan called for the agents to assume the identities of French prisoners already dying of typhus in the hospital ward, but Ding-Schuler felt he could not hide more than a few substitutions, and decided he would only help three men. Balachowsky brought the news to Yeo-Thomas, and told him that Ding-Schuler had placed a further condition on the scheme. He had demanded that as 'Dodkin' was the obvious leader of the agents, and therefore the most potent voice in later pleas for clemency, he was to be one of the three men saved. He was quite unmoving in this condition, and so it was left to Yeo-Thomas to select the other two men – a fearful decision to place on any person. Who should be saved, and who should die?

Yeo-Thomas went into seclusion to ponder his decision, and select the two men who he felt might have the best hope of survival. Finally he sought out Balachowsky and gave him the names of two men who spoke fluent French, thereby giving the scheme the best possible chance of success. Balachowsky nodded gravely and went off to see Ding-Schuler with the news. The men Yeo-Thomas had chosen were Henri (Harry) Peulevé and Stéphane Hessel.

The French prisoners terminally ill with typhus had recently arrived in the camp as part of a large group and were in a special ward of the Revier (sick quarters). A German Kapo by the name of Arthur Dietzsch had also been promised confirmation of his actions to save the men should he be brought to trial, and he arranged for some prisoners to be transferred to Block 46. Among them were three desperately ill men by the names of Marcel Seigneur, Maurice Chouquet and Michel Boitel. These brave men, who knew they were dying, agreed to the substitution. Meanwhile Yeo-Thomas, Peulevé and Hessel were given injections which would produce a high fever and they were transferred to Block 46 after Dietzsch had 'diagnosed' typhus.

The deception was carried out just in time. On 4 October the tannoy blared again and the names of a further fifteen from

Yeo-Thomas's group were read out, including that of Captain Peulevé. He was immediately injected with more drugs to simulate typhus. When Kommandant Pister was told that one of the condemned fifteen was desperately ill with typhus he ordered Ding-Schuler to release the man so that he could be eliminated along with the others. Fortunately for Peulevé, Ding-Schuler was able to convince the Kommandant that to do so might cause an epidemic throughout the camp. Pister reluctantly compromised, saying that Peulevé had to be killed immediately by injection.

An NCO was despatched to carry out Peulevé's execution, but Dietzsch managed to waylay the man with a bottle of schnapps, and when the soldier was drunk enough, showed him a typhus-racked patient and identified him as Peulevé. Dietzsch dismissed the use of a lethal injection, saying it was a waste of medicine – the man would obviously be dead by morning. Agreeing with Dietzsch, the drunken NCO left and reported that the execution had been carried out.

The other fourteen agents whose names had been read out were taken to the mortuary block, knowing their last moments were upon them. With no hope of salvation, they elected to be shot, and this mass execution was carried out.

By the following morning, Marcel Seigneur was found to have died, and Peulevé assumed his identity, while Seigneur's body was cremated as that of the SOE agent. It had been a close thing. Maurice Boitel died on 13 October, and Chouquet five days later, following which Yeo-Thomas and Hessel took their respective identities. Again this was none too soon, for their execution orders had come through.

Now in the guise of Frenchmen, the three agents still had to survive until the Allied liberation, but Kogon was able to help once again by having the men transferred to work parties on outside Kommandos. All three men would survive the war.

Sadly, the memories of Fresnes and Buchenwald would haunt Peulevé through the post-war years. He married and had two children, but was later divorced. He took on a position as the overseas manager for a light engineering company, but a deep melancholy had set in and he died a broken man in Seville on 18 March 1963.

The other four surviving agents, twin brothers Henry and Alfred Newton, Maurice Southgate and Christopher Burney, lived in constant fear of following the other thirty men to their deaths, but somehow their execution orders never came through.

Kapo Dietzsch later missed the gallows because of the written testament promised to him by Wing Commander Yeo-Thomas, but was sentenced to fifteen years imprisonment. He was released from prison in 1950 and died in Burgdorf, Germany, on 26 August 1974. Major Ding-Schuler took his own life in September 1945, before going on trial.

For his courage and insuperable example, 'Tommy' Yeo-Thomas was awarded the George Cross on 15 February 1946, and the words of his citation perhaps best relate his movements after Buchenwald.

> Wing Commander Yeo-Thomas was later transferred to a work Kommando for Jews. In attempting to escape he was picked up by a German patrol and, claiming French nationality, was transferred to another camp near Marienburg for French prisoners of war. On 16 April 1945 he led a party of 20 in a most gallant attempt to escape in broad daylight. Ten were killed by fire from the guards. Those who reached cover split up into smaller groups. Wing Commander Yeo-Thomas became separated from his companions

> after three days without food. He continued alone for a week and was recaptured when only 800 yards from the American lines. A few days later he escaped with a party of ten French prisoners of war, whom he led through German patrols to the American lines.
>
> Wing Commander Yeo-Thomas thus turned his final mission into a success by his determined opposition to the enemy, his strenuous efforts to maintain the morale of his fellow prisoners, and his brilliant escape activities. He endured brutal treatment and torture without flinching and showed the most amazing fortitude and devotion to duty throughout his service abroad, during which he was under the constant threat of death.

Yeo-Thomas returned to Paris after the war, becoming a representative of the Federation of British Industries, but the treatment he had received at the hands of the Germans meant that he was never physically the same person. Gradually his health deteriorated and he died on 26 February 1964.

It would be certain that his widow Barbara mused a little as the grand tributes flowed during his Memorial Service at London's St Clement Danes Church on 30 April that year. When her husband died at the age of 62, he had never been compensated for the evil perpetrated upon him. The British government had granted their famed White Rabbit a disability pension, but this barely covered his medical expenses. At the time of his death his own government had done virtually nothing towards obtaining just compensation from the Germans.

During the compilation of the original version of this book, Barbara Yeo-Thomas spoke to the author at length about her husband, and mentioned the manner in which he was portrayed in the book *The White Rabbit*.

> If I may make just one comment on Bruce Marshall's characterisation of Tommy; to me Tommy was sunshine and laughter; he had a wonderful sense of humour and quick repartee. I don't think this comes across somehow. Admittedly there was the icy steel side to his nature, but one man who was with him in Buchenwald told me, 'We would be feeling as miserable as Hell, then Tommy would come along, looking awful, but with a broad grin on his face, and somehow we all felt better, although there was absolutely nothing to laugh about!' I understand what this man meant – Tommy had a sort of charisma; it was impossible to be depressed or unhappy when he was around.

SOE operatives Burney, Peulevé, Southgate and Hessel have since died. Stéphane Hessel, who passed away at the grand age of 95 in February 2013, went on to become a French Ambassador, and during the research for this book he too requested a few lines from the author in order to pay tribute to his former colleague.

> Of all the qualities that made up the exceptional figure of Wing Commander Yeo-Thomas, the one that remains most unforgettably in my memory is his sense of humour; in the truly dramatic situations we faced together, at times when life and death, torture or salvation were in the most precarious balance, he would smilingly bet for success and take us with him with a joke. From him I have learnt not only courage and determination, but the courteous bow to the Goddess of Fortune without whose help our thriving meets frustration. He had needed her often and she never failed him, and we who fought by his side felt through him her protection and goodwill.

> As a Frenchman I should have been doubly grateful for the way he, as a Briton, chose to save my life. But it seemed natural since his belonging to France as much as to his own country was part of his nature and, may I say, part of his charm.

On 27 September 1944, Flying Officer Philip Derek Hemmens succumbed to septicaemia, rheumatic fever and pneumonia, and died in his sleep. When he had first developed septicaemia he was placed in the camp hospital, but nothing was done apart from having his joints opened up using a knife. He didn't have the strength left to fight off the subsequent infection, while the constant damp and cold only served to compound his illness. His body was cremated and the ashes stored in a vault already crammed to overflowing with small labelled bottles.

Philip, the son of the Reverend Ernest Hemmens, had served with No. 49 (Lancaster) Squadron, RAF, before being shot down over France. Ron Leverington, in hiding at the time with fellow crew members Douglas Eagle, Reg Joyce and Don Leslie at the Lisors home of their helper Madame Huguette Verhague, recalls that Hemmens, who had suffered a broken arm in the crash of the Lancaster, often paid them a visit.

> Philip's arm seemed to be progressing satisfactorily while we were in hiding, and on occasions he accompanied myself and Huguette on night sorties in the forest nearby, looking for likely landing and dropping points in the clearings. He did manage to get hold of a plan of a V-1 site, which was very sketchy, on a piece of paper which he hid in his sack. We ate this in Gestapo headquarters before being searched. He was a great guy.

When he entered Buchenwald the month before his death, Hemmens was, apart from his broken arm, a picture of physical fitness. He lost his life not only through illness, but through the criminal neglect and incompetence of those who manned the so-called hospital. When his fellow airmen were notified of his death, a memorial service was organised and held outside Hut 58, conducted by one of the Danish fathers before a solemn group of prisoners with shaved heads bared, standing respectfully at attention. All 1,700 of the Danish prisoners attended the service and Flying Officer Tommy Blackham gave a memorial address in English. A minute's silence was then observed, following which the hymns 'Abide With Me' and 'Nearer My God to Thee' were sung in an emotional mixture of French, Danish, Norwegian and English, which lent a sweeping poignancy to the service for the gallant young flyer.

A week after Hemmens' death, conditions began to improve a little for the men. Their shoes were returned and they were issued with some short coats. This was certainly the work of several of the more seasoned inmates, and not the SS. The clothing was not officially issued, but as the longer-serving Communist prisoners practically ran day-to-day administration within the camp, small concessions could be made in exchange for favours or gifts.

Time lay heavily in the men's hearts as the weather grew colder. October brought with it bone-chilling winds and constant, driving rain. The men spent most of their time inside the barracks, and by night, although packed tightly together, they still suffered from the biting cold. Stanley Booker echoed a common fear from those days of uncertainty.

> Our main worry was that nobody knew we were there. None of us had been caught by the Luftwaffe in the first place, and there had been no contact with the International Red Cross at Paris, or anywhere else. We all knew the war was going well, but we could not contemplate that anyone could possibly know where we were, and thus we might simply disappear without a trace.

In order to address this constant state of apprehension and feelings of insecurity expressed by the KLB airmen, it was decided that they should hold formal meetings to give them a sense of purpose and order in their lives. And so in October 1944 the KLB [Konzentrationslager Buchenwald] Club came into being. Elected representatives of each nationality held separate meetings to collate the previously scattered efforts of those who had proposed address lists, meetings after the war and other pursuits. The meetings were held in accordance with strict protocol and were well attended. More than anything else they displayed the airmen's militariness and solidarity, and though few of their recommendations were adopted after the war, they formed a bond that brought the men together for decades after the liberation of Buchenwald.

The man elected as the East Canada representative, Flying Officer Art Kinnis, carefully compiled a list containing the names, ranks, service numbers, Buchenwald numbers and private addresses of all the airmen.

Thirty-five years later, in 1979, Kinnis saw a newspaper photograph of four former Buchenwald Canadians and hauled out his almost-forgotten address list. The four men's wartime addresses were there, and one by one he managed to make contact with Jim Stewart, Stan Hetherington, Ed Carter-Edwards and Bill Gibson.

Art and his wife Betty packed themselves into their mobile motor-home and crossed Canada, meeting the men and picking up new contact addresses along the way. By the time he returned home to Victoria, British Columbia, he had decided to embark on the vast and complex task of tracing as many of the airmen as possible – men who had relocated themselves all over the world. While his list would never be completed, and sadly bore the notation 'deceased' against several names, a spirit of comradeship and a shared hardship had been rekindled, and men who had not met or corresponded for nearly fifty years were back in contact.

For the sake of posterity, it is worth recording here the minutes of the meetings attended in the concentration camp and noted by Art Kinnis, for they trace the origins of the group that became known as the KLB Club.

Meeting held in Block 58, Buchenwald
Date: 12th October 1944, 1630 hours
Chairman: F/O A. Kinnis

Following in the footsteps of the USA and British members, the Canadians present at Buchenwald decided to get together and do whatever was possible towards the formation of a Canadian club which would keep alive the comradeship shown in the last three months. F/O J. Prudham was nominated for President by F/O C. Willis and seconded by F/O C. Hoffman. Motion carried unanimously.

At this point it was suggested by the Chairman that as members could be divided into three main groups, namely 15 in the east, 6 from the central and 6 from the west, that one member from each regional group be on the Central Committee. This being agreed upon, the following members were duly elected by the respective groups:

EAST Montreal: F/O J. D. Harvie
Toronto: F/O E. C. Watson
CENTRAL Winnipeg: F/O T. R. Hodgson
WEST Vancouver: F/O A. G. Kinnis

Suggestions were requested by the committee and members were told that further meetings would be held in which any ideas would be greatly appreciated. It has been suggested that in view of the great distance that Canadians would have to travel for a central meeting that all would find it more practical to have regional meetings, with the local leader in charge. Full cooperation with American members as well as affiliation with the Canadian Legion will be one of several aims.

Meeting adjourned.

The Committee of the British members is:
President: F/Lt T. Blackham
Secretary: F/O R. Taylor
Members: F/O M. Mutter, F/O E. Jackson, F/O K. Chapman

The problem of the Australian members are (*sic*) such that one member only was elected, said man being F/Sgt E. L. Johnston. They will keep in touch with all chapters through him.

The Committee of the United States members is:
President: 1st Lt W. Powell
Secretary: 2nd Lt R. H. Brown

Meeting held in Block 58, Buchenwald
Date: 13th October 1944, 1000 hours
Chairman: F/O J. Prudham

At this meeting the Committee approved of the following constitution which will be subject to the Club's approval:

1. That the name of the Club shall be the KLB Club, and that membership shall include flying personnel who were prisoners at Buchenwald.
2. That the Committee shall consist of:
   a) a President, whose duties shall be to call and preside over all meetings.
   b) a Vice President who will act in the absence of the President.
   c) a Secretary/Treasurer who will be the Managing Director.
   d) Regional Managers – elected in the following manner: 2 from the east, 1 from the central, and 1 from the west.
   e) An NCO member.
3. As seen by Section 2d, Canada has been divided into three regional groups – east, central and west. This is due to the small membership, and their distribution, and the great distance all would have to travel. It is proposed that each regional chairman be responsible for his own region's gatherings.
4. A pin and a membership list shall be sent to all members, said list to have the name, address and occupation of all Allied personnel. The list will be revised as necessary.
5. An initiation fee of $15.00 shall be charged, with an annual fee of $1.
6. A souvenir booklet shall be issued to all members.

7. Full cooperation with the American Club will be attempted, and the Canadian Branch will strive to affiliate itself with the Canadian Legion.
8. A bank account shall be opened in the name of the KLB Club, and the Secretary or President shall be authorised to sign checks up to the sum of $15.00, and by the Secretary and President if over that amount.

It is proposed that a national meeting be held every five years for the purpose of selection of officers. If possible this should be held in conjunction with the American Club. The purpose of the Club is to perpetuate the comradeship already shown by the flying personnel of Great Britain, Australia,. United States and Canada by the interchanging of pamphlets, ideas and visits.

Meeting held in Block 58, Buchenwald
Date: 13th October 1944, 1400 hours
Chairman: F/O J. Prudham

The second meeting of the Club was for the ratification of the proposed constitution. Full approval was obtained.

Members were asked to contribute sketches or ideas for the international pin.

It was further suggested that a gathering be held in London as soon after our return as possible. All members should leave their full address (home and abroad) at BC House, Waterloo Place, London. The Secretary will pick up all information at that point.

The meeting adjourned.

1st International Committee Meeting
15th October 1944
Chairman: F/Lt T. Blackham

It has been suggested that a book in the nature of a history of our life from Fresnes prison to our stay in Buchenwald be compiled as a souvenir.

The Committee drew up the following rough plan:-

1) Cover of blue leather with the club pin embossed in silver or gold.
2) A flyleaf dedicated to F/O Philip Hemmens.
3) A list of club officers.
4) Editorial.
5) Photograph of all aircraft flown by the various club members.
6) History of all our activities from Fresnes.
7) History of the various sections (humorous).
8) Photographs of all members in uniform (no hat).
9) Photograph with prison number underneath; name and nickname; rank; service number; position in type of aircraft flown; date shot down and captured. Date of birth, married or single, address and occupation.
10) Motto: 'Appell is Appell'.

International Committee Meeting
17th October 1944

Full approval was obtained in the selection of a pin design. All members expressed themselves as well pleased with the design.

The pin design formulated in Buchenwald is now a symbol that binds the airmen. It shows a naked, winged foot, symbolising their barefoot condition while in the concentration camp. The foot is chained to a ball bearing the letters KLB, with the whole mounted on a white star, which was the crest of the Allied invasion forces.

The Russians, through Phil Lamason's friendly overtures to their leaders, were supplying the airmen with some bread and wooden clogs. Doctor Balachowsky was meanwhile able to supplement the men's meagre diet; among experiments in which he was involved at the medical block were studies on rabbits, which were injected with various disease germs. When the rabbits died, and if the experiments had not rendered the animals uneatable, he secretly passed the carcasses on to the airmen who furtively cooked them.

It was about this time that specific orders from Berlin reached the desk of Kommandant Pister, who reluctantly set the process in motion. The orders stated that all of the airmen, including the bedridden and desperately ill, were to be exterminated within the week.

This terrible news was conveyed to Phil Lamason by a German Communist who had been given the information by a friend who worked in the administrative area. Lamason sought out Tommy Yeo-Thomas, Christopher Burney and Jan Robert, a Dutch patriot who had been an Olympic training masseur. The four men discussed the information at length, but concluded that there was precious little any of them could do to avert the mass execution. Talks with the Russians regarding weapons and armed resistance were coming along, albeit slowly. It was an inch-by-inch process, and a sudden demand for help would probably see the shutters go down on any further negotiations.

Burney told Lamason that, through contacts within the camp, he would try to pass a message concerning the airmen's plight to the outside world, but their only real hope at that time was to pray that the dire news was wrong. Lamason kept the information to himself, and in fact did not reveal the closeness of the airmen's escape from extermination until a KLB reunion in Canada in 1985.

There is little reason to doubt that the orders were issued, but the administration involved in carrying out such a vast and complex operation was massive. The airmen were certainly an embarrassment to the Germans, but their deaths would have enormous ramifications if the British found out. The killings would have to be concealed by the issue of false certificates stating that each death was the result of natural causes. Fortunately for the sake of the men, such documentation would require a great deal of time. Unaware of their pending execution, the airmen went about their daily routine.

Around this time, as Lamason could vividly recall, there was a day when he was approached by two no-nonsense guards. He was instructed to accompany them, following which they escorted him out of sight of the other airmen. He was not sure what was happening, but went along with the guards as they hustled him away from the Little Camp and into a sparsely-grassed clearing. He began to sense that all was not well. 'They marched me in and I think they were going to shoot me,' he recalled many years later to interviewer Mike Dorsey. This concern was borne out when he saw a group of soldiers armed with rifles standing nearby. Next, a young German officer stood right in front of Lamason and began angrily berating him, implying that he was a troublemaker and the airmen under his command were disobedient and rebellious. It was his fault, the officer insisted, and it had to stop.

'I said with a bit of irony, "I didn't realise it took about twenty guys to shoot me." And there was this dog jumping up and snapping at my throat. But I would not step back. I could smell the dog's breath on my face . . . and I just knew that any movement backwards at all and all hell would break loose. I could not step back . . . and it saved my life and the life of my men.

'In those moments I stressed to the officer that my mother was a widow, my mother-in-law was a widow, and how, if I was shot, my wife too would be a widow. I stressed to him that the Germans were losing the war and that I would vouch for him as being an honourable officer in any war court hearings if he released me.'

It was an agonising few seconds as Lamason stood his ground and defiantly watched the young officer weighing up what he had just said. 'I was looking straight at him and he looked at me and I thought he looked quite a decent guy. He looked for another minute and then he gave the order to "ground arms" and marched them out again.'

Lamason stood there gathering his thoughts for the next couple of minutes, suddenly trembling and weak-kneed, knowing just how close he had come to being executed. Shortly after, a guard escorted him back into the Little Camp. As he walked he was wreathed in thought, but decided to keep news of this close encounter with death to himself. Once again, however, it demonstrated the mettle and fine leadership of this great man.

How then did the miracle happen? How did the airmen secure a transfer from Buchenwald when the records clearly state that they were not to be transferred to another camp? The man to thank was Christopher Burney, the SOE agent and official camp interpreter. Burney, a former commando subaltern, was captured at Caen in August 1942 after being parachuted into France by SOE's 'F' Section. His German captors knew his identity, but despite interrogations and torture, he refused to divulge anything beyond his name, rank and service number. He was cast into a solitary confinement cell for eighteen months, but managed to survive this terrible ordeal and was sent to Buchenwald. For fifteen months, until the liberation of the camp, he was fully engaged in plans to seize control from the Germans.

His plans were continually frustrated by the German Communist prisoners who were forming their own resistance movement, and who thwarted his every attempt to obtain arms. These the International Camp Committee kept to themselves, and even regarded the young Englishman's plans with considerable mistrust and even contempt.

As interpreter, Burney had free access to the Little Camp, and he was both a solace and an inspiration to the Allied airmen. He was in frequent contact with Yeo-Thomas, and was instrumental in organising the substitution affair for the Wing Commander and his two companions, following which they hid out in Hut 46 until their transfer out of Buchenwald on a working party.

Being officially confined to the Little Camp, the airmen were not permitted into the Main Camp except for ration collection and various other fatigues or for administrative reasons. However, as the men's senior officer, Lamason was able to move into the Main Camp where he would meet and liaise directly with Burney and members of the powerful International Camp Committee. They decided to smuggle out a note, to be delivered to the Luftwaffe hierarchy, letting them know that aircrew personnel were being illegally held in a concentration camp.

With the aid of a trusted prisoner on an outside working party at the nearby Luftwaffe airfield, the Committee managed to get their message out of the camp, with a request that an officer pass the information to Berlin, and for the Luftwaffe to intercede on behalf of the men.

The message apparently got through. Soon after, a small group of Luftwaffe officers including a staff officer later identified by former prisoners from photographs as Johannes (Hannes) Trautloft, arrived at the camp from Berlin to investigate the claim. Trautloft was a decorated fighter pilot who had flown and fought in the Battle of France and the Battle of Britain. On the orders of Hermann Goering, commander-in-chief of the Luftwaffe, Trautloft had earlier been given responsibility for inspecting and reporting on the condition of the Luftwaffe's fleet of daytime fighters at different airfields. While carrying out this task, it is believed (but cannot be verified) that he heard rumours of a large group of Allied airmen being held captive in Buchenwald concentration camp. He decided to investigate and travelled to the camp, ostensibly to check out the bombing damage from the August raid.

After completing his inspection, Trautloft and his aides were about to leave the camp when German-speaking American airman Bernard Scharf called out to him from behind a fence in the Little Camp and beckoned him over. He told Trautloft that more than a hundred Allied airmen were being held under atrocious conditions in the camp, and begged him to intervene on their behalf. After making official enquiries, he was satisfied that there were indeed Allied airmen being held illegally in the camp. On his return to Berlin, it is believed Trautloft reported his findings to his superior officers, including Reichsmarschall Goering. An enraged Goering then made stern approaches 'at the highest level' (presumably Adolf Hitler), as he feared possible reprisals against German prisoners of war if news of this atrocity managed to reach Allied ears. His protestations brought the desired result, with Hitler apparently giving permission for the airmen to be immediately transferred to a regular prisoner of war camp under Luftwaffe control.

It had been a flimsy and perhaps risky chance, but it had paid off. Phil Lamason would recall the time Yeo-Thomas informed him that the information had not only made it through to the Luftwaffe, but had in turn reached London.

'How on earth could you know it has reached England?' he enquired with disbelief.

Yeo-Thomas had smiled. 'We heard it on the BBC news last night, courtesy of our secret radio,' was the laconic reply. 'You must learn to trust me, Phil. We'll soon have you and the other chaps out of here. Must go – talk with you later.' With that he walked off, leaving Lamason open-mouthed with incredulity.

*

On the morning of 14 October 1944, a tall, sharp-looking civilian arrived from Dulag Luft in Oberursel, the Luftwaffe's interrogation centre and transit camp for captured Allied aircrew, situated on the outskirts of Wiesbaden.

In the Little Camp, the puzzled airmen were ordered to assemble after being told they were to be addressed in the Main Camp. With the exception of those in hospital, they were marched down through the camp and taken to the large canteen building. The men were understandably nervous following the gruesome murders of the SOE operatives. Following on the heels of Phil Lamason, they were herded into the canteen building where the civilian stood facing them, accompanied by two Luftwaffe officers. For most of the men it was their first sight of a Luftwaffe uniform, and their desultory conversation swelled with speculation. The civilian held up his hands and called for silence.

'Gentlemen,' he began, 'I would ask that you listen very carefully to what I have to say. I am here from Dulag Luft. Do you all know where that is, and what it means?' He looked around as a few of the men murmured and nodded. They'd all heard of the centre where downed and captured airmen were sent for interrogation prior to their transfer to more permanent POW camps.

'Recently, it came to the attention of the Luftwaffe that all of you were being held in this place and were brought here, so the SS tells me, by mistake!' A derisive howl greeted this statement, but the men quickly fell silent as the civilian raised his hand once again.

'Now I have brought you here for two reasons. The first is to tell you that you will all be released from this place and transferred to a prisoner of war camp – this time under Luftwaffe control.' The statement created an instant hubbub and this time it was Lamason who stood and requested silence.

'Thank you, Squadron Leader,' continued the civilian. 'I am also directed to inform you that this transfer is conditional on you completing the required information on some Red Cross forms. This is necessary to prove your identity and status, and must be fully completed. I am instructed to inform you that should any of you choose not to complete this formality you will remain at Buchenwald as a political prisoner, and I need hardly remind you what that might mean!'

It was apparent that the speaker could barely contain his disgust with the concentration camp and its administrators. Together with the uniformed officers, he brought forward a small stack of forms embossed with the Red Cross symbol and some pencils, both of which were passed around. As the men read the questionnaires they groaned in exasperation – these were the spurious forms they had been briefed on by the Intelligence people back in England. The forms not only required personal information but asked for details on their squadron, aircraft and operational movements. Several of the men addressed themselves to Lamason.

'Sir, we've already been told not to fill out these bloody forms. What should we do?' Phil Lamason had already pondered the question and made his decision.

'We all know the origin of these forms,' he said to the small crowd now pressed around him. 'I will certainly not instruct any of you to go against orders. I'll just say this; that it is up to each man as to how much information he puts down, and how much of it is correct. I must however remind you that we are in an extremely dicey situation here.' Only Lamason knew of the extermination order at this time, and he was not about to share this information with anyone, but it was a vital element in what he was now trying to impress upon the men. 'However, as we have been prisoners for several months now, any information required on these bits of paper is most likely not only known to the Germans, but is out of date.' He paused. 'For my own part, I intend giving them nothing but my name, rank and number.'

The mood was one of confusion and anger, and one man confronted the German. 'It is against our orders to fill out a lot of the information on this form. You know that as much as we do!'

The civilian's eyes blazed momentarily. 'You are not, repeat *not*, in a position to argue, young man. Either you fill in that form or you stay here. I am trying to help, but that depends entirely on each of you.'

It was a sticky situation. The men had no uniforms, no dog tags – nothing in fact to prove who they were. Was this German bluffing? The thought of remaining where they were appalled the airmen, but how far could they go against King's regulations and very specific orders? Name, rank and service number only, the authorities in England had said. But had they ever envisaged a predicament such as the one in which they now found themselves? The nightmare memories of their time already spent in the camp plus the prospect of trying to survive a savage winter finally convinced the majority of them and they complied with the German's request. Most of them followed Lamason's advice, which by now had been passed around. They wrote in their names and numbers and filled out the other information, for the most part with bogus addresses, squadrons and types of aircraft flown.

Texas-born Stratton Appleman was quite against Lamason's recommendations. Appleman, who had flown a glider into Normandy during the D-Day beach landings on 6 June, was captured in full uniform and made a prisoner of war. Two weeks later he escaped his captors by leaping from a moving prison train bound for Germany, landing in an orchard. He and fellow airman Ralph Dearay were hidden by the Resistance in the village of Rosay. The two men, now dressed in civilian attire, were arrested while attempting to make their way to Épernay and an Underground escape route. Thus Appleman had once been an officially recognised prisoner of war in Germany, but he too had lost all military status when joining the group bound for Buchenwald. Now, as he told the author, he was adamant that the men should follow his example and only give the required name, rank and number.

> As the senior officer, Lamason was taking a position now recognised by military authorities as the proper role for the senior officer among a group of POWs. His first concern was the welfare of his men. As a very junior officer who had seen that to follow my original military orders had seen me well through innumerable interrogations, I chose to challenge his order. I announced that I would do everything possible to report anyone who cooperated with the Germans in what I considered a violation of our standing military orders.
>
> Several of the men sided with me in refusing to complete the forms. The German major present explained that those who cooperated would depart Buchenwald the following day, and that he could not be responsible for those who didn't.
>
> If Lamason remembers the incident I describe, I hope he will remember my youth. My position during the past eighteen years as spokesman for the US Veterans' Administration has required me to become involved in an extensive study of POW behaviour, and I recognise mine as a rather typical case of trying to restore

> self-esteem lost as a result of being a prisoner by trying to over-comply with my own interpretation of military orders, and by drawing attention to my exploits as an escapee. With all that experience behind me, I know now that the KLB Club was fortunate to have had Lamason as its leader.

For thirty of the men, the thought of aiding the Germans in any way, shape or form was repugnant, however dated the information they were asked to disclose might be. They stood firm and either gave only names and numbers, or totally refused to fill out the forms, enraging the civilian and his cronies, who separated those dissenters from the rest of the men as they handed back their uncompleted forms. Phil Lamason's countryman Malcolm Cullen was one of this number.

> After the interview, we were isolated from the remainder of our companions, and that night we turned and tossed in unaccustomed beds wondering if what we had done would prove to be our undoing. Next morning, however, we were more cheerful and decided amongst ourselves that we would hold to our first decision. Late that afternoon we were taken back and harangued again, this time individually. Finding that he still only received a polite negative from each of us, he finished up and informed us that it was the last we would see of him, and that he thought we would have had more sense.
>
> I must say that as we marched away this time, back to our old barracks, our spirits had reached a low ebb, and the thought of staying behind while most of the others were sent to a proper camp made me shudder.

The next few days passed slowly for the airmen, who waited impatiently for news of their fate. For those who had partially or totally refused to fill out the bogus form, the days were filled with agonies of uncertainty.

Nothing was heard until 3 pm on the afternoon of 18 October when a list was sent to the block, naming those who were to report to the main gate the following morning. Only fourteen in hospital, who were too sick to move, were listed to remain behind. Malcolm Cullen and his fellow dissenters heard their names read out together with the others. The men could barely contain themselves at the thought that this might be their last night in the concentration camp.

No one slept very well that evening, and the following morning many were up early, endeavouring to shave themselves with the two or three well-used razors some men had managed to retain. The blades were blunt and it was raining outside, but they were too excited to care about such minor inconveniences. Not even the march to the Effektenkammer in the cold driving rain could dampen their spirits.

As sentries in the nearby watchtowers stood close to their machine-guns and looked on with interest, the men were handed their old civilian clothing, together with most effects taken from them on arrival at Buchenwald. Once again they shook their heads at German efficiency, although the clothes now hung like sacks from their far slimmer forms. Outside, the SS guards stood them in files of five and conducted a headcount in the rain, which had now slackened off to a drizzle.

Not long after, the gates beneath the dreaded tower were swung open and a Luftwaffe Hauptmann (Captain) in full uniform was ushered in. The relief felt by the men on seeing that uniform was almost tangible. The Hauptmann stood in front of the men, looked up at the leaden sky and grunted.

'Gentlemen,' he said, 'please break your ranks and go back inside out of the rain.' The men could scarcely believe their ears. Civility – and from a German. They quickly scattered and made their way back into the shelter of the Effektenkammer, where the Hauptmann addressed them. It was like a dream to the men as he spoke in soft but precise terms. The Geneva Convention – Red Cross parcels – prisoner of war status – beds with sheets. He was describing things they had hardly dared to think about while in the Little Camp.

When the rain had finally eased, the men were formed up once again, ready to march out through the camp gates. As the steel barriers with the despised 'Jedem das Seine' motto closed behind them, not a single one of the 153 looked back as they tramped along the Caracho Way, back to the railhead where they had arrived amid such chaos back in August. They had left behind fourteen hospitalised members of their group who were far too ill or diseased to travel, but had received assurances that these men would not only be well treated, but transferred to their new camp once they were well enough. In fact the fourteen would receive little or no special treatment at all, but as they recovered sufficiently to leave Buchenwald they would be packed off to join the others at their POW camp. It was not entirely a day for overt celebration for the airmen. As well as the fourteen remaining behind, the transfer had sadly come too late for young Philip Hemmens.

Passing by the shattered ruins of the Gustloff Werke, they finally reached the railhead and saw the waiting evacuation train. Their hopes sank somewhat when they noted the familiar '40 hommes/8 chevaux' on the sides of the cattle trucks. This time, however, there was none of the appalling overcrowding they had endured on the inbound journey. The men were now spread out over ten cars, with fresh straw on the floor, a stove, two guards, and an open door. It was almost first-class travel.

They had not been told their ultimate destination, but the airmen were not worried so far as they would soon be leaving Buchenwald far behind. After a long wait, the train pulled away from the platform and gradually built up speed as Buchenwald, its stink and its terror receded in the distance.

Victorian Tom Malcolm was one of those left behind in the camp hospital at Buchenwald. He was delirious with erysipelas, a severe and highly contagious infection of the skin causing high fever and often grave complications such as pneumonia and inflammation of the kidneys. The potentially fatal malady could have been treated easily, and even eradicated, by the use of sulphonamides, but this disease was quite common in the hospital, where no medicines were dispensed. He had to endure the most primitive of treatments – he was simply wrapped in wet blankets. It was a kill or cure method administered by indifferent attendants. Fortunately he survived and later joined the rest of the airmen in their POW camp, bunking in with fellow Australians Ray Perry and Jim Gwilliam, but any recollection of his latter days at Buchenwald were lost to him.

> To this day I have no memory of what happened to me during the time I was seriously ill in hospital, nor of my move across to the air force camp to join the others. What I do remember, quite vividly, is being cocooned for what seemed an eternity in sopping wet blankets.

Another of those too ill to be moved was Ed Carter-Edwards. He had developed pneumonia and pleurisy and was segregated with the other thirteen airmen who required intense medical treatment. The so-called hospital they occupied was Block 61, designated to hold the seriously ill and dying. It was a large hut, 25 metres long by 7 metres wide, holding nearly 800 patients from the Little Camp. It stank of death, putrefaction and defecation. Carter-Edwards was delirious for almost two weeks, his fever aggravated by the unsanitary conditions. The only treatment he received was from a sympathetic inmate – a doctor and former professor from the University of Paris – who managed to locate a syringe. At great personal risk he carefully inserted it into Carter-Edwards' back, draining the fluid from his lungs.

That was the only treatment the Canadian received for his illnesses. There was no medication, no aspirins, no antibiotics. The inmates either survived or died. If they lived they were lucky; if not, their corpse would be dragged out the next day. Some operations were performed by prison doctors on a table at one end of the hut, carried out in full view of the other patients, and performed without the use of any anaesthetic.

Every morning Russian prisoners would enter the hut and haul out those who had died during the night, sometimes as many as three dozen at a time. They would strip the bodies and write the deceased's name on his leg. Why they bothered to do this was a mystery to Carter-Edwards, as the Russians were simply taking the corpses to the crematorium, but someone along the way must have entered the names in what would have been a very lengthy book. The Russians piled the bodies on a homemade stretcher like cord-wood and bore them off. Some of the men suffered terribly before they died, crying out the names of loved ones, their bodies racked with pain, their eyes rolling and their mouths gaping. They were dying in such numbers the Germans could not cremate the bodies fast enough.

The conditions were inhumane and the patients were that in name only. They had to sleep on thin straw mattresses without any blankets. Paper bandages were applied to open sores, but these were quickly eaten by the starving prisoners at the first opportunity. Every few days the Russians would be sent through with a hose to wash the whole place down – walls, floors, and even patients in their beds – which surely hastened many a death. Dysentery was rife, and the resultant mess saturated the blankets, leaking through onto those unfortunate enough to be on the bunk below. The Russians were brutal, they had no mercy for anyone, even though they knew many of those in the hut were their allies, and the patients were all treated in the same disgraceful manner. One can only assume that they were more concerned for their own survival.

Carter-Edwards' fellow patients lived and died in these terrible conditions and his time in the hut stood out most in his memories of Buchenwald. Death was all around him; he witnessed it, heard it, felt it, and came within a whisker of experiencing it.

After nearly six weeks in this death-house, Ed Carter-Edwards was considered well enough to be turned out, despite the fact that he was so weak he could barely stand, let alone walk. But with his release from that purgatory came the full realisation that he was essentially on his own – merely one of almost 40,000 doomed men whose sole preoccupation was survival as they shuffled aimlessly around the dusty compound, dazed and generally uncomprehending.

Two days after his release from the hut, he was forced to work on a thirteen-kilometre railway line the Germans were laying outside the camp, labouring as part of a group for anything up to fourteen hours a shift. The original track, laid in mid-1943, ran down to Weimar with a 300-metre difference in elevation. He was made to work, sometimes up to his knees in mud, in his debilitated condition. At one time he took it upon himself to complain to his guards. They merely laughed at the Canadian and one of them jerked his thumb towards the crematorium. 'You don't want to work?' he scoffed. 'Then perhaps you would prefer to report to the crematorium and go up the chimney?' Ed kept working.

The group dug an embankment on top of which the guards stood, kicking stones and dirt down onto the workers to compound their misery in the cold, wet conditions. The Germans also had several guard dogs on long leashes, and they would gather up these leashes in their hands before advancing menacingly towards some terrified prisoner. They would then shout an order and partially release the leash. The dog would leap straight at the prisoner's face and the guards' game was to see how close it came before the leash became taut and held the snapping beast at bay. The guards considered this a huge joke, and laughed at the misery of their victims.

Ed Carter-Edwards was eventually able to contact a friendly fellow prisoner by the name of Kurt Barrs, who had been training to be a doctor before joining the Dutch Underground. Barrs' work at the camp entailed keeping a headcount of the dead, and he somehow manipulated his lists to show that the Canadian had died. Barr then told Carter-Edwards to keep out of sight as much as possible, but there was no real need to hide in such a huge camp filled with so many similarly-dressed, emaciated people.

By this time, he had been moved to the middle compound and by making discreet enquiries he found out, to his horror, that the rest of the airmen had vacated the camp and been sent to a regular prisoner of war camp. He was now in a quandary. According to the records he was dead, and yet somehow he had to join his air force colleagues. He felt miserable, forgotten, and all alone.

Carter-Edwards lived under terrible conditions, on a bed in a stack like bakers' shelves. Each bed was two metres wide, with four tiers against each wall, and the prisoners were jammed in like sardines. Movement was all but impossible. They slept in their clothes – the only clothes they had. There were no toilet facilities, no washroom and no soap, and his discomfort was worsened by the fact that he couldn't speak the language of those around him.

Towards the end of November, a high-ranking German air force officer came into the camp and started asking after Carter-Edwards. He knew that Ed was still alive, so word had somehow been smuggled out of the camp, probably by Kurt Barrs, as the records showed that he was deceased, but Ed never did find out. Eventually the news that he was being sought reached Ed, who decided to take a chance that the man asking for him was genuine. He surrendered to a guard and was immediately taken to the officer. With surprising swiftness, he was taken under guard to be reunited with his aircrew colleagues in their POW camp, where he received an emotional welcome from the other airmen.

He found life at the Luftwaffe camp tough, with very little food and constant harassment from the guards, but in his own words, 'It was heaven compared to Buchenwald!'

7

DEATH MARCH

WITH THE WARMTH OF A stove to comfort them, the rocking movement of the train and the hypnotic click-clacking as it rolled along the rails, exhaustion soon took its toll on the group of airmen as Buchenwald was being left far behind. Before too long most had fallen into a deep, undisturbed sleep.

The following morning they were handed a chunk of bread and a tough but palatable piece of sausage meat. A little later, after the train had stopped and the men had been permitted to relieve themselves by the rails, they were each given a mug of ersatz acorn coffee.

With most of their earlier suspicions now gone, some of the men actually began to enjoy the journey, particularly as they could talk freely with each other. They even sang to express their feelings of relief. Jim Gwilliam remembered one of his guards as an elderly fellow from the Great War who was trying to play a mouth organ but was only succeeding in making a woeful noise. Through gesticulation, Jim asked if he might be able to have a go, and the guard handed over his instrument. Within seconds Gwilliam had launched into a melancholy version of 'Lili Marlene' and the guard's face lit up with pleasure. Every time he tried to change the tune, the guard would give him a pitiful look and beg him for another encore of what was obviously his favourite song. By the time they reached Sagan station around noon on the third day, the guard had become friendly and was singing along with gusto. He and the other guards had given the prisoners some cigarettes, which they had all smoked together.

At Sagan the doors of the cattle trucks were rolled open to reveal an armed guard company dressed in the field blue of the Luftwaffe. Seeing these uniforms was a great relief for the airmen, many of whom had cringed on hearing the sudden blows on the doors. The new guard company ordered the occupants to detrain, and as they stood on the platform and stretched cramped limbs, they looked around at the bordering pine forests. The forest air was sweet, clean and cool. Their former guards wished them all a sincere 'Guten abend', following which the Luftwaffe detail counted the men before marching the long column along a narrow track to their new camp, Stalag Luft III. Soon the trees thinned out and they saw their new 'home' for the first time. The massive air force camp was sprawled over several hectares in a clearing hewn from the pines, encircled by a high, double barbed-wire fence. Placed at intervals around the fence were a number of high watchtowers, each containing a guard, a spotlight pointed into the camp and a fixed machine-gun. Within the compound was a series of single-level wooden huts.

Arriving at the main gate, they were halted, counted and re-counted before being ushered through the large wooden gate and into the camp. Their reception was overwhelming. The Luftwaffe authorities, who had no love for the SS and Gestapo, were genuinely shocked at the condition of their latest prisoners. Once again the airmen were photographed and registered, given hot showers and kitted out with a complete airman's uniform and a set of underwear, their first in months. They could scarcely comprehend the difference between this place and Buchenwald. Here they were being treated as true prisoners of war and not as caged animals. To top it all off they were each given an entire Red Cross parcel. They quickly withdrew to a quiet corner somewhere to examine the contents of their parcel in seclusion. Stanley Booker vividly recalls the ecstasy of having such luxury all to himself.

> Needless to say it was quickly devoured, and many of us were violently sick shortly afterwards. At last we felt secure, into a proper organised routine, with the delight of a clean bunk with sheets and two clean blankets. However the greatest thrill was not the food, as relatively little as it was, but the sheer joy of being able to write that first Red Cross letter home, to hopefully let our loved ones know we were alive and well.

Joe Moser recalled their arrival at Stalag Luft III, the Luftwaffe POW camp originally designed and set up to hold Allied airmen, which earlier in the war would have – and should have – been their destination.

> Our Buchenwald group would not stay together. We were just assigned barracks rooms according to where there were openings. I was sent to the barrack identified as Block 104 in the North Camp. As it turned out, Block 104 was the most famous barracks of the entire war in the most famous POW camp of the entire war, and possibly any war – and certainly not because I lived there! It was

> in this very barracks, underneath the very stove on which I helped cook my meals for the next several months, that the tunnel called 'Harry' was started. This is the tunnel from which 76 Allied airmen escaped on March 24, 1944.

The tunnel break from Block 104 came to be known as 'The Great Escape', with three of the 76 escapees making successful home runs. The fact that so many downed airmen had fled captivity completely enraged Adolf Hitler, who demanded that all of those recaptured were to be shot. Hermann Goering and other high-ranking German officers were understandably appalled at this directive and managed to convince Hitler that such an unwarranted massacre might cause similar reprisals against German POWs held by the Allies. Hitler finally saw a degree of reason in this, but stubbornly insisted that 'more than half' of those recaptured were to be executed – an order that he passed on to the brutal head of the SS, Heinrich Himmler. As a result, 50 of the 73 airmen eventually rounded up were shot in cold blood, either singly or in pairs. As the escape and reprisals had taken place just two months before the arrival of the Buchenwald airmen, the residents of the camp were understandably still in a state of profound distress and confusion, while harbouring a deep-rooted rage against their captors.

In the first edition of his later-revised book, *Escape From Germany* (Air Ministry Publication, 1956), RAF fighter pilot Aidan Crawley made the following observations.

> When [the prisoners] arrived the most distinctive sign of the treatment they had received was their shaved heads, but it was noticed on the first parade that as the German NCO who was

> counting the prisoners passed them they instinctively stiffened as if expecting a blow. A question they all asked the first day of their arrival was how many men went for 'the chop' each week. When their fellow prisoners did not understand they were surprised and explained that 'the chop' in Buchenwald meant execution . . . The story of Buchenwald and the other concentration camps is now well known. When these airmen first described what they had seen, the endless beatings, the starving and dying people lying on the floor in their own filth too weak to move, the stench, the lampshades made of human skin, the hospital where human beings were treated as guinea pigs, their fellow prisoners found their story hard to believe.

One of the prisoners at Sagan, Kevin Murphy, told of his shock at the first sight of a friend, one of the Englishmen recently arrived from Buchenwald.

> It was late 1944 and the usual blanket of low cloud covered the pine trees that ringed Stalag Luft III. We no longer expected to be home for Christmas and were reconciling ourselves to yet another winter of wrestling with the weather and the 'goons' [a derogatory term for their guards]. I was walking with a friend around the 'circuit' that afternoon to keep warm and to pass the time until dinner, when I was accosted by a slight figure in a nondescript uniform. I stopped and looked uncertainly at this stranger who said, 'Don't you know me, Spud?' Peeling off the balaclava, he revealed a shaven head and a very pale face which I began to realise resembled an old friend, Ian Robb, a fellow navigator, missing presumed dead since August 1943! I was completely flabbergasted, but recovered enough to take him to my hut for a cup of Nescafé. There I presented him

with a letter from his mother and his fiancée – his first news for eighteen months. We had a lot to say to each other. In addition to his obvious undernourishment he had lost the use of his left arm, having been operated upon for boils with a razor blade in Buchenwald. Fortunately Red Cross food and treatment by an Australian physiotherapist named Byrne restored him to the Ian I had known!

In late November, word reached Stalag Luft III of the death of an airman forced through illness to remain at Buchenwald. First Lieutenant Levitt Clinton Beck, Jr, a fighter pilot with the USAAF, had finally succumbed to purulent pleurisy.

Beck, a fresh-faced 24-year-old, had been born and raised for the first twelve years of his life in Houston, Texas. His family later moved to Huntington Park in California and on 23 March 1942 he enlisted in the Army Air Force at March Field, becoming an outstanding pilot on P-47 Thunderbolts. He was shot down near Dreux in France on 29 June 1944, and while hiding out for three weeks at the Café de la Marie in the small village of Anet, he began writing the outline of a book based on his experiences. Madame Paulette Mesnard, the sympathetic owner of the café, tried to persuade Beck to stay there until he could be liberated by Allied troops, but he was determined to get back into the fighting. He asked if she would bury his completed and sealed manuscript under a shed behind the café until it could be retrieved after the war. She agreed, and Beck was then moved south to the home of Rene Farcy, in Des Vieilles Ventes, Sorel-Moussel. A week later he was picked up by the double agent Jacques Desoubrie and his companion Madame Orsini, who drove him to the Picardy Hotel on the Boulevard Saint-Michel in

Paris, where they said arrangements were being made for his return to England. Instead, his trust in the pair was shattered when, the following day, he was sold out and handed over to the Gestapo.

In 1945, as promised, Beck's manuscript was recovered at war's end by Madame Mesnard and later forwarded to Beck's parents by the Military Intelligence Office in Paris. It spoke of his youthful aspirations, his joy at being chosen as a pilot, and his plans once he got back to England. His parents Levitt and Verne added the sad ending to the young American's story, and the manuscript was later published under the title *Fighter Pilot*, an absorbing, emotional book about a young man's experiences and thoughts on war.

An accomplished musician, Beck's cheerfulness and stoical defiance had been an inspiration to others. While in Buchenwald he managed to obtain a tenor sax from a Green (criminal offender) prisoner and formed a small jazz trio, but the days and nights sleeping in wet clothes out in the open gave him pneumonia. He fought the disease, refusing to accept the dubious help offered by the camp infirmary. The rumoured news of a move to a regular POW camp gave Beck the strength to take his place at rollcalls, although he was growing weaker by the day. Finally his body could no longer support him and with the transfer a bare two days away he collapsed and was taken to the hospital where, as feared, he received no assistance or medication. Pleurisy set in, and his resistance weakened. He became delirious as a result of the beatings he had endured and the pain which now racked his body, but nothing was done to alleviate his suffering.

The day before Beck died, he sent a note to Joe Chopp from Antwerp, a trusted Belgian friend in the compound. In it he expressed the fear that he would never recover from his illness, and if the worst should occur he was to let Beck's parents know that his last thoughts were of them.

Levitt Beck slipped into the final oblivion on the evening of 29 November 1944. His body, like that of Philip Hemmens, was wheeled directly over to the crematorium and fed into one of the ovens. In a post-war letter to Beck's parents, fellow KLB prisoner Donat Dauteuil remarked:

> L.C. was one of the finest boys that I have had the pleasure of knowing. When our group of Allied prisoners at Buchenwald were in the lowest of spirits, L.C. was always there with some jazz to cheer us up. He had talked someone into getting him an old saxophone and he really knew how to put it to good use. He was always a source of good cheer and high spirits and quite frankly, we all needed it at that time. His popularity was proven by the fact that 100 per cent of the original group were present at the Memorial Service which was held for him, when we learned of his death, at Stalag Luft III. Some of our best men stayed over there. Believe me when I say that your son was tops. A man to ride the river with.

On 12 January 1945, General Georgi Zhukov's Russian army group had built up its strength around a number of key bridgeheads south of Warsaw on the upper Vistula and headed towards Silesia. To the north his armies crossed the river from both sides of Warsaw, which fell on 17 January. Joseph Stalin had thrown 180 divisions into East Prussia and Poland alone, creating the greatest Russian offensive of the war. Fifteen days later the Russian advance had turned into an unstoppable tidal wave which swept all German resistance before it.

By now East and West Prussia had been cut off from the rest of the Reich and General Zhukov triumphantly crossed the Oder near Lüben. In two weeks he had advanced 350 kilometres and reached German soil just 160 kilometres from Berlin. Shortly after, General Dwight Eisenhower's 85 divisions began to close in on the Rhine, and by the end of February they had reached the river at several positions north of Düsseldorf, meeting rapidly diminishing resistance from the German forces.

According to Ray Perry, the consensus among the POWs at Sagan by 25 January was that they would soon be evacuated.

> Rumours were rife around the camp that we were going to be moved towards the west. For those of us who had been in Fresnes prison, we wondered if we would be moved away from liberation again.
>
> Although it was illegal to do so, many of us converted our kit bags to rucksacks by sewing on a pair of braces for straps. Being mid-winter and very cold, we knew we would want to carry as much clothing and food with us as possible – the Germans were by now so disorganised that we knew it would not be easy to survive any march in this weather. We were getting frequent falls of snow. Some of us thought that if the snow continued and froze we would be able to carry our gear easier if we made a sledge from a wooden box, with wooden runners underneath.

On the morning of 27 January the prisoners' news service brought welcome tidings of Russian army advances less than 30 kilometres to the east, and the men hoped that the guards would move out and leave them to their eventual liberation. The rumbling thunder of Russian artillery attacking Breslau brought hope to the men, while creating fearful anticipation amongst the Germans. The prisoners were placed on a one-hour standby to leave. Despite the freezing cold and sweeping snowstorms, they moved amongst themselves out in the compound, talking over the prospect of freedom or evacuation. The men's kits and sledges were packed and ready for either event, and an air of nervous expectancy warmed the men despite the chill and the whirling snowflakes.

At seven-thirty that evening the American Senior Officer of the camp's South compound was given 30 minutes to have his men at the front gate ready for evacuation. The POWs hurriedly donned their backpacks, tightened kits securely to their rough sledges (some of which had once been barracks doors) and formed up in lines at the gate according to their blocks. The wind whipped at their faces but the men waited pensively, wondering what fate lay beyond the familiar wire gates. Then the gates swung open and they were on the move.

The West and Centre compounds were given their marching orders shortly after and the camp began to empty rapidly. The remainder of the men cooked and ate the biggest meal they could manage but still had to leave precious food behind, unable to fit it into their kit bags or knapsacks. Next to be called out were the prisoners from the North and Belaria compounds, and they tagged onto the long string of apprehensive marchers filing out into the countryside.

At 8:45 pm orders came through for the last of the prisoners, those from East compound, to prepare for immediate evacuation. Time dragged on as delay followed delay, and the fully-clothed men dozed off in their barracks as they waited. Finally, at six o'clock the following morning, the men were ordered to line up outside their blocks. Ninety minutes later, on Sunday, 28 January, the final group of POWs steadily moved out of the East compound, becoming the last Allied servicemen to evacuate Stalag Luft III. Even though few guards remained behind at this time, the Senior British Officer ordered the men not to make any escape attempts. It was essential that they stay together, not only for mutual support and assistance, but because the murder of fifty officers from the camp following the ill-fated Great Escape ten months earlier was still fresh in the minds of the long-term Sagan residents. Ray Perry, one of the last to leave, describes the final minutes of the evacuation:

> It was snowing lightly over the camp. We moved towards the Red Cross store to get a parcel each, which I stacked on my sledge and, as we were the last, we started throwing some parcels over the fence to some Russian prisoners in a nearby compound. There was still quite a bit left in the store when we moved out.

A weak dawn had begun to streak the eastern horizon as they pulled out, at the end of a long centipede line stretching more than 12 kilometres. The road, once covered with 20 centimetres of snow, was now just a muddy quagmire bordered by metre-high snow drifts. The men were wearing every available piece of clothing and carrying as much kit and food as they could. Every hundred metres or so along the column trudged the unhappy guards, machine-guns at the ready.

With the Russian and Allied armies now exerting the squeeze on Germany from two fronts, the prisoners were forced into a meandering westerly direction. They slept in barns, open fields, churches and schools. They bartered for bread with German people along the way, using cigarettes as currency. They endured freezing winds and blizzards. Many died from a combination of exposure and exhaustion, and others, worst of all, as a result of ground strafing by Allied aircraft. The roadsides became littered with kit items and even food as the weary marchers found their loads too heavy to bear. Precious diaries and treasured souvenirs were discarded by desperate men whose sole thought was survival, and trodden into the slush by those who followed. The distances they travelled varied between 20 and 30 kilometres daily.

At Spremberg, a railhead between Muskau and Cottbus, the long column was split in two and the prisoners taken in different directions. Some moved south-west to Moosburg, while others were marched north-westward to keep ahead of the rapid Russian push. The route was eventually diverted eastwards – this time to avoid the oncoming British forces. Hundreds of marchers were herded off to the former naval prison camp of Marlag-Milag near Bremen, while others were entrained for a one-day journey to Stalag IIIA at Luckenwalde.

Suddenly it was all over. The victorious Russian, British and American forces finally overwhelmed the remaining pockets of German resistance, liberating many thousands of exhausted but exultant POWs. For those whose freedom came at the hands of the Russians, however, the last lap home was held up for several weeks. Negotiations between the Americans and the stubborn Russians delayed their final release and the war was over before many of them planted their feet on British soil once again.

Back in England, the men were given a quick delousing, an advance in pay (one pound for officers, ten bob for NCOs), blank telegram forms with which to notify their next of kin they were safe, some clothing and food coupons. For many their first meal back home was an occasion – the culmination of months and even years of starvation. Before being allowed to return to their homes, many headed off into nearby towns and villages to fulfil some long-held dreams, and to eat the fish and chips smothered in salt and vinegar they had talked of so lovingly and longingly as prisoners of war, washed down with a pint from the local pub. This, more than anything else, made them feel they were finally home, and free men once more.

Buchenwald concentration camp remained in operation for only six months following the departure of the bulk of the airmen. The story of its fall only became known to them after their return to England.

In mid-1943 an International Camp Committee had been formed in Buchenwald, the main purpose of which was to coordinate military and sabotage operations by all nationalities represented in the camp. The men of these nations, particularly the powerful German Communists, finally came to an agreement over such activities and began to work in concert. The resultant acts of resistance and covert operations worked far more smoothly. The ICC provided a common front of all inmates prepared to work against the SS, to build evidence against traitors, and to arm themselves for self-preservation in the event of German treachery at the time of liberation.

Countries represented at frequent secret meetings included Germany, Russia, France, Italy, Austria, the Netherlands, Czechoslovakia, Yugoslavia, Poland and Belgium, and the absolute authority of the ICC was respected by all nationalities. Meetings were held in the camp hospital, while trusted inmates provided the necessary security lookouts.

Several radio receivers were hidden within the huts, and broadcasts were carefully monitored and transcribed. By March 1945 three transmitters had also been constructed in the camp, but due to the high risks involved, had not been operated. None of the hidden radio receivers or transmitters were ever discovered by the Germans.

It is astonishing to note that by the spring of 1945 the resistance movement within Buchenwald possessed a vast array of weapons. These had either been smuggled into the camp or manufactured within it. The remarkable inventory listed one light machine-gun, 96 rifles and a similar number of pistols, 16 hand grenades, 107 camp-made grenades, 1100 petrol incendiary bombs and about 50 hand-made knives, slashing weapons and bludgeons.

Secret training in the use of firearms and grenades was carried out in a disinfection room. Other prisoners had discovered the means by which they could shut off power to the electrified fence, and wooden planks were prepared in the event the gates had to be stormed.

On Wednesday evening, 4 April 1945, Kommandant Pister ordered his guard company to commence the immediate and total evacuation of the 8,000 Jews still remaining in the camp. These Jews were told to present themselves for rollcall, but none obeyed. They stayed defiantly in their huts knowing that evacuation would mean almost certain death. Meanwhile, the leaders of the camp resistance decided to bring delaying tactics into effect at the massive rollcall, which caused its postponement by the SS until the following day. By this time, and according to the scheme, the Jews had intermingled with the Aryans, destroyed all personal means of identification, and removed the hated yellow star from their sleeves.

The next day the guards began to hunt out the Jews, but their task was a difficult one, for all 8,000 of them were spread throughout the camp. Sporadic shooting rang out during the day. Eventually 1,500 of the Jews had been rounded up and were forced to evacuate the camp under guard. The fears of these men were later realised; hundreds died or were murdered during the forced march that followed.

That same day, 5 April, Christopher Burney and his three surviving SOE colleagues, Southgate and the Newton brothers, received reliable information that they were about to be seized by the SS. Before they could be taken, the four men were hidden in a cramped cellar less than a metre high beneath Hut 56 in the Little Camp.

With extraordinary confusion occurring outside the Little Camp the following day, and with most of the SS concentrating on the Jewish evacuation, Burney and his companions felt it safe enough to leave their tiny hiding place and mingle with the other prisoners. They returned to their cellar that night and towards ten o'clock word reached them that the Gestapo had presented a list of 47 names to the SS, with orders for their immediate execution. The ICC spy system was now operating so efficiently that the list of names became available to the conspirators eight hours before the SS could act upon it, and the men named in the list were hurriedly moved into the cellar. The four SOE men felt it safe enough for them to return to Block 50. During the night they learned that another 8,000 men, those that the Germans regarded as the worst troublemakers in the camp, were to be evacuated and transported to the concentration camps at Flossenbürg, Dachau and Theresienstadt in Czechoslovakia. This was carried out on 7 April.

The next day, with American fighter planes roaming openly and unchallenged across the skies and with land forces just 12 kilometres away, Kommandant Pister announced that the entire camp was to be evacuated by the following Monday, and 10,000 inmates were to leave immediately. Using a hidden radio transmitter installed in the camp cinema, a Polish member of the ICC named Gwidon Damazyn transmitted a message in Morse code intended for General George Patton, using the 36.8 m wavelength identified to the operators by the Allied airmen. The message, sent in both English and German, was received by the American forces and acknowledged, with an added assurance that the camp's liberation was at hand. This promise of freedom was short-lived for many, as the Germans successfully evacuated half of the remaining inmates – Russians, Czechs, Poles and Frenchmen. Despite this massive drain of prisoners, over 20,000 of them still remained in Buchenwald.

On Wednesday, 11 April, the camp's prisoner defence force readied itself to take over the guard company. By now most of the SS contingent had either left with the other prisoners or in their own transport. An eerie silence reigned throughout the camp; there was no shooting, and very few guards had been left in attendance. Confusion was rampant. The Kommandant was clearly in a quandary, knowing that the Allied tanks were near, but not wishing to relinquish his control over Buchenwald. Prisoner lists and orders had either been destroyed or diverted by the camp insurgents, and false orders were finding their way into Pister's office. Matters were not aided by the constant wailing of air-raid sirens and the desertion of many of his guards into the woods. They had absconded with half of the camp's food supplies, leaving the remaining prisoners with a meagre 250 grams of bread apiece.

The Leipzig-Halle-Magdeberg area had been given a fearful pasting by Allied bombers and fighters and the prisoners knew the end, whatever it might bring, was near. It was rumoured, apparently with some foundation, that a squad of SS troops armed with flamethrowers had arrived at Weimar with orders to burn the camp and incinerate the remaining inmates. They were to be aided in this gruesome task by a large squad of Hitler Youth who were to take control of the camp, thus releasing the guard company for urgent combat assignments. Fortunately the SS death squad moved out of Weimar in the face of the American advance, and the train transporting the Hitler Youth unit was captured.

Pister finally admitted defeat and fled the camp. Two months after the liberation of Buchenwald, he was discovered hiding among other German prisoners of war at an Allied detention camp near Munich, along with several members of his staff. They were arrested and placed on trial by the American Military Tribunal at the former concentration camp of Dachau in April 1947. Pister was found guilty of all charges and sentenced to death by hanging. He was subsequently transferred to Landsberg Prison, west of Munich, where he suffered a massive heart attack on 28 September 1948 and died before his sentence could be carried out.

Gunfire now rang out in the woods outside the camp and the prisoners could see long convoys of German artillery and lines of soldiers evacuating the area. Very few guards now remained at their posts, and the united camp defence forces decided that the time was ripe to take over control of Buchenwald.

At 2:30 pm, brandishing guns, grenades and makeshift weapons, the prisoners' defence force stormed out of their huts in rapidly swelling numbers. Witnessing this uprising, the few remaining guards clambered out of their towers and fled, closely pursued by hordes of vengeance-seeking inmates. Within the hour a huge white flag, hoisted on the mast above the main tower, was flapping triumphantly in the breeze. The victorious prisoners had captured 220 of their former guard company and returned them to the camp, where they were housed under close watch in a barracks building before later being handed over to the American liberators. They also seized nearly a thousand rifles. Guns were fired into the air and men went berserk in a delirium of freedom, cutting the barbed wire fences, breaking into German offices, and generally running amok after years of confinement and the ever-present spectre of death.

As five o'clock neared, the din in the camp suddenly died and the men's voices became hushed as a heavy clanking noise could be heard approaching along the road. Then a huge cheer went up as the first of several American tanks roared into the camp compound and hundreds of enraptured men swarmed their way, striving to touch these imperious machines and greet their liberators.

One of the delirious prisoners greeting the Americans that day was French teenager Robert Widerman, who later recalled that: 'We tore off our shirts and waved them . . . Inmates hugged each other, jumping up and down, dancing, laughing with tears running down their cheeks, and shouting with incredible joy. Those too ill and weak could only smile; they understood what was happening. It was almost impossible to fathom that this day had actually arrived, that our miseries had come to an end, that we had survived.' Widerman would later change his name to Robert Clary, become an actor, and find fame as one of the stars of the television situation comedy *Hogan's Heroes*, ironically set in the fictional World War II POW camp, Stalag 13.

The Americans, for their part, were appalled at the ghastly scene confronting them. They had already driven past countless hundreds of bodies in the Weimar woods, where groups of evacuees had been massacred, but none of them was ready for the massive wave of hysterical living skeletons surging towards them. Shock followed shock for the Americans as they moved further into the camp. Beyond the filthy hordes of emaciated survivors were the corpses, piled haphazardly in mountains of putrefying flesh. It was a sight none of them would ever forget. Gone was the sensation of triumph, to be replaced by despair and a rage beyond comprehension. Having tasted the sweetness of a hard-fought victory over the might of Hitler's Third Reich, they were hardly ready for the grim legacy of his most vicious doctrines.

The battle for Weimar was not fully resolved at this time, and to the dismay of the camp inmates, the tanks were forced to withdraw temporarily. The Germans had launched a last-ditch counter-offensive in the area and Buchenwald was right in the middle of the battle.

For hours, shells roared overhead from both sides, several landing in the camp itself. The terrified prisoners lay on the floor of their huts or out in the compound, hands clasped over their heads in fear. After what seemed an eternity, the Americans secured the area. Once again tanks rolled into the camp.

Buchenwald concentration camp was officially liberated on 12 April 1945, following which teams of military doctors and nurses moved in to tend to the sick and dying. Unbelieving inmates were given food and clothing, cigarettes, sweets, and other small luxuries. A sad after-effect of this kindness was that several prisoners died from a too-rich diet after years of meagre, bland food. Their stomachs just could not cope.

For many of the liberating US troops, the sickening sights they encountered would never be forgotten. Sergeant Leon Bass was a

19-year-old African-American soldier serving with Patton's Third Army as a member of the all-black 761st Tank Battalion, known as the 'Black Panthers'. Bass entered Buchenwald six days after the camp was liberated and later recounted the horrors he witnessed.

> The day that I walked through the concentration camp gates of Buchenwald, and I saw what I saw, I can never say that I'm callous about human life. It made me know that human life is sacred, because when I walked through those gates in the spring of April of 1945, I was totally unprepared for what I saw. And I saw what I can refer to now as the walking dead. I saw human beings there that had been beaten and starved and tortured and so mistreated that they were nothing but human skeletons. They were skin and bone and they had those skeletal faces with the deep-set eyes, and their heads had been clean-shaved. And they were standing there holding on to one another, and they were so thin. They had sores on their bodies that were brought on by malnutrition. And [a] man held out his hands, and his fingers had webbed together with the scabs that come from malnutrition. And I just said to myself, 'My God, what is this? This is some kind of insanity! Who are the people? What did they do that was so wrong?' And that's when I found out that they were Jews and gypsies, some were Jehovah Witnesses, they were trade unionists, they were Communists, they were homosexuals. He went on and told us there were so many different groups placed in that camp by the Nazis. And what did the Nazis use as a yardstick as to who would be chosen to go there? They said those people who were not good enough, those people who were inferior, they could be segregated.

In a 1985 letter to the *New York Times*, a former Buchenwald prisoner wrote: 'The recollections are still vivid – black soldiers of the Third Army, tall and strong, crying like babies, carrying the emaciated bodies of the liberated prisoners.' Another survivor, David Yeager of Poland, said of the 761st: 'I thought they had come down from heaven.'

Accompanied by two mates from his unit, the US Army's Fifth Ranger Battalion, PFC Harry Herder, Jr – also 19 years old – was another of those who ventured through the main gate and entered the appalling hell that was Buchenwald.

> The bodies of human beings were stacked like cord wood. All of them dead. All of them stripped. The inspection I made of the pile was not very close, but the corpses seemed to be all male. The bottom layer of the bodies had a north/south orientation, the next layer went east/west, and they continued alternating. The stack was about five feet high, maybe a little more; I could see over the top. They extended down the hill, only a slight hill, for fifty to seventy-five feet. Human bodies neatly stacked, naked, ready for disposal. The arms and legs were neatly arranged, but an occasional limb dangled oddly. The bodies we could see were all face up. There was an aisle, then another stack, and another aisle, and more stacks. The Lord only knows how many there were.
>
> Just looking at these bodies made one believe they had been starved to death. They appeared to be skin covering bones and nothing more. The eyes on some were closed, on others open. Bill, Tim, and I grew very quiet. I think my only comment was, 'Jesus Christ.'
>
> I have since seen the movie made about Buchenwald. The stack of bodies is vividly displayed in the movie, just as I saw it the first

day, but it is not the same. In no way is it the same. The black-and-white film did not depict the dirty grey-green colour of those bodies, and, what it could not possibly capture was the odour, the smell, the stink. Watching the movie was, in a way, a reliving of the first walk through those stacks of bodies.

The three of us looked, and we walked down the edge of those stacks. I know I didn't count them – it wouldn't have mattered. We looked and said not a word. A group of guys from the company noticed us and said, 'Wait till you see in there.'

They pointed to a long building which was about two stories high, and butted up tightly to the chimney. It had two barn-like doors on either end of the building we were looking at, and the doors were standing open. We turned and walked back to the building where we found others from our company, along with some of the prisoners milling around in the space between the bodies and the building. We moved gently through those people, through the doors and felt the warmth immediately. Not far from the doors, and parallel to the front of the building, there was a brick wall, solid to the top of the building. In the wall were small openings fitted with iron doors. Those doors were a little more than two feet wide and about two-and-a-half feet high; the tops of the doors had curved shapes much like the entrances to churches. Those iron doors were in sets, three high. There must have been more than ten of those sets, extending down that brick wall. Most of the doors were closed, but down near the middle a few stood open. Heavy metal trays had been pulled out of those openings, and on those trays were partially burned bodies. On one tray was a skull partially burned through, with a hole in the top; other trays held partially disintegrated arms and legs. It appeared that those trays could hold three bodies at a time. And the door, my God, the door.

I had enough. I couldn't take it anymore. I left the building with Bill and Tim close behind me. As we passed through the door someone from the company said, 'The crematorium.' Until then I had no idea what a crematorium was.

For Americans involved in the military operation, that momentous 12 April would come to mean more than the occasion on which they freed the inhabitants of a notorious death camp. Their triumph was quickly tempered by the devastating news from home that their beloved president, Franklin Roosevelt, had died.

Omar White was a war correspondent with General George Patton's Third US Army as it moved through southern Germany. Some time in April 1945 he filed a report on what he saw, experienced and was told during a post-liberation inspection of Buchenwald. He titled his report 'Deepest Pit of Hell That Hitler Dug: Dreadful Scenes in Notorious Buchenwald Prison Camp'.

I saw Buchenwald and moved among its living dead. I cannot now, nor ever will be able to write objectively of what I have seen. One cannot observe war for three-and-a-half years as a newspaperman and remain either a sentimentalist or be supersensitive to spectacles of human suffering. Yet what I saw at Buchenwald last week moved me to physical illness. It moved me to a conviction that never again can civilisation trust the German people, as they are, to determine their own social and political destiny.

Before the civilised world dare grant again this people the power of self-determination, the civilised world must be assured – more, convinced by unchallengeable proofs – that the Germans have been severed completely from their inheritance of a past which is not only their shame but the shame of all humanity. One day last week, in the morning, I left the city of Weimar, loved home of Goethe, Schiller and Liszt, and drove three miles through forests, fields, beautiful with spring. I came to a fence of barbed wire and an entrance lodge of brown wood over which on a pole limply hung a great black flag.

This, they told me, was Buchenwald – the deepest pit of hell that Hitler dug. I said to myself, 'One more concentration camp, tighten up your nerves, get ready to look at torture hooks and corpses.' They told me there once were 50,000 people here. Now there are only 20,000.

I went through the iron gates looking at people who walked about on concrete and gravel courtyards. Most of them showed signs of slow starvation. They were clad in ragged, ugly prison suits. They were unshaven. The lines on their faces were etched there by long suffering and the death of hope. They wore little coloured badges to indicate the nature of their 'offence' and their nationality.

For six weeks now I have been seeing people like these on roads all over Germany, answering their salutes until my arms tired, and their smiles until my answering smile became meaningless. These were the same sort of slaves – not yet quite free, and a little hungrier – a little uglier and more brutalised.

Doctor Hugo Mortelmans, lecturer in Pathology at Antwerp Medical School – a small, round-faced man with bright eyes – came forward and offered himself as guide and interpreter. He was taken by the Gestapo because of his resistance activities, and given employment in the SS Department of Histology. He led the way to a concrete court, where the day's dead were being loaded onto an iron-sided truck. There were about 100 blue-white, stiff bodies, with shaven skulls and purple bruises from beatings still on the skins. They were most horribly emaciated from starvation and disease. Atop them was a limp, fat corpse of an SS guard, who had hanged himself in his cell.

We went to the crematorium, where six furnaces still contained the blackened frames of what once were men. Above the door was a verse beginning: 'Worms shall not devour me, but flames can consume this body. I always loved the heat, and light . . .'

From there we descended to the death room in the basement, where holes which had contained 20 to 30 hooks upon which men were garrotted had been hastily plastered up and whitewashed in a vain effort to conceal the room's purpose. An attendant showed me the club with which those who did not die quickly enough had their brains beaten out. Dr Mortelmans said he believed that between 30 and 40 Allied airmen had been executed, and it was estimated there had been 48,000 executions in the last five years.

From this place we were taken to [the] SS Museum of Pathology, where magnificently-prepared sections of diseased organs of the human body were displayed. Here, Doctor Mark Klein, Professor of Histology at the University of Strasbourg, interned at Buchenwald since May 5 last year, said he had been forced to work in the preparation of sections. So many cases of all kinds of disease in all their stages were available as material that the work done here has scientific value. Much of the work also done here had no scientific value. It was indulged in solely to satisfy the sadistic mania of those in control.

Dr Klein produced sections of human skin bearing elaborate tattoo marks which, he said, were prepared and preserved by a

German doctor who had written and published a paper on the subject. Dr Klein produced two human heads on wooden mounts, and explained that the technician who prepared them had carefully followed the process of the Jivaro Indians in South America. They were the heads of Poles or Russians. They were so perfectly preserved that they still bore the expression with which the men died.

I was then taken to 'Block 50' where a slave scientist, Professor Maurice Suard of Angers Medical School, explained the work there. The chief work had been the development of anti-typhus serum, and after experiments with animals, Nazi physicians had deliberately inoculated healthy prisoners with typhus virus to observe the course of the disease and the efficacy of various sera. Dr Suard stated that on his own knowledge batches of 49 and 50 prisoners were executed by toxin injections. He demonstrated the excellent scientific equipment with which the block was furnished, and stated that the work undertaken there was of objective scientific value, but that the experiments had been undertaken with a complete disregard for human life and suffering. Countless prisoners had been murdered by Nazi scientists in the course of experiments. Dr Suard stated that slave scientists had not been required to make these experiments. They were employed solely to prepare sera and do work in which there was danger of infection – of which the Germans were almost ludicrously afraid – and keep records, which were sent to Berlin.

Doctor Joseph Brau, a physician who is now acting as chief physician of all prisoners remaining in the camp, conducted me to the quarters of the Poles and the Russians. I first inspected the barracks of 'normal' prisoners. They were in an advanced stage of malnutrition, sleeping and lying in filthy three-tier bunks, 10 men to a compartment. The hut was swarming with vermin and the occupants were all suffering from dysentery.

Many men were obviously insane. As the party walked by a hut and British uniforms were recognised, a low growling noise broke out. I did not recognise this as a kind of applause until someone started clapping hands. Men crawled weakly from bunks and stood at attention and saluted. Among them were children of 11 and 12 years. Dr Brau said the children mostly were sent to gas chambers, but one man had concealed his son in this jungle of indescribable suffering for three years. We saw the child. He was five years old and tolerably nourished. The father was washing his hands, which were delicately formed.

Dr Brau then conducted me to the 'sick house'. I cannot picture for you what I saw here. I can only say that the dead walked or stood stark naked outside in the sun, shivering in uncontrollable rigors, or lay in the filth of their diseases. I can only say that their voices sounded like wind in a dark deep place, that the image of their eyes and their teeth as they smiled will, until the day of my death, remain my most terrible recollection.

I said to Dr Brau: 'The only humane thing the Germans did here was when they strangled them.' Dr Brau replied, 'That is true.' After this inspection I did not go to the brothel kept by the guards for prisoners who had money and to which women were assigned as a final punishment. I went back to town, where Goethe, Schiller and Liszt lived and worked.

Following their liberation, the former inmates broke into the German storehouses and helped themselves to provisions long denied. The Americans, appalled at the magnitude of the German atrocities, initially turned a blind eye to several acts of revenge carried out by uncontrollable prisoners who had lost friends and loved ones to the followers of the Nazi doctrines. The day after the second liberation they reluctantly took steps to prevent the Germans from being attacked by the vengeance-seeking prisoners. Nevertheless, the Russian prisoners wanted further revenge, so they commandeered as many vehicles as possible and sped off in the direction of Weimar, seeking out victims.

Hard lessons had to be learned, and the following report appeared in a London newspaper on April 17: 'Escorted by American military police, 1,000 citizens of Weimar, in batches of 100, were conducted on a tour of the Buchenwald concentration camp today to let them see the truth about their countrymen's brutality,' says a correspondent of *The Times* at Weimar. 'They were shown the crematorium, with the blackened frames of bodies still in ovens, and two piles of emaciated dead in the yard outside. They were taken through huts, where living skeletons were too weak or too ill to rise. They lay packed in three-tier bunks. The Germans were also shown the riding stables where 1,000 were shot before even reaching the inner camp, and the research block, where doctors tried new serums on human beings with fatal consequences for 90 percent of them.

'It was an experience which they will never forget. Most of the women and some of the men were in tears as they were conducted from block to block. Many were crying bitterly. Some of the women fainted, and could be taken no farther.

'Substantial help has been sent to the 21,000 inmates since the Americans overran the camp, but men were still dying at the rate of 40 a day because they were beyond help. Scores of first-aid men and doctors have arrived, and two complete evacuation hospitals, camp hospitals and 18 barrack buildings have been taken over for the 5,000 sick, more than half of whom are suffering seriously from dysentery, tuberculosis, typhus or starvation.'

At the behest of General Dwight Eisenhower, a British Parliamentary delegation left London bound for Weimar on the afternoon of Friday, 20 April, in order 'that they may themselves have ocular and first-hand proof of these atrocities'. They arrived at Buchenwald the following day, toured such areas as the mortuary and crematorium, saw the rotting heaps of emaciated corpses awaiting a more dignified funeral, and talked with many of the inmates. Extracts from their subsequent report reflect the difficulty they had in coming to terms with the terrible inhumanities perpetrated at the camp.

> A detailed report presented to us by representatives of an anti-Fascist committee stated that, up to 1st April, the total number of those who had died or been killed at Buchenwald, or immediately on removal therefrom to subsidiary 'extermination camps' was 51,572 – at least 17,000 of them since 1st January, 1945. The camp has now been thrown open, and a certain number of its inmates must have left independently. Detailed camp records, including nominal rolls, were left behind by the Nazis; but, at the time of our visit, it had not been possible to start drawing up rolls of those still in the camp, the American medical and sanitary authorities being naturally preoccupied with the cleaning of the camp (a task performed partly by German civilians from the neighbourhood, parties of whom are also brought daily to see what had been done in their name and in their midst), and with problems of feeding and medical attention.
>
> Although the work of cleaning the camp had gone on busily for over a week before our visit, and conditions must therefore have been

improved considerably, our immediate and continuing impression was of intense general squalor; the odour of dissolution and disease still pervaded the entire place. One of the first of a number of huts that we entered was one of the best; it was divided into small rooms with cement floor and windows, four of which had been used, the American authorities informed us, as a brothel to which the higher-grade prisoners – those employed in various supervisory jobs, with extra rations and other privileges – were allowed to resort for 20 minutes at a time. When the Americans arrived, fifteen women were found in this brothel. This hut was one of those now used as transit hospitals for some of the worst cases of malnutrition. Many were unable to speak; they lay in a semi-coma, or following us with their eyes. Others spoke freely, displaying sores and severe scars and bruises which could have been caused by kicks or blows. They lay on the floor and under quilts. All of them were in a state of extreme emaciation. We were told by the US authorities that, since their arrival, the number of deaths had been reduced from about a hundred a day to 35 on the day before our visit. One half-naked skeleton, tottering painfully along the passage as though on stilts, drew himself up when he saw our party, smiled and saluted.

In preparing this report, we have endeavoured to write with restraint and objectivity, and to avoid obtruding personal reactions or emotional comments. We would conclude, however, by stating that it is our considered and unanimous position, on the evidence available to us, that a policy of steady starvation and inhuman brutality was carried out at Buchenwald for a long period of time; and that such camps as this mark the lowest point of degradation to which humanity has yet descended. The memory of what we saw and heard at Buchenwald will haunt us ineffaceably for many years.

On 11 April 1947, two years to the day after Patton's victorious Third Army had stormed into Buchenwald, 31 defendants from the former concentration camp were brought before an American war crimes trial convened at Dachau. Prosecutors at the trial charged the male and female defendants with responsibility for the deaths of 53,000 inmates and the torturing of thousands of others. All 31 were eventually convicted of violating the laws and usage of war by their systematic cruelties and mass murders. A total of 22 were sentenced to hang, five including Ilse Koch were sentenced to life imprisonment, one to 20 years, two to 15 years and one to 10 years.

Among those receiving the death penalty were the last Kommandant of Buchenwald, Hermann Pister, and Max Schobert, the former camp leader. Included in those given life sentences was Prince Josias zu Waldeck-Pyrmont, a confidant of Hitler and the first German of royal blood to be tried for war crimes. Edwin Katzen-Ellenbogen, 64, a former resident of the United States and one of the camp physicians, was another given a life sentence. He had started out as a Buchenwald prisoner, but later opted to serve his Nazi captors.

On 3 May 1944, a 14-year-old German Jewish girl named Anne Frank, who was to die at Belsen-Bergen concentration camp the following year, penned a few words on the appalling and disastrous effects of totalitarianism in her secret but subsequently world-famous diary while hiding from the Nazis with her family in Amsterdam. Her simple, innocent words reflect on the cruelty of those times.

> I don't believe that the big men, the politicians and the capitalists alone are guilty of the war. Oh no, the little man is just as keen, otherwise the people of the world would have risen in revolt

> long ago! There is an urge and rage in people to destroy, to kill, to murder, and until all mankind, without exception, undergoes a great change, wars will be waged, everything that has been built up, cultivated and grown, will be destroyed and disfigured, after which mankind will have to begin all over again.

The Frank family was sent to Auschwitz in September 1944. The following month Anne and her sister Margot were transported to Belsen-Bergen, where both died of typhus in February or March of 1945. Their mother Edith never left Auschwitz, but their father Otto managed to survive until the camp was liberated. Post-war, Anne's handwritten diary was discovered in their former hiding place, and Otto had it published in 1947. In it, she had written, 'I still believe, in spite of everything, that people are really good at heart.'

The eventual return to the comfort of their homes and families did not bring about an end to the conflict for many of the KLB airmen. Within the home environment, the mental scars of Buchenwald which went unnoticed and certainly unheeded as prisoners, came as a shock to the men's wives and close friends. The ghosts of the past would reach out to haunt them for the rest of their lives, and the fears they brought home were to manifest themselves in many different ways and to varying degrees.

Painful memories of the past still lurked within many of the KLB airmen, occasionally rising to the surface when a familiar sight, sound or experience opened an unwanted door to the past. The sound of someone speaking German, for instance, or a child screaming, could create nervous distress in them, or they might become fretful when certain evocative images appeared on their television screen. It was an inescapable facet of their remaining years.

The majority of the Australian and New Zealand airmen confessed to their own post-war traumas, but for Mervyn Fairclough there was little doubt that the tentacles of black horror reached out for him after the war, carrying him back inexorably to the hell camp. Despair would finally claim him as a victim and cause his premature death at the relatively youthful age of forty.

Returning to Australia outwardly fit and well, Mervyn Fairclough resumed life on the farm at Dumbleyung with his wife Elaine and baby son Brian. The young West Australian didn't talk much about his war experiences, and even years after his death his widow said she knew only the barest of details concerning his capture and imprisonment. He preferred to keep his memories to himself – a silence Elaine respected, but tried hard to understand. She knew he had lived through quite severe traumas in France and Germany, but to all intents and purposes they had resumed their married life together, and there was great joy when baby Rhonda was born in 1946.

Curiously, it was an act of official courtesy two years after his return that caused the first visible disturbance in the gentle, doting father. That day a card arrived from the local post office, advising him of a parcel to be collected. He claimed the small package, which contained a familiar gold ring and a letter. The ring, inscribed with his and Elaine's names, was the one which had been torn so violently from his finger by a guard at Fresnes prison. An accompanying note from the American Embassy informed him that the ring had been found amongst the thousands of effects abandoned by the Germans when they were swept from Paris, and Fairclough's name and address had finally been located in the records.

He stuck the ring in his pocket and never mentioned it at home, although Elaine noticed he had become more pensive, and she would often see him looking at the ring, obviously brooding over the past.

The next jolt came when they decided to take in a film. The feature that night happened to be *Odette*, a black-and-white film based on the wartime experiences of Odette Samson, the SOE agent parachuted into France who was later captured and brutally tortured by the Gestapo at their headquarters and at Fresnes prison. Mervyn watched the film in complete silence until the setting changed to the corridors of Fresnes. A sudden panic overwhelmed him as he sat there, seeing once again the familiar passageways and cells. Then, almost hysterical, he leapt to his feet and cried, 'No, no! I've been there! I've been there!' He left the theatre a badly shaken man.

The nightmares came more frequently to him after this, mostly dreams of being blown out of his aircraft, the savage beatings, and the inhumanities he had witnessed. In his late thirties the former airman, whose children remember him as a caring and interested parent, took to rambling on about the strangest subjects. He destroyed and discarded almost everything pertaining to his wartime service.

One Saturday in late 1963 he went to see his son Brian play football for Claremont League in Perth. Although he was not feeling well, he would not miss the pride he always felt in watching his son take the field. At home, Elaine was doing some housework as she listened to a live broadcast of the match. Suddenly the radio announcer reported that a spectator had collapsed in the Members' Stand and was being taken away by ambulance. Elaine's blood ran cold. Instinctively she knew it was Mervyn, and this was confirmed just two hours later when a staff member from the Royal Perth Hospital rang to say that her husband was in Casualty with a severe heart condition. Brian drove to Perth, only to find his father standing stubbornly on the footpath, demanding to be taken home. Fortunately he allowed himself to be taken back inside for treatment, but when he eventually came home he had lost any inclination to work on the farm again. Physically he was in reasonable shape, but his nerves were shattered by the chronic nightmares. After this he was in and out of the local hospital at Katanning, and Hollywood Repatriation in Perth.

Near the end, when he was home he would often be found wandering around outside the house at night, and Elaine would quietly watch over him until he returned to bed. Sometimes he would grab her shoulder and shake her, asking who she was, and then his mind would wander and he would babble on about having to get away from the Russians. Mervyn knew there was something terribly wrong with his mind, and in his less-frequent lucid times he would plead with Elaine, 'Don't let the children see me like this!'

Finally, on Thursday 23 July 1964, a specialist from the Repatriation Hospital called Elaine in to see him and explained that it would be better for everyone if her husband was given specialist care in the hospital. He added that intense psychological help was needed. Returning home, Elaine put all their affairs in order prior to Mervyn's admittance. While waiting for the specialist to call back with an admission date, she tended her husband at the local Katanning Hospital. Then a week later, and without warning, Mervyn Fairclough died. His end was quick and peaceful.

He had been an active young man, one who loved his wife and children, and he had experienced the wonderment of holding his first grandchild. But there was little doubt that his experiences in

Fresnes and Buchenwald had unhinged a corner of his mind, almost indiscernibly to begin with, but in the end consuming him until he could no longer cope with living or life.

Following her husband's death, Elaine Fairclough became deeply involved in charity work. In 1985 she was awarded the Order of Australia, of which she was justly proud, and in 1995 received the Red Cross Services Award. She passed away on 2 October 2016.

And what of the other KLB airmen today? While many are loath to reflect on those days, and often with good reason, others such as Ian Robb, from Chalfont St Giles, volunteered the following candid comments:

> Those of us who survived the experiences of living with the Resistance of all nationalities, Fresnes prison and Buchenwald, and who incurred no physical or mental disability were in fact privileged. That may seem an odd statement, but we saw men and women prepared to risk prison and even death to help those who were complete strangers with the sole purpose of ridding their country of the invader, and displaying cool courage of the highest order.
>
> On the other hand, we witnessed the real horror and brutality of Nazi tyranny. Despite all the reports in newspapers and books, on film, television and radio, I believe the scale of the Holocaust was such as to make it impossible for those who did not experience it to comprehend the full horror. We who did have no doubts that, despite all the suffering and loss of life, there was no alternative but to fight the war to the bitter end, and to make sure we are never again left defenceless and at the mercy of other aggressors.

Ed Carter-Edwards from Hamilton, Ontario, was shot down on 7 June 1944 while acting as a wireless operator/air gunner with No. 427 Squadron, RCAF. He too described the lingering after-shocks of his weeks in the concentration camp:

> After I got home, I still suffered the effects of Buchenwald and had to receive help at a convalescent hospital in Ancaster. I was there about three months and finally got straightened out and went back to work.
>
> Luckily the years have cast some shadows over my mind, blacking out much of the Buchenwald experience. But the mental pictures remain, and are sometimes triggered easily by a war movie or if I hear a German accent, or even a siren or planes flying overhead. These things are not as bad as they used to be, but they are still there. I'm very happy to have survived but I still feel that it should never have happened. Not only that I shouldn't have suffered all those inhumanities and indignities, but also that for a nation, even a nation like Germany, it was totally wrong to develop the camps. What purpose did they serve other than to cause suffering and indignity to human beings? I'm sure men and women deserve more than that, no matter what nationality they are and under what circumstances. These circumstances of degradation are totally unnecessary in the twentieth century. It's the one thing that will live with me and die with me.
>
> I have great difficulty now warming to any Germans, no matter how friendly they are or how far removed from the scene. They are still basically of that heritage; it's happened once, it's happened twice, and it could happen again – and this is one of the things I fear.

Bill Gibson of Halifax, Nova Scotia, a Canadian rear gunner on a Lancaster shot down on 4 July 1944, also spoke openly of the anguish he still felt:

> I'm terrified of dying . . . we saw death in some horrible ways and these things frighten me. In the first year I was home I could not sleep without a light on and every morning I'm scared when I wake up. I know another chap who tells me it's in the afternoon he's scared. I think we all of us have a psychiatric reaction to those years, I have found, and other people have found, that it's difficult to have people believe you; that you were there and those things happened.

Under an agreement signed with West Germany in June 1964, one-million pounds became available to British victims of Nazi persecution. The British KLB airmen received a basic compensation payment of £183.50 for the time they spent in Buchenwald. Some of the former airmen gave media interviews at the time and many, including Bob Harper of Warrington, Lancashire, were critical of the payment:

> I was an RAF warrant officer flying as an observer and I was shot down over France in November 1943. I was with the Resistance for six weeks and then I was picked up by the Gestapo. I was in three different French prisons for about ten months. Later I was sent to Buchenwald and spent three months there before going to a prisoner camp. I don't get any compensation for the months I was imprisoned by the Gestapo. The £184 is for the time in Buchenwald. I think it's shocking. It's as if the Foreign Office has allowed the Germans to put us off with a token payment.

Londoner George Watmough's weight fell from 80 to 37 kilograms in Buchenwald:

> Fortunately I was sent to a prisoner of war camp after three months in Buchenwald. I'm not bitter about the scale of the compensation. After all these years I didn't really expect to get anything, but I can see why some of the former prisoners are disappointed. I'm lucky – my health wasn't affected so badly, but when you think of it, £2 a day isn't much for being in Buchenwald.

John Clarke from Leicestershire was able to receive a little more money from the compensation fund:

> I was in Buchenwald for three months and doctors say my health is permanently affected. It seems I had TB when I was in the camp. Even now if I get a cold I just collapse. I've had more from the fund than many of the others. I've had £1,100, but I think this may be because I've never had any disability allowance. Compared with some of the other lads in Buchenwald, I've been lucky!

From his cosy home in Victoria, British Columbia, Art Kinnis told the author of the problems faced by many of his KLB friends over the half-century since the war ended:

> The fact that no one knew where we were was always in our thoughts. We existed, and those who could block out their surroundings fared better than those who couldn't. To this day much that happened has become hidden in our minds, and now can only be recalled with difficulty. After we were released, and for many months, nightmares

and sleepless nights were our constant lot. Some required more help than others, but we're all aware of the enormous help our wives gave us. Every man amongst us will be grateful to his wife till the day he dies for the moral and spiritual help they gave us when we returned home confused, angry, and filled with the terrors of that place. We truly bless them one and all.

Nervous breakdowns were not uncommon. It has only been over recent years that we have been able to resurrect some of the happenings to our sympathetic friends and those who were there. It was something of the past that we were afraid to disturb because of the consequences that might result.

Chest conditions, sinus and other problems that started then are still with us, and many still show the scars of the bed bugs. The mental scars do not show, but they're like that part of an iceberg which lays below the surface. Some have required medication and psychiatric help for extended periods.

Former KLB Senior Officer Phil Lamason always remained proud of the men under his command at Buchenwald:

I haven't talked very much about my experiences during the war. No, I've hardly mentioned it since. But although we witnessed some particularly horrible things, New Zealand is a long way from Germany, and Malcolm Cullen is the only chap here from those days, and he lives some distance away from me. Apart from my family, people don't know of my involvement in these things, although I suppose I gained a little notoriety in Bruce Marshall's book, *The White Rabbit*. Sure there are the nightmares, but not many at all now, and in any case I'm a light sleeper. If little else, I suppose my experiences made me far more tolerant in many ways and not quite as dogmatic, but then we all naturally mellow over the years.

I hold no particular grudges from those days, but I still find it quite unbelievable that a civilised race like the Germans could behave in such a manner. I found them to be a very disciplined people who, if they're told to do something, will do it. He mightn't like it, but he'll do it. What they did was inexcusable, whatever their philosophies, and far too horrible to ever describe. I'm sorry, but it was something you had to see – you had to have been there to have any sort of comprehension of the gross atrocities they went on with, day after day.

Following my eventual liberation and return to England, I was asked to consider commanding one of the Okinawa squadrons for the final attack on Japan, but the New Zealand Air Force said no, I was to return home. In fact I arrived back in New Zealand the day after they dropped the bomb on Hiroshima, so the war was all but over, and I returned to the land.

Through this book, I'd like to pay tribute to the entire group of fellow airmen in Buchenwald. They were from different countries, living together in one of the most horrific places on God's earth, but to a man they gave me their unquestioning loyalty, which meant a lot to me at the time. If there is any singularly good recollection of those days then that is it. They were, and are, a tremendous group of men, and I feel deeply honoured to have been their Senior Officer during that period.

8

MAN OF A GHOST

STANLEY BOOKER, MBE, LEGION D'HONNEUR, from Bracknell in Berkshire was one of the English contingent in Buchenwald, and he undertook a pilgrimage with his wife to the site of the notorious camp in September 1984. They returned in April 1985 to commemorate the fortieth anniversary of the liberation of Buchenwald.

Stan Booker was the sole British representative, and his homage to his fellow airmen and the SOE group is gratefully recorded as a fitting finale and tribute to those who endured and died within the barbed wire of Buchenwald. His words were written prior to the fall of the Berlin Wall and the unification of Germany, when movement around the German Democratic Republic, or East Germany, was certainly restricted, but could be achieved with a little patience.

> At the Hotel Elephant in Weimar we were made genuinely welcome, especially when they learned that I had been a former guest up on the hill all those years before. Weimar itself has a cultural link with the past, and the classics (Goethe and others dominate the place),

but they have not tried to hide the grimmer association with its more evil past. There are conspicuous signposts indicating the route to the Nationale Mahn und Gedenkstätte [National Reminder and Memorial], Buchenwald, and a regular bus for visitors runs from the main railway station. However, on the day we made the visit there were a series of roadblocks which made the route rather vague and confusing. Being a very large Soviet garrison town, with numerous bustling army barracks very much in prominence, I had no wish to loiter too much, so I used my navigator's natural instinct and headed for the main station. I reasoned that during the war we had set off from there to mount the steep wooded hill the five or six miles to the camp, so the obvious thing would be to find the route of the rail spur, which we eventually did. Although the track had been lifted, there was no problem in taking the road through the culvert, and after climbing up through the lovely beech woods we came out onto the site of the former Gustloff Werke, and the shabby old railhead, and the platforms that had struck so much terror into so many thousands of hapless souls in the past.

Following the route of the old 'Road of Blood', the Caracho Way, we came upon the five large multi-storeyed brick barrack blocks that were the former SS Headquarters on the southern perimeter track, and which are now used as administration offices and a tourist hotel/restaurant for the many thousands of visitors they have from all over the world. Out of politeness, not having written to say we were coming, we reported to the Reception Centre, asking for the Museum Director, Dr Trostorff, who was unfortunately away in Moscow on a conference. We were greeted, almost overwhelmed, by Herr Rothmann, the Deputy Director, who was very moved to meet us, and settle us in to what he appreciated could be quite a traumatic occasion. He immediately cancelled all his engagements for the day, giving us his complete personal attention. There were a million things to talk about; fortunately I speak fair German.

Being the first former British prisoner, and having read a personal account that I had submitted to the Museum, we almost seemed like old friends – not at all the reception I had somehow expected, for the hurt, even after all these years, has never healed, and I think somehow, perhaps because we were behind the Curtain, I didn't appreciate what a common bond of understanding there was.

We seemed to talk about everything, and time was going too fast – it all seemed unreal; there we were in the former dreaded SS Kommandant's office – SS Sturmbannführer Koch and his equally infamous successor, Pister, who was in charge during our sojourn there. We were taken to the briefing room where there was a vast scaled model of the former camp, on which every feature suddenly became real, and moved on down through the remarkably well preserved and original SS buildings until we came up to the gateway – the entrance to the former camp. The camp remained, preserved, just as it was when functioning at the close of the Second World War. The clock over the gateway was stopped at 3:15 pm – the time the white flag went up and the camp freed itself from the yoke of the SS tyrants, back on the 11th of April, 1945.

The electrified perimeter wire, the raised guard towers surmounting the fence, the evil crematorium (no longer belching out its foul smoke), were all completely intact and preserved for visitors to examine, even to the complete gas ovens, the furnaces, the gallows and the lethal syringes. The conspicuous main entrance, with adjoining dark and fearful bunker cells were open for inspection. All that was missing were the row upon row of the long low huts that were packed in the space between the perimeter wires – they were burned for sanitary reasons after the war, but their foundations are there, calling out to be seen in their geometrically precise rows, grim reminders of their former function.

Beyond the crematorium was the huge three-storeyed Effektenkammer [storeroom], now the new museum, alongside of which was the low reception building where the induction process took place – the showers and the barbers with their electric clippers and the mountains of hair. On the horizon, beyond the wire, was a wired gate – the entrance to our own private hell – the former Little Camp, now mercifully returned to nature. Beyond the former 'Kanteen' building, now used as a cultural centre, was the dreaded quarry. Taking the narrow path down into its depths was like treading on hallowed ground – oh, the ghosts that must have been close to me, now so silent and still, but sending that shiver down one's spine at the terrible events only history can preserve.

Passing through the gates into the former camp was perhaps one of the most traumatic moments I have ever experienced. There was such a vast contrast between the lovely natural woodlands, the proud beeches that surround the outer perimeter fence. Within, everything was so utterly stark and barren. It was so still, so quiet, so completely lifeless; no birds sang, not a blade of grass – it was as if nature had turned its back on the evil establishment as its own form of protest. I uttered a silent prayer that I had been spared the cruel fate that had befallen so many thousands of those nameless inmates who never lived to see their loved ones, their homes and freedom.

As you would expect from a German national memorial, this once infamous establishment is very well organised and most efficiently run. Quite unbelievably everything is intact – there has been no vandalism – the place is not guarded in any way, and visitors can come and go just as they please without any control of entry or restriction. There are no police or uniforms of any kind, except the occasional visiting Soviet soldier wandering around the various internal features, all of which, not unnaturally, carry display signs in both Russian and German. At various main features there are guides who remain discreetly in the background, but who carry linguaphones, giving helpful commentaries and assistance when required.

The day we were there, there were very few visitors, but those who were walked almost with reverence, and spoke in low voices as if in church. Later, parties of school children arrived, aged between twelve and fourteen, accompanied by their elderly school teachers. Apparently, in the GDR, every school child at a certain age has to attend one or other of the former concentration camps, now established as national memorials (Buchenwald, Sachsenhausen and Ravensbrück) for a full day of indoctrination. They are given a series of lectures, shown films and given conducted tours of the entire encampments and the respective museums. Nothing is held back; they receive the full treatment of the evil of the Nazi dynasty and how the camps were run.

Within the main camp area, on the site of the former Block 17 (where the few Allied SOE inmates were housed), there is a simple stone slab, commemorating the murder of the Allied parachutists in 1944. Other simple memorial tablets are located elsewhere, at various sites where other nationals had been incarcerated.

Approximately one mile from the original camp site, on the edge of the escarpment overlooking Weimar, the woodlands have been cleared, and a most impressive and imposing bell tower memorial has been set up to commemorate the fate of the thousands of former inmates of the camp during its eight years of infamy. Three immense circular massed grave sites, each contained within high walls, display very explicit wall murals depicting daily scenes within the camp routine, and linked by an impressive 'Road of Nations', along which have been set up eighteen huge solid stone pylons, with oil flames burning on the tops. Each pylon is dedicated to one of the many nations who had their nationals incarcerated within the camp, and whose country was occupied by the Germans – thus there is not one for the United Kingdom.

Once a year, on the anniversary date of the liberation of the camp, the whole area comes alive with thousands of visitors from all countries, making their pilgrimage to this national centre, carrying their national flags and wreaths to lay on their pylons.

The day went very quickly, and before departing we were given various original booklets and mementoes to associate our visit with the past. We were also given a warm invitation to return the following springtime to attend the fortieth anniversary of the self-liberation of the camp, which was to be a special effort to gather as many original surviving inmates as possible, as it was appreciated that age was critical and many wouldn't be alive for the fiftieth anniversary.

After our return to England, the Royal Air Force Museum at Hendon requested that I prepare a special commemorative cover associated with the involvement of the small party of RAF who were imprisoned in the camp during 1944, to be taken back and cancelled on the 11th April 1985 at the fortieth anniversary celebrations. Accordingly, on the 9th April 1985, my wife and I set off laden with six boxes of covers, all stamped ready for overfranking, a very large boxed poppy wreath, and of course our own luggage. We crossed over the Channel to Paris, taking the overnight express to Frankfurt where we changed trains, joining an East German train for the remainder of the journey. Once again we received a warm welcome at the hotel, though this time we had to stay in Erfurt, about ten miles the other side of the camp, as Weimar was packed full with overseas visitors long since booked in for the occasion.

At Weimar the postal authorities went to considerable care to individually hand cancel each stamped cover, whilst another endorsement was put on with the Buchenwald camp identification. At Buchenwald, the long-awaited three-day celebrations were somewhat harrowing – we were the sole British visitors in the midst of ten-thousand others, many of them frail old former inmates, proudly displaying their ragged coloured triangles and their tattered camp registration numbers on their chests. We laid our poppy wreath with quiet dignity on the SOE memorial tablet, providing a great source of interest to the very many visitors who made their way down the roadway from the bunker block, past the crematorium to the new museum in the former Effektenkammer. It was very moving, my wife and I being embraced by complete strangers, making their sincere messages known in a mixture of broken German, Russian, French and English – all so genuine in their sincere greetings and concern for the events of the past. So many people wished to convey their admiration at the conduct of the brave 'parachutists' who had gone to their fate with such dignity.

Everywhere, we met genuine regret for events that had brought us, as Englishmen, into the camp, and for the events we witnessed with shame to their nation. We met no hostility, and no attempt was made at any time to embarrass us with anti-Western propaganda.

The local police were very helpful; with so many vehicles bringing visitors to the camp from hundreds of miles around, the area within four miles of the camp was completely sealed off. We had a hired East German car, yet when we made our identities known, we were given special escorted clearance through each road check, and allocated a special parking lot, right outside the headquarters building itself. Had we been the British Ambassador, we couldn't have received more respectful treatment.

I feel these events of the past must be recorded – I feel guilty that I haven't done more in some ways to do my share. However, I feel that I have done my duty in other ways. The modest little SOE memorial tablet is now recognised by the government departments concerned, and is being improved. Our British Military Mission makes its annual visit on St George's Day, with the full cooperation of the local Soviet military authorities, and the Union Jack now flies, after all these years, over the camp and in the Avenue of the Nations. The RAF commemorative cover was a success – the world now knows about the little band of young, perhaps a little apprehensive, but brave airmen.

Epilogue

THE FINAL VICTORY

In 1963 Britain announced that it had reached agreement over the claims of its servicemen who were, according to International Law, held illegally in Nazi concentration camps, and claimed compensation on their behalf from the West German government. As a result, reparation was made to British service personnel in 1965, but when Australian servicemen lodged their claims they met with a firm rebuttal. The West German government would not investigate their claims for compensation, they declared, until a Peace Treaty to end the war – a war which finished in 1945 – had been signed between East and West Germany. Such a forlorn hope ended with the unification in 1990, the year after the hated Berlin Wall had been torn down.

Worse still, when the Australians appealed to their own federal government leaders, they were told their claims could not be verified. The Australian and New Zealand governments consistently denied that any of their service personnel were ever held in concentration camps, and refused to investigate the claims made by a mere handful of men. The same denial applied in Canada.

In the United States, iniquity still prevails over the plight of the Buchenwald airmen, and it seems true recognition will never be afforded that nation's remaining military personnel who were illegally held in Hitler's concentration camps. Despite overwhelming documentary and anecdotal evidence, the story of the Buchenwald airmen sadly continues to the present day, with the US government yet to acknowledge that it ever took place.

As far back as 1945, a Congressional report categorically denied that any American military personnel had been held in concentration camps, and this has never been subject to change. Half a century on, in 1993, 1995 and 1997, some determined former Buchenwald airmen attempted to have their wartime experiences and service recognised, if not compensated like other British and Allied nations. The latter two attempts passed through the House, but hit a roadblock in the Senate Judiciary Committee.

On Tuesday 10 June 1997, the Hon. Dave Weldon of Florida, speaking in the House of Representatives, spoke up on behalf of the few surviving members of the American branch of the KLB Club.

> Mr Speaker, fifty-two years is a long time to wait, but the Federal Government should finally recognize the bravery and sacrifice of a group of World War II airmen who were held as German political prisoners. These airmen were different from other Allied prisoners because they were held at Buchenwald, a Nazi concentration camp, and therefore not subject to the protections of the Geneva Convention. Today I am submitting a bill that would give these airmen their long-overdue recognition, and I am proud to say that it has already garnered the bipartisan support of twenty-one of our House colleagues. Representative Peter Deutsch assisted me in

this important effort, and I thank him for his early support of this bill. An identical bill will be introduced this week by Senators Tim Hutchinson and Joseph Lieberman.

The Nazi concentration camps will forever occupy an ignominious place in our human history, and we have long recognized the bravery and daring of many prisoners who fought their Nazi oppressors and struggled to win political and religious freedom. But tragically, the United States has never formally recognized the service, sacrifice, and bravery of these American airmen while they were held as political prisoners at the Buchenwald Concentration Camp. My bill, which is endorsed by the American Ex-Prisoners of War and the Veterans of Foreign Wars, would recognize these 82 American airmen and ask that the President issue a proclamation commending them, by name, for their service. I have also included a list of these airmen, by name, that I would ask be inserted in the Congressional Record. I encourage all of my colleagues to join us in support of this important measure, so that those veterans still living, and the families and friends of those who have passed on, can fully realize the public recognition these brave men so surely deserve.

On Wednesday 10 September, Senator Tim Hutchinson followed through in Congress, beginning with an impassioned plea on behalf of and in memory of former KLB airman William Powell.

Mr President, I rise today full of sadness. Mr William Powell of Bella Vista, Arizona, has recently passed away. I came to know Mr Powell as one of the eighty-two American airmen that were held prisoner of war at the Buchenwald concentration camp during World War II.

During my tenure in Congress, I have introduced two resolutions that would have given appropriate and well-deserved recognition to this group of World War II prisoners. These brave airmen were different from other Allied prisoners, because they were held at Buchenwald – a Nazi concentration camp – and therefore not subject to the protections of the Geneva Convention. Tragically, Mr President, the United States has never formally recognized the service, sacrifice, and bravery of these American airmen while they were held as political prisoners. Even more tragically, the United States and this Congress will never have the opportunity to express our admiration to Mr Powell.

When I introduced Senate Concurrent Resolution 32 in this Congress, on Thursday, June 12, I contacted Mr Powell. He responded by saying, and I quote: 'The recognition is long overdue. For decades, the Department of Defense and the International Red Cross have stated that there were no military personnel in Buchenwald. Yet as someone who was imprisoned there for four months, I know of at least fifty-five other American soldiers who endured the hardships of this camp. Two men even lost their lives there. And nearly all suffered diseases later in life because of the treatment they received while in Buchenwald. In the late 70s/early 80s, I joined with the other survivors of Buchenwald to push this government to recognize our service. We never wanted any money; we just wanted the United States Government to say, "Yes, you were there, and we appreciate what you went through."'

Mr William Powell was a good man, a true patriot, and while this resolution that I spoke of earlier, Senate Concurrent Resolution 32, has yet to pass this body, I urge my colleagues to join with me in passing it, in honor of Mr William Powell. My thoughts and prayers are with his family.

By that time, so few of the Buchenwald airmen were still living and any further appeals to correct the record for the elderly survivors were deemed energy-sapping and unworkable, and that is where the situation in Congress rests today. However, in a completely separate development, the German government decided in 1999 to pay 34.5 million deutschmarks in reparation to US survivors of the Holocaust, both military and civilian, who had been once interned in Nazi concentration camps during World War II. The American airmen who had been sent to Buchenwald were among those receiving this German compensation, but – gallingly – there would never be any official recognition from their own government.

As Frederick Martini, son of one of the KLB airmen, observed: 'The US Air Force has acknowledged the Buchenwald airmen with an exhibit at the Air Force Museum. However, the airmen are shown in uniform, rather than in civilian clothes, and there is no mention of the decades-long denial of their experiences by other branches of the government.'

While the passing years never diluted the memories of what these men witnessed and experienced, their protracted pleas for some form of recognition and just compensation fell on deaf ears and were totally rejected or ignored by a succession of chronically slow and indifferent governments. In the more extreme cases, this failure to act caused a tragic alienation of their former servicemen, who felt betrayed by their own political leaders. They had donned their country's uniform and left their homes to fight in a world war, and yet they were being told there was no evidence of their having been held in Buchenwald and other Nazi death camps. The author would suggest that this evidence has always been readily and easily obtainable, and in most instances is a matter of public record. No one, it seemed, gave a damn about the men's claims.

Finally, in light of irrefutable evidence that these servicemen were indeed held in such camps, the Federal Labor governments of both Australia and New Zealand were stirred into belated action. However, the pressure on these governments and their ministers had to be maintained, as they remained strong on perorations and light on results. In the process of researching this book, the ongoing plight of the Australian servicemen was described to me by a disappointed and frustrated former KLB airman, Ray Perry, who died in 1997:

> During a visit to the United Kingdom in 1963, considerable publicity appeared in the press concerning proposed compensation for people who had suffered Nazi persecution during the world war. I wrote to the office of the High Commissioner for Australia regarding compensation and, following a reply, wrote to the British Foreign Office, who advised that they were looking into the matter with the Federal Republic of Germany, but that Australians would not be covered.
>
> On my return to Western Australia in 1965 I took up this matter with the Australian government, who were not interested and obviously didn't want to know me. I gave up following replies to my letters. In October 1979 there was a report in the newspaper of other Australian servicemen who were illegally interned during the war, in Theresienstadt concentration camp. So I wrote to Dr Klugman,

MHR, who had raised the matter in parliament, asking him if he was aware of RAAF men having spent time in Buchenwald concentration camp. He was not aware of this and pursued matters further in parliament, but with little success. Dr Klugman's speeches did, however, attract the attention of Paul Rea of the *Newcastle Herald*, who wrote up my story.

I again took up the matter with the Australian Government through my local member, but again met with all sorts of excuses being brought forward. I had to obtain proof from the International Red Cross in Switzerland, which was time-consuming, and then I was asked to provide the names of all the Australians and New Zealanders who were illegally interned in Buchenwald, together with their present addresses. I would have thought the government, if they had wanted to, would have been in a better position to do this, and felt that had I achieved success, another obstacle would have been put forward . . .

In March 1983 the Department of Foreign Affairs replied that, 'While servicemen interned in concentration camps do have claims in International Law, these claims cannot be settled in the absence of a peace treaty with Germany.' The English servicemen, although Britain does not have a peace treaty either, did receive compensation for their illegal internment.

Over a period of nine years, unrelenting pressure was applied on successive Federal governments by journalist Paul Rea, whose dedication to the plight of the Australian servicemen held in Theresienstadt culminated in a moving television documentary, *Where Death Wears a Smile* (later turned into the best-selling book *Voices from the Fortress: Stories of Survival from Terezin Concentration Camp*).

A significant breakthrough finally came when a more compassionate Minister for Foreign Affairs, Bill Hayden, set up a special committee to investigate the claims of the servicemen from Theresienstadt and Buchenwald, in conjunction with the New Zealand government. In February 1986, Senator Kerry Sibraa raised the question of compensation in parliament with the then Minister for Veterans' Affairs, Senator Arthur Gietzelt. His response, which follows, was the first clear indication that a claim for compensation was being pursued.

> It is true that an endeavour has been made by Australian ex-servicemen who were placed in Nazi concentration camps in Germany and Czechoslovakia during World War II to seek some form of reparations or compensation from the West German government. It was not until 1982 that the previous government, the Liberal–National Party government, decided to make representations to the West German government in respect of these matters and it received no assurances that compensation would be paid.
>
> However, since the change of government in 1983, Mr Hayden and I have had several discussions with respect to this matter and an interdepartmental committee has been established under the chairmanship of the Department of Foreign Affairs with representatives from other interested parties, such as the Department of the Prime Minister and Cabinet, the Department of Finance and the Department of the Treasury, for example, as well as the Department of Veterans' Affairs. We recognise that there is a substantial case for some form of compensation for the dwindling number of ex-prisoners of war who were placed in concentration camps because they were considered too unreliable by the Nazis for

ordinary POW camps. Their unreliability by Nazi standards was determined by their attempts to escape and to organise against the Nazi regime.

There is no question that some equity should be available to Australian ex-servicemen. The government believes that there is a prima facie case for some form of recognition. The difficulty is that the West German government is not sympathetic to the proposals. Constant endeavours are being made to try to shift the West German government in this respect. All I can tell Senator Sibraa is that the government is determined to press on with the matter. We are not prepared to accept the negative attitude that is being taken by the West German government. We are hopeful that some progress will be made, even if finally it has to come down to some form of ex gratia payment to the dwindling number of Australian prisoners of war. As Senator Sibraa suggests, the film *Where Death Wears a Smile* shows the degree of persecution, torture and other inhuman activities that were carried out in the concentration camps. We believe that there is a very genuine case for the West German government's accepting some responsibility for reparation in these matters.

It was a time of waiting, and the only assurances coming from Canberra were those suggesting patience. The author meantime had supplied the Minister for Veterans' Affairs with a current address list for the eight surviving Australian KLB airmen, having successfully tracked them down all over the country. It took some time, but as Ray Perry had surmised, any government instrumentality with the incentive to locate these men and their present address could have done so with relative ease. Additionally, copies of certain documents which gave irrefutable proof that the men had indeed been in Buchenwald were passed to the Minister. For their part, the men ensured Canberra remained aware that they were waiting in the wings, by repeatedly pressing their local MPs to check on the progress of their claims, and by writing to the Minister for Veterans' Affairs.

Then, in a policy speech for the upcoming federal election in 1987, Prime Minister Bob Hawke stated that a compensation sum would be paid to Australian ex-servicemen held 'in Nazi concentration camps or like institutions'.

In February 1988 it was all over. The claimants from Buchenwald and Theresienstadt concentration camps, and others such as Auschwitz and Dachau, each received an ex gratia payment of $10,000. The New Zealand government followed suit, and similar compensation payments were made.

In total, 27 payments were made to surviving Australian ex-servicemen; seventeen to former soldiers and ten to former airmen. Peter Thorp, Secretary of the Concentration Camp Committee, revealed to the author that these Australians had been held in the following camps:

AUSCHWITZ: Seven (of whom two were held in auxiliary work camps, and one who for a period had been held at Belsen)

DACHAU: Two

BUCHENWALD: Eight

THERESIENSTADT: Six

LUBLIN: One

STUTTHOF: One (who was held in an auxiliary work camp)

FLOSSENBÜRG: Two (both held in an auxiliary work camp)

For most, it was a huge relief after years of denial and rebuttal, but the years of empty words and false promises would never be forgotten.

On the weekend of 24/25 June 1988, six of the eight surviving KLB Australians and their wives met in Canberra for a long overdue reunion, and to celebrate their compensation payments. For Tom Malcolm and Kevin Light in particular it was an opportunity to meet aircrew colleagues they had not seen for 40 years, while for Elaine Fairclough it was a chance to talk at last with the men who had shared the events of Buchenwald with her late husband. Due to unavoidable circumstances Ray Perry and Les Whellum had been unable to make the trip, but Bob 'Lofty' Mills and his crew members from Buchenwald were all there; he, Jim Gwilliam, Keith Mills and Eric Johnston had stayed in touch over the years and seemed to almost enjoy the novelty of media interest in their story. Another member of their wartime crew, Ian Innes, was also in attendance. Unlike his friends he had made a successful escape back to England following the crash of their brand-new Halifax bomber. It would prove to be the last get-together for the crew; two years later, on 8 August 1990, Bob Mills was tragically killed in a car accident.

Prior to a dinner at the National Press Club, Major-General Alan Morrison, representing the newly-incumbent Minister for Veterans' Affairs, Ben Humphreys, formally welcomed the group to Canberra and took them carefully and succinctly through the history of the compensation story. Later, over dinner, Bob Mills eloquently proposed the toast: to absent friends. Elaine Fairclough silently shed a tear.

Suddenly it seemed everyone wanted to know the story from these elderly survivors of Hitler's Holocaust. The press, radio and television people badgered them over the weekend for interviews – all graciously given.

As the weekend wound down late on the Sunday afternoon, and having made my farewells to the others, I stood outside the High Court building with Jim and Pam Gwilliam, with whom I had become great friends, reflecting on a weekend of triumph for the KLB group.

'Well, I guess your book has its ending now,' Jim remarked as we watched the other men and their wives saying goodbye to each other. 'You know, it's funny how these things turn out. I'd already accepted the fact that nobody cared, and that any thought of compensation was just a bloody pipe dream. Of course it's nice to get the money after all this time, even though it wouldn't buy much more than a second-hand car and a packet of smokes, but it was nice to have someone go in to bat for us. And seeing those blokes again – crikey, that's made it all worthwhile. Forty years – it's been a long time!'

We shook hands, Jim took Pam's arm, and they strolled away together as I opened my car door. Pausing for a few moments to look back at the cluster of KLB men and their wives, I felt mixed emotions of sadness and pleasure. They had finally won their long battle for recognition and compensation, but the motive for their reunion had its origins half a world away in the bloodied dust of a despised place in Germany, and in the inhuman excesses of their captors. Apart from their experiences as wartime aircrew, Buchenwald was their common bond, yet it was quite noticeable that talk amongst them of Hitler's hell camp, set amid Goethe's beloved beech trees, had little place in their weekend of celebration and remembrance.

There are those today who would admonish us to disregard the more horrifying aspects of wartime history and others whose emphasis is one of trivialising such matters, but the memories should remain strong, and we should never forget the barbarism perpetrated in the name of war and conquest.

During my research for this book I happened across some appropriate words penned by Samuel Taylor Coleridge, and they came back to me as the Buchenwald airmen drifted off on their separate paths once again.

> If men could learn from history, what lessons it might teach us! But passion and party blind our eyes, and the light which experience gives us is a lantern on the stern, which shines only on the waves behind us.

I settled into my car, started the engine and engaged low gear, then crunched across the gravel of the car park onto the roadway. Pensively I drove off, as a blood red sun slowly dipped below the Canberra hills.

Appendix

THE POEMS

These two poems by former KLB airmen were penned on either side of their Buchenwald experience. In the first, Canadian Willie Waldrum presents some emotional post-war reminiscences, while Texan Levitt Beck, who died under appalling circumstances at the concentration camp, seemed to sadly prophesy his own tragic and lonely death in a poem he wrote prior to captivity.

KLB (Konzentrationslager Buchenwald): A Reflection

I'll think of you, dear KLB,
Again some future day,
When the world is gay and free
And I am so far away.

Of those long appells in pouring rain
With neither boots nor shoes,
And the SS guards who counted us
Hitting whom they choose.

When I bounce my children on my knee
I'll think of those gypsy kids
Who, instead of wearing ball and chain,
Should have been wearing bibs.

When I lay in my cosy bed at night
I'll think of your hard boards,
With a single blanket to cover us,
And fleas and lice in hordes.

Ironically, I'll think of how
You took our dog-tags from us,
'Nix soldat – civil' you said
Smiling fanatically at us.

Yes, you gave us soup and enough black bread
To etch out a mere existence,
Enough to keep us wanting more
And weaken our resistance.

How two of our number lost their lives
For lack of medical aid,
You wouldn't even give them food
To help save them from the grave.

And then: after eight weeks spent in your filthy soul,
Which seemed to me like years,
The Luftwaffe came, took us away,
I felt like shedding tears.

And so to all you Konzentrators,
A toast I offer thee;
Here's to wishing you a happy life,
And to Hell with KLB!

Willie Waldrum, Ex-RAF, Ex-KLB

I See it Now

(Written in 1940)

I watched the day turn into nite,
Creeping shadows reached the sky;
Birds flew to their nests,
Still singing as they went;
All mankind lay at rest,
As though heaven sent.
Quiet ne'er before was like this –
Even wind hung softly about the trees,
As if afraid of waking birds,
Sleeping in their nests;
'Twas like another world to me,
And I found myself wishing –
Wishing it were true.

I've suffered – and have hated it,
But in my mind a thought was born,
Making a new path for me –
On which I now find my way.

I see it now –
While I suffer here
I must not question of it;
It is the way of life –
Too much happiness would spoil me;
I'd grown too fond of life on earth
And the afterlife I seek
Would not be sweet –
We must have our troubles here;
– Our hearts torn by loss
– Our hands made bloody by war
– Our future left unknown.

First Lieutenant Levitt C. Beck, Jr, USAAF
Born: Houston, Texas, 2 January 1920
Died: Buchenwald, Germany, 29 November 1944

THE 168 AIRMEN IN BUCHENWALD

New Zealand

Cullen, F/Lt Malcolm Ford: 257 (Burma) Fighter Squadron

Lamason, S/Ldr Phillip John: 15 Squadron

Australia

Fairclough, F/Sgt Mervyn James: 51 Squadron

Gwilliam, F/Sgt James Percival: 78 Squadron

Johnston, F/Sgt Eric Lyle: 78 Squadron

Light, F/O Kevin William: 9 Squadron

Malcolm, F/Sgt Thomas Alexander: 463 (RAAF) Squadron

Mills, F/Sgt Keith Cyril: 78 Squadron

Mills, P/O Robert Neil: 78 Squadron

Perry, F/Sgt Raymond Walter: 466 (RAAF) Squadron

Whellum, F/Sgt Lesley Keith: 102 (RAAF) Squadron

Jamaica

Guilfoyle, P/O Michael A.: 12 Squadron

Canada

Atkins, F/O Harold A.: 427 (RCAF) Squadron
Bastaple, F/O Harold D.: 640 Squadron
Carter-Edwards, P/O Edward: 427 (RCAF) Squadron
Clark, W/O Don: 76 Squadron
Compton, F/Sgt G. A. Edward: 424 (RCAF) Squadron
Crawford, Sgt John: 106 Squadron
Fulsher, Sgt Frederick H.: 100 Squadron
Gibson, Sgt William R.: 419 (RCAF) Squadron
Grenon, F/Sgt Leon T.: 433 (RCAF) Squadron
Harvie, P/O John D. M.: 433 (RCAF) Squadron
Head, W/O Leslie F.: 419 (RCAF) Squadron
Hetherington, F/O Stanley G.: 433 (RCAF) Squadron
High, Sgt Dave: 419 (RCAF) Squadron
Hodgson, F/Sgt Thomas R.: 625 Squadron
Hoffman, F/O Charles Richard: 432 (RCAF) Squadron
Kinnis, F/O Arthur G.: 106 Squadron
Leslie, Sgt Donald E.: 102 Squadron
McLenaghan, F/Sgt J. Ralph: 514 Squadron
Prudham, F/O James Ewart: 419 (RCAF) Squadron
Scullion, P/O Patrick: 433 (RCAF) Squadron
Shepherd, F/O Ernest G.: 640 Squadron
Smith, F/O James A.: 419 (RCAF) Squadron
Sonshine, W/O E. R. (Joseph): 12 Squadron
Walderam, Sgt Willie A.: 106 Squadron
Watson, F/O Earl Carruthers: 432 (RCAF) Squadron
Willis, F/O Calvin E.: 640 Squadron

United Kingdom

Angus, F/Sgt Jack Wilson: 78 Squadron
Barham, F/Sgt Leonard P.: 207 Squadron
Baxter, F/O Stuart: 514 Squadron
Bennett, F/Sgt Geoffrey: 57 Squadron
Blackham, F/Lt Thomas Henry: 50 Squadron
Booker, F/O Stanley Albert: 10 Squadron
Bryden, Sgt Robert: 76 Squadron
Chapman, F/O E. W. (Ken): 15 Squadron
Chinn, F/Sgt Albert J.: 207 Squadron
Clarke, Sgt John: 514 Squadron
Davis, F/Sgt Eric: 83 Squadron
Dowdeswell, Sgt Philip: 158 Squadron
Eagle, F/Sgt Douglas: 102 Squadron
Fernandez, F/Sgt Ivan: 158 Squadron
Gould, F/Sgt Terrance: 10 Squadron
Harper, Sgt Robert: 622 Squadron
Hegarty, Sgt Patrick W.: 51 Squadron
Hemmens, F/O Philip D.: 49 Squadron
Hughes, Sgt Ronald R.: 76 Squadron
Jackson, Lt Edgar: 100 Squadron
Jordin, Sgt Douglas F.: 12 Squadron
Joyce, Sgt Reginald W.: 102 Squadron
Kay, P/O William: 100 Squadron
Leverington, F/Sgt Ronald L.: 102 Squadron
Lucas, Sgt Leslie J.: 106 Squadron
MacPherson, Sgt Alexander J.: 207 Squadron
Marshall, Sgt Wilfred: 12 Squadron
Measures, F/Sgt Derek K.: 101 Squadron

Mutter, F/O Neville E. S.: 65 Squadron
Nuttal, F/Lt Cyril Worsley: 158 Squadron
Osselton, Sgt John N.: 10 Squadron
Peirson, F/Sgt Frank: 76 Squadron
Percy, F/O Douglas C.: 630 Squadron
Phelps, F/Sgt Edward K.: 207 Squadron
Reid, Sgt John David: 514 Squadron
Robb, F/O Ian A.: 218 Squadron
Rowe, Sgt Andrew: 640 Squadron
Salt, F/Sgt Frank: 35 Squadron
Sharratt, F/Sgt William D.: 78 Squadron
Spierenburg, F/O Splinter Adolph: 582 Squadron
Stewart, F/O James A.: 609 Squadron
Taylor, F/O Peter D.: 10 Squadron
Taylor, F/O Ralph John: 10 Squadron
Vincombe, Sgt Frederick S.: 419 Squadron
Ward, Sgt John D.: 576 Squadron
Watmough, Sgt George F.: 433 Squadron
Wesley, W/O Laurie: 207 Squadron
Williams, F/O Llewelyn: 102 Squadron

United States

Alexander, S/Sgt William Joseph: 489 Bomber Group, 845 Squadron
Allen, 1st/Lt Roy Walter: 457 Bomber Group, 750 Squadron
Appleman, Lt Stratton Mayfield: 437 Troop Carrier Group, 85 Squadron
Bauder, Lt Warren Floyd: 44 Bomber Group, 506 Squadron
Beck, Jr, 1st/Lt Levitt Clinton: 406 Fighter Group, 514 Squadron

Bedford, 2nd/Lt Richard Lawrence: 353 Fighter Group, 350 Squadron

Bowen, S/Sgt Chasten Leroy: 91 Bomber Group, 323 Squadron

Bozarth, S/Sgt James Walter: 401 Bomber Group, 615 Squadron

Brown, 2nd/Lt Robert Harold: 384 Bomber Group, 544 Squadron

Carr, 2nd/Lt Frederick Walter: 489 Bomber Group, 845 Squadron

Chalot, Lt John André: 355 Fighter Group, 358 Squadron

Chapman, 2nd/Lt Park: 322 Bomber Group, 450 Squadron

Chesshir, S/Sgt Douglas Murrell: 489 Bomber Group, 845 Squadron

Coats, S/Sgt Basil Arthur: 390 Bomber Group, 571 Squadron

Coffman, 2nd/Lt J. D.: 489 Bomber Group, 845 Squadron

Cowan, T/Sgt Frank Kirby: 96 Bomber Group, 339 Squadron

Crouch, Jr, Lt Marshall Combs: 392 Bomber Group, 579 Squadron

Dauteuil, 2nd/Lt Donat François: 391 Bomber Group, 547 Squadron

Dearey, 2nd/Lt Ralph H.: 339 Fighter Group, 503 Squadron

Denaro, 2nd/Lt Joseph Charles: 801 Bomber Group, 850 Squadron

Duncan, 2nd/Lt James Harold: 390 Bomber Group, 568 Squadron

Edge, Sgt William Littleton: 394 Bomber Group, 585 Squadron

Fix, S/Sgt Earl Ellsworth: 489 Bomber Group, 845 Squadron

Fore, Lt James William: 91 Bomber Group, 323 Squadron

Freeman, 2nd/Lt Elmer Clayton: 397 Bomber Group, 596 Squadron

Friel, Sgt Edward Joseph: 491 Bomber Group, 852 Squadron

Granberry III, 2nd/Lt William Langley: 801 Bomber Group, 850 Squadron

Hanson, S/Sgt John Patrick: 385 Bomber Group, 548 Squadron

Hastin, 1st/Lt James Dale: 361 Fighter Group, 374 Squadron

Heimerman, S/Sgt Lawrence Albert: 487 Bomber Group, 838 Squadron
Hilding, 2nd/Lt Russ Duane: 447 Bomber Group, 709 Squadron
Hoffman, 2nd/Lt Robert Bruce: 55 Fighter Group, 38 Squadron
Horrigan, T/Sgt Roy Joseph: 493 Bomber Group, 862 Squadron
Horwege, 2nd/Lt Glenn Lorensen: 362 Fighter Group, 377 Squadron
Hunter, 1st/Lt Harry Floyd: 353 Fighter Group, 351 Squadron
Johnson, S/Sgt Robert Thayer: 448 Bomber Group, 714 Squadron
King, 1st/Lt Myles Anthony: 355 Fighter Group, 357 Squadron
Larson, Capt Merle Elmo: 474 Fighter Group, 429 Squadron
Little, S/Sgt Bruce Scott: 379 Bomber Group, 526 Squadron
Ludwig, S/Sgt Everett Franklin: 390 Bomber Group, 571 Squadron
Martini, S/Sgt Frederic Cosmo: 385 Bomber Group, 551 Squadron
Mauk, Jr, Sgt William Emmanuel: 489 Bomber Group, 845 Squadron
McClanaham, S/Sgt John Howard: 384 Bomber Group, 544 Squadron
McLaughlin, 1st/Lt Daniel G.: 457 Bomber Group, 751 Squadron
Mikel, Jr, 2nd/Lt George L.: 92 Bomber Group, 327 Squadron
Mitchell, 2nd/Lt Gerald E.: 801 Bomber Group, 850 Squadron
Moser, 1st/Lt Joseph F.: 474 Fighter Group, 429 Squadron
O'Masters, Sgt Lovell: 457 Bomber Group, 751 Squadron
Pacha, T/Sgt Arthur M.: 385 Bomber Group, 549 Squadron
Pecus, Sgt Steve: 489 Bomber Group, 845 Squadron
Pederson, 2nd/Lt Joseph W.: 306 Bomber Group, 367 Squadron
Pelletier, S/Sgt Arthur J.: 487 Bomber Group, 838 Squadron
Pennell, S/Sgt Sam: 385 Bomber Group, 551 Squadron
Petrich, 1st/Lt Michael Robert: 391 Bomber Group, 575 Squadron

Phelps, Jr, 1st/Lt Byron Forbes: 367 Fighter Group, 393 Squadron
Powell, Lt William: 385 Bomber Group, 549 Squadron
Reynolds, Sgt Leo J.: 385 Bomber Group, 549 Squadron
Richey, S/Sgt Glenn Thomas: 390 Bomber Group, 571 Squadron
Ritter, S/Sgt Edwin W.: 93 Bomber Group, 328 Squadron
Roberson, S/Sgt Charles William: 384 Bomber Group, 544 Squadron
Ryherd, 1st/Lt William Henry: 397 Bomber Group, 598 Squadron
Salo, T/Sgt Laurie A.: 801 Bomber Group, 850 Squadron
Scharf, S/Sgt Bernard T.: 91 Bomber Group, 323 Squadron
Scott, Sgt George Wayne: 416 Bomber Group, 668 Squadron
Shearer, T/Sgt Donald Ross: 391 Bomber Group, 573 Squadron
Smith, 2nd/Lt James Henry: 493 Bomber Group, 862 Squadron
Stanley, Keith Paxton: 493 Bomber Group, 862 Squadron
Stralka, Jr, S/Sgt Paul A.: 801 Bomber Group, 850 Squadron
Suddock, T/Sgt Dwight Elmer: 351 Bomber Group, 510 Squadron
Sypher, 1st/Lt Leroy Henry: 361 Fighter Group, 375 Squadron
Thompson, 2nd/Lt Warren Archie: 410 Bomber Group, 647 Squadron
Vallee, S/Sgt Edward Joseph: 303 Bomber Group, 360 Squadron
Vance, 1st/Lt Ira E.: 397 Bomber Group, 598 Squadron
Vincent, 1st/Lt Edwin L.: 381 Bomber Group, 534 Squadron
Vratney, 1st/Lt Frank: 487 Bomber Group, 838 Squadron
Ward, 2nd/Lt Robert W.: 91 Bomber Group, 323 Squadron
Watson, S/Sgt John Paul: 487 Bomber Group, 838 Squadron
Williams, S/Sgt William J. (Bill): 385 Bomber Group, 549 Squadron
Wilson, S/Sgt Paul J.: 391 Bomber Group, 574 Squadron
Wojnicz, 1st/Lt Raymond E.: 447 Bomber Group, 709 Squadron
Zander, 1st/Lt Arthur: 448 Bomber Group, 14 Squadron
Zeiser, S/Sgt James F.: 91 Bomber Group, 323 Squadron

Glossary of Rank:

1st/Lt = First Lieutenant

F/Sgt = Flight Sergeant

F/O = Flying Officer

Lt = Lieutenant

P/O = Pilot Officer

2nd/Lt = Second Lieutenant

Sgt = Sergeant

S/Sgt = Staff Sergeant

W/O = Warrant Officer

SELECT BIBLIOGRAPHY

Beck, Levin C., *Fighter Pilot*, Wetzel Publishing, Los Angeles, 1946

Blackham, Thomas, 'I Survived Buchenwald', *Flying Review*, May 1954

Burney, Christopher, *The Dungeon Democracy*, William Heinemann, Portsmouth, 1983

Dencocks, G. (ed.), *In Enemy Hands*, Hurtig Publications, Edmonton, 1983

D'Harcourt, Pierre, *The Real Enemy*, Scribner Books, New York, 1967

Foot, M. R. D., *S.O.E. France*, HMSO, London, UK, 1966

Harvie, John D., *Missing in Action*, McGill-Queen's University Press, Montreal, 1995

Kinnis, Arthur and Booker, Stanley, *168 Jump Into Hell*, Privately published (Kinnis), Victoria, 1999

Kogon, Eugen, *The Theory and Practice of Hell*, Farrar, Straus & Cudahy, New York, 1950

Marshall, Bruce, *The White Rabbit*, Evans Bros., London, 1952

Martini, Frederick H., *Betrayed: Secrecy, Lies and Consequences*, Rugged Land Publishing, New York, 2018

Moser, Joseph and Baron, Gerald, *A Fighter Pilot in Buchenwald*, All Clear Publishing, Chicago, 2009

Neave, Airey, *Saturday at M.I.9*, Hodder and Stoughton, London, 1969

Pederson, Hilary (et al.), *I Would Not Step Back*, The Phil Lamason Heritage Trust (Inc.), Danniverke, 2018

Poller, Walter, *Butchers of Buchenwald*, Souvenir Press, London, 1961

Richey, Robert J., *My Brother Glenn: A Prisoner of the Gestapo During World War II*, Authorhouse Publishing, Bloomington, 2011

Strachan, Anthony (ed.), *In the Clutch of Circumstance*, Cappis Press, Victoria, 1985

INDEX OF NAMES

ABOUT THE AUTHOR

Colin Burgess was born in suburban Sydney, Australia, in 1947. In 2002, after 32 years of in-flight service with Qantas Airways in a variety of roles, Colin took an early retirement in order to concentrate on his writing career.

His first published book was *The Diggers of Colditz* in 1985, co-authored with Colditz veteran Jack Champ. Since then, he has had numerous non-fiction books published on a wide variety of subjects. In recent years he has not only turned his attention to writing books on the history of human space exploration, but was appointed series editor for the Outward Odyssey series of books on that subject, published by the University of Nebraska Press in the United States.

To date, he has written or co-authored nearly 40 books and is currently working on a biography of Sister Betty Jeffrey OAM, the Australian nurse who was interned in a Japanese prison camp during the Second World War.